The Coming Age of Woman Power

OTHER BOOKS BY KONRAD KELLEN

Battle in the Wilderness
Khrushchev—A Political Portrait

The Coming Age of Woman Power

by Konrad Kellen

PETER H. WYDEN, INC. / PUBLISHER
New York

THE COMING AGE OF WOMAN POWER

LIBRARY OF CONGRESS CATALOG CARD NUMBER: 72–85995

MANUFACTURED IN THE UNITED STATES OF AMERICA

ACKNOWLEDGMENTS

I am deeply indebted to Margaret Carpenter, who collaborated with me on this book. By conducting the interviews—only a fraction of which appear in the Appendix, but which were the principal source from which I drew my conclusions—she provided a large number of the materials on the woman's movement and other relevant subjects. Her patience in many conversations made it possible for me to shape and test my own emerging opinions. The final result is mine alone—and as Miss Carpenter puts it, "a man's point of view"—but the book could not have been written without her.

I am indebted as well to Rachel Whitebook, who did an extraordinarily sensitive and intelligent job of editing, clarifying, and otherwise civilizing the manuscript. I have been around books and other written materials for a quarter of a century and have never known a better editor.

Finally, I am grateful to Ruth Young, who typed and otherwise cared for the manuscript during its genesis, for her patience, speed, and accuracy.

K. K.

CONTENTS

"It is very difficult to predict—especially the future."

—Niels Bohr, Nobel Prize-winning physicist

The Coming Age of Woman Power

INTRODUCTION: THE COMING AGE OF WOMAN POWER

A LONG time from now people will probably look back upon our era as one of the few great turning points—and perhaps the greatest turning point—in history. They will perhaps look at it as the age when the human race rescued itself from collective madness and self-destruction by the skin of its teeth. How? By *woman power,* entering into all its affairs, its concerns, its ideas in entirely new ways. In retrospect our century will not be regarded primarily as the time of communism or fascism challenging democracy—such distinctions will appear hazy and idle to future historians, insignificant. What they will identify as decisive will be, first, the rise of woman power in human affairs, beginning in the United States, and, second, the human control of atomic energy.

The latter will give future historians a point of departure for their analysis of the ultimate bankruptcy of male-dominated society in the 1970s: more than a quarter century after harnessing nuclear energy "man"—incredibly—had not been able to do anything with it except build his bombs and a few aircraft carriers and submarines powered by such energy. Nothing could symbolize and illustrate more glaringly the utter mismanagement and immobility in all of man's affairs. The other point of departure for future historians in their analysis of our time will be the profusion of genocidal wars fought in our century: nothing could symbolize and illustrate better the futility and brutality with which "man" finally came to administer his affairs. And the calamitous state of society, of science, of politics in the pre-woman-power age will be further proof to future observers that woman power came to the rescue only in the nick of time.

Actually, the future historian will not conclude that the human race was about to blow itself off the globe with nuclear weapons, as little old ladies of both sexes warn us in their stereotype letters to editors, or as shallow demagogues tell us in their stereotype speeches we will, unless we elect *them* and hand over to their insolent control our individual powers and resources. The future historian will conclude instead that the human race, shortly before the decisive rise of woman power in the last third of the twentieth century, was on the verge, not of killing itself physically, but of driving itself insane, turning the earth for all except a small and pampered minority into a living hell. The future historian will conclude, with a certain awe, that woman power materialized just as "man" was about to use his new technology to create for the many the most intolerable living conditions ever known on earth; to perpetrate, with its help, the grossest injustices; to damage permanently, with his propaganda technology, the minds of the race; to exhaust, in the name of conservation, his best resources; to commit, with the help of electronics and force, the greatest iniquities, killing people by the million abroad, taxing them into the ground at home, depriving them of all civil liberties in the name of civil liberties, robbing them of all personal safety and dignity.

Yet at the very moment when "man" was about to perpetrate his ultimate political, scientific, technological, social, and military idiocies and atrocities, woman power—future historians will discern—appeared and firmly said, "No, friends, it's enough now. From here on we will do things quite differently. Together, we hope, if you wish." Man, his bluff called, his back against the wall of his government and industry and labor and church fortresses, will be seen as having changed course—perhaps not even unwillingly, because of his inability to suppress the rise of woman power with his customary tactics. And it is quite probable that future historians will count the last third of the twentieth century, and not the Reformation, as the end of the Dark Ages and the beginning of humankind's civilization.

The human race, the human individual, bothersome though this may be, cannot choose whether it wants to be civilized. It *must* be civilized, at least up to a point, to be able to solve or at least live with the many difficulties the "Naked Ape," as Desmond Morris has styled him, will always face. Yet male power today keeps suggesting that we need more organization, more force, more money, rather than more civilization—that is, more man power rather than woman power. Wielding eternally its sledgehammer of coercion, threats, ultimata, bribery, blackmail, propaganda, man power "attacks" contemporary problems as a gorilla might a sensitive watch for having stopped ticking. Faced with a growing crime rate, runaway drug addiction, rebellion of the young and of women, an arms race, inflation, recession, racial strife, social unrest, ecological problems, and so much more, man tightens his grip on that sledgehammer and ensconces himself deeper in the "philosophy" that has brought him to the current profusion of impasses. He is ready, not to blow himself off the earth, but to demolish what little human civilization, what little truth or kindness or understanding there is, with his politics, his "policies," his lies, his wars, his greed, his fears, his science—particularly his "social" science.

But when a higher degree of civilization became necessary to prevent disasters much more hair-raising than the physical end of the human race (which, like the dinosaur, will have to disappear in any event some day), the task obviously fell to women. Can anyone deny that women are more civilized than men, that they have had and have a more civilizing influence on the human race than man? What is it to be "civilized"? It is to be sensible, compassionate, fair, kind, tolerant, understanding; it is also to be intolerant of vileness in all its forms. Seen from that perspective, man seems to be somewhere between animal and woman. In all of the many socially and legally sanctioned forms men kill and suppress, rob and lie. They behave when thrown together, as in the army, with grossness and brutality. And the feebler they have become physically under the impact of modern life, the more they exhibit their hairy-chest syndrome on all occasions. They are rude, crude, and coarse in their tastes and habits. Conversely, all that is encompassed by the word "civilization"—a certain refinement, sensitivity, compassion, self-restraint, gentleness—is possessed mainly by woman. Yet at the very time when civilizing influences are needed more than anything else, man is in command.

Perhaps it was not always that way. In *The First Sex* Elizabeth Gould Davies says that "the further back one traced man's history, the larger loomed the figure of woman. If the gods and goddesses of today are but the heroes and heroines of yesterday, then unquestionably the goddesses of historical times were but the reflected memory of the ruling hierarchy of a former civilization"—a civilization in which women were dominant in all spheres of life and men were servants and studs only.* A drama reconstructed by Mrs. Davies' imagination—woman's rule of the prehistoric era—comes to an end when man suddenly rebels: "Led perhaps by the queen's consort, the rebellious males burst onstage, overturn the queen's throne, and take her captive. Her consort moves to center stage. He lifts his bloody sword over the

* Mrs. Davies also claims that women are physically on a higher level of civilization too, being "three-holers," while men are only "two-holers" (and the lowest animals "one-holers"). An interesting theory.

heads of courtiers. The queen's subjects—Democracy, Peace, Justice, and the rest—flee the scene in disarray."

The deterioration in the status of women, Mrs. Davies believes, went hand in hand with the Dark Ages that followed. And "the implacability with which Western Man (after the triumphant rise of Teutonic-Semitic patriarchy) has retaliated against woman serves only to confirm the truth of her former dominance—a dominance that man felt compelled to stamp out and forget." Mrs. Davies concludes the introduction to her book: "Recorded history starts with a patriarchal revolution (against the earlier, gynocratic system). Let it continue with the matriarchal counter-revolution that is the only hope for the survival of the human race." [1] *

Future historians will probably see that things did not work out quite as Mrs. Davies hoped. Rather than revert to gynocratic patterns in the form of a counter-revolution, the world is more likely to see a synthesis, a new life style altogether, a fruitful and reasonably harmonious symbiosis between the sexes or, more mundanely, a partnership society.

That partnership, however, is not likely to appear as some men are already envisioning it as the ultimate fallback position for themselves. It will *not* be a partnership in which women, having simply been "granted" the same rights and privileges and jobs as men and paid the same salaries, would then for equal pay proceed with equal folly, and merely do things side by side with men in the same heedless, destructive, corrupt fashion as men have become accustomed to doing everything. Rather, once they start seeping into the (male) establishment in large numbers, women will bring with them, as their dowry, their own way of doing things, based on their own feelings and views. And many men, as a result, are likely to be liberated, just as women these days predict they will be, by women, first from their archaic view of

* Superscripts refer to bibliographical information contained in Notes (pp. 353–356).

themselves, their he-manism; then from their distorted view of the world around them; and finally from the worst forms of social and economic bondage they have brought upon themselves and must bear today, regardless of their positions on the social and economic scale.

Thus, though the chemical comparison is surely limping, woman power will be both the additive and the catalyst in the new life force that will take over the stalling and flailing machine. All this is much nearer than many women think, including many who are militant or liberated. One reason is that the human race and human society, usually so slow in effecting the slightest changes, can move quite quickly when its self-preservation is at stake. And the ice is already breaking, particularly in the United States.

There are two other reasons that the change will be swift and drastic. The first is that the men generally seem to have no idea of how strong the women's movement, the new woman power, already is or at what rate it is growing, because they do not seem to know what it *is*. The (male) establishment underestimates woman power because it is not an old-style revolutionary movement—with a formalized ideology, cells, an organized conspiracy, weapons, and the limited aim of "taking over." It thus seems weak. The opposite is true: a traditional revolutionary movement would be easy to beat back. But the women's movement is rather like a flood rising along the crumbling ramparts of an obsolete fortress: it will have no trouble flowing in everywhere.

Changes are also likely to be more swift and dramatic than anticipated because woman power underestimates its own strength. Not being really conversant with man's affairs and their sorry state, woman power probably does not realize its *relative* strength; and not realizing yet how well suited woman's gifts, woman's ways, woman's aims are to help humanize the human race and its society, and how avidly the system will want to use these qualities once it has become accustomed to the idea, woman power probably does not realize its *absolute* strength.

What do women want? When America's great labor leader Samuel Gompers was asked a long time ago what he really wanted for his people, he gave his answer in a single word: "More." To some extent that is also true for women today. But they want "more than more," more than just a bigger share of the society in which they live. They want a different society. Regarded by frightened business leaders as a wild revolutionary and subversive, Gompers was a staid traditionalist as compared to the contemporary liberated woman. For labor wanted only a *share;* women want a *change.*

The Western world, and particularly the United States, will be a very different place to live in a decade from now. And it will be very different from what today's pseudoprophets (who, significantly, are all males who puff themselves up with their "scientific method") say it will be. For while these prophets see only more gadgets, more space travel, more competition between nations, more experimentation with genetics—all, of course, under firm male control—a genuine and thorough change in values, a true reordering of priorities, entirely different from the one now called for by machine politicians and their sidekicks, the machine scientists, will gradually bring about a basic change.

Because of woman power's entering upon the stage in the coming decade, all that the establishment futurologists now prophesy is likely *not* to come to pass, for they do not even look at one of the dominant factors, or, as they call it, variables, to be put into the equation: woman power. They therefore see only extensions, more of the same, while life is likely to run in truly different channels a decade from now. They may go so far as to think: So, Mrs. X will be a lawyer like Mr. X and they will share an office and win a big case for General Electric while the kids are in the day-care center, and that's all there is to it. But that is not all there is to it.

In this book, as an experiment in forecasting, *the quality of life,* what the mad scientists in our mad day call "software," but to which they actually pay little attention in their forecasts, will be sketched out. To do this it is necessary, first, to acquaint the reader with some of the current ramifications of institutionalized prophecy.

1

THE FUTUROLOGIST AND THE FOOL

THE contemporary futurologist winks at the fool: "Wanna sire a couple of Einsteins? We got the genetics for it, you know, almost." And the fool is excited. "That'll be the day," he says. And the futurologist continues, "We got something that's perhaps even better. Far out, man. By the year 2000 we'll wire your brain to some console with buttons. If you push one button, you get the sensation of sex. If you push another, it's beer, sausage, and sauerkraut." The fool quivers with anticipation; he begins to wonder whether maybe he can push both buttons at the same time. "And of course," says the futurologist, "once we have your brain wired to that console, you no longer *need* to sire those Einsteins. You can push buttons that will give you the same pride you'd feel if you *had* sired them, see?" And the fool thinks, "Wow, I can have it either way!" He is not fully convinced yet, perhaps; in fact, he cannot quite place himself in such a wondrous world. But he is elated at the prospect, happy to see the human race make such rapid progress, and grateful to the prophet. And he wants to hear more.

Never in history, it seems, has the future held more promises, but also more threats, than in this time of rapidly accelerating change. Do we overestimate the uniqueness of change in our era? In Goethe's famous novel *The Elective Affinities*, which appeared in 1805, Eduard complains, "It is awful that we no longer can learn anything that remains valid throughout life. Our ancestors kept to what they had learned. But we must relearn everything every five years if we do not want to fall out of fashion completely." And *he* probably underestimated the rate of change in the earlier times of which he spoke. Still, change in our day is much greater than it ever has been, covers more territory, progresses at a fiercer pace, opens newer and stranger perspectives. No wonder more people are more interested in what the future will bring than they have ever been, and no wonder that there are more people ready to tell them than there have ever been.

But the greed to know the future always has existed and so has the blindness such greed tends to beget. As a result prophecy has been a relatively easy and profitable business, lending great status to the prophet. Not everyone, of course, can be a prophet: it takes a special knack and a great deal of gall. Particularly in past ages, when individual personal safety was not as assured as it seems to be today in our country, prophets ran great risks; kings and other rulers, when crossed up by evolving reality, thought little of beheading a prophet who failed. Perhaps this was not such a bad system, considering contemporary prophets and their products.

To insure his safety to some extent and also to safeguard his reputation of infallibility, without which the prophet could no more work than could the barber without his scissors, the prophet often resorted to ambiguity or imprecision. Joseph of Egypt told Pharaoh—whose slumber was disturbed by a dream of seven skinny cows—that there might be a drought that would last seven years. It is not clear whether the meager years were five or seven or nine. But there was some sort of drought and, as Joseph had also predicted, it came eventually to an end and was followed by many rich harvests. And Joseph became Viceroy over Egypt.

The Sphinx did not merely use imprecision or ambiguity as a

fallback position, but is reported to have spoken in riddles. That is a safe way to proceed, but cannot satisfy the modern fool, who clamors for "facts." Anyway, not much is known about the Sphinx. The famous oracle at Delphi, on the other hand, said much that is recorded, and we must pay the oracle tribute for its skillful use of ambiguity. When some proud king—we have forgotten his name—prior to a campaign of aggression rulers always so eagerly undertake, asked the oracle what the campaign's outcome would be, the oracle said, "When you cross the big river, you will destroy a great army." The king went forth in fine spirits, crossed the big river, engaged the enemy, and was totally defeated. The oracle had been proven right: the king had indeed destroyed a great army. It just happened to be his own. The oracle was as clever a semanticist as any contemporary political candidate.

Throughout history prophets continued to fascinate the human race, whether they worked with the entrails of chickens or other tools of their curious trade. There was the famous Nostradamus, who predicted in the sixteenth century a variety of disasters, all of which occurred on time, depending on one's interpretation of what he said; and then there is the Bible, which abounds with prophecies. To the extent that we can verify, prophecy was generally in greater demand in bad times than in good. Apparently people are more anxious to learn something about the future when times are bad. One wonders whether that can be turned around: When people demand so much from their prophets, are the times bad?

What makes prophets so eagerly sought out is the aura of mystery surrounding them. Charles Dickens' Barnaby Rudge says that "to surround anything, however monstrous or ridiculous, with an air of mystery, is to invest it with power of attraction which to the crowd is irresistible. . . . Curiosity is, and has been from the creation of the world, a master passion. To awaken it, to gratify it by slight degrees and yet leave always something in suspense, is to establish the surest hold that can be had on the unthinking portion of mankind." And the prophet, who has always been surrounded by that air of mystery, is today so more than ever, perhaps because he often has access to top-secret materials, as in think tanks. This makes the modern prophet's hold on the fool all the greater. Little does the fool know that these classified documents rarely contain anything of importance to him.

The modern prophet, of course, is different from his predecessor, who could be anything from a holy lamb foaming at the mouth to an invisible oracle, a priest, a medicine man. The modern prophet is a scientist, and not a prophet at all; he calls himself a futurologist. And his predictions are not inspired, they are not revealed knowledge; they are the result of his brilliant mind applying some rigidly scientific methodologies (which he has invented) to the "data" (which he has selected). Another difference between him and his predecessors is that he usually looks farther into the future and deals with a wider range of events. The fool wants to know, and so the prophet predicts, what will happen in the year 2000, in the twenty-first century, and so on. This makes it convenient for the prophet, who can target a date not likely to arrive during his lifetime, or at least not while he still conducts his business that is so sensitive to reality. And the contemporary fool wants to know other things than the fool of yore who wondered mainly about wealth and love. The contemporary fool wants to know whether people with cancer will be frozen alive until a cure has been perfected or whether he will inhabit the moon. Contrary to what the fool thinks, the experienced futurologist does not find such questions hard to answer.

The fool also likes his predictions big, radical, exciting. The experienced futurologist thus tells the fool of the incredible progress he will make, flashing fantastic technological images upon the latter's mental screen. That, at least until recently, was the futurologist's principal stock in trade. Now, however, he also sends shivers down the fool's spine by conjuring up untold and entirely novel disasters that may yet be the price the fool will have to pay for his progress. The prophet threatens the fool that if he continues with his foolishness and persists in his slothful ways, he will be deprived of what even the cavemen had in abundance, such as fresh water and air, and the fool feels that he is already suffocating. In fact, the contemporary prophet is now pretty adept at tormenting the faithful fool with gruesome imagery: satanic urban blight over what will be a single rotting megalopolis from Brooklyn to Santa Monica, poisonous food in every pizzeria, traffic jams from which many may never return, the death of the oceans, standing room only in a world that is one gigantic fume-filled subway car in rush hour, and still more (almost audible) population explosions. Where the projection of a technological miracle world was until recently the futurologist's Sunday punch, the capstone of his far-flung intellectual enterprises now appears to be disasterology. And the fool, though he shakes in his boots, is satisfied; a first-class apocalyptic vision can be more stimulating and liberating than a dull day at the office. In fact, it can vie as escapism with any vision of Paradise. But on balance the more dire predictions engender great anxiety in the heart of the fool, who loves to drive in his car with the 300-horsepower engine but fears death from the emissions. And he begs for more forecasts from the master.

One group of people who have reaped an unexpected windfall from all this forecasting (other than the forecasters themselves who saw their trade flourish beyond their wildest expectations) are the politicians. Politicians thrive on issues, and issues are not easy to manufacture. The greatest danger facing a politician is that he might bore people, and historically he often has. But today's futurologist has prepared much of the ground for the politician, he has created and formulated the issues, and the fool watching the speech on TV is already very hot under the collar about ecology, race relations, limited war. The politician has only to pick up any one or several of these burning issues, and the fool is fully engaged. The politician owes this largely to the futurologist, and the futurologist is well aware of this.

The futurologist is similar to the prophet of old in that he has his own vocabulary, of which he is extremely proud and of which the fool stands in reverence. His whole "scientific terminology," his "methodologies," his scenarios, parameters, paradigms, extrapolations, regression analyses, his multicolored charts and graphs, his "models" of futures, future futures, future wars, future worlds, fascinate the fool and are heady wine as well for the prophet himself, who intoxicates himself and his fellow prophets with them. This terminology is the prophet's equivalent of the sorcerer's abracadabra, of the medieval Latin that the clergymen and medicine men of that era used as status symbol and device to extort admiration and even submission from the fool, who could neither speak nor understand it. Except, of course, that the contemporary futurologist's semantic paraphernalia are infinitely more modern and involved.

The futurologist is in many ways similar to the quack known throughout history. This does not mean that the modern quack is a mere swindler—far from it. To varying degrees the quack always believes his own creations, but to a considerable degree he does not (the fool would be astonished to know to what degree). But mostly the quack does believe in his methods and results, and in fact trains new generations at universities to become quacks in his image. The futurologist, actually the social scientist, has largely taken over the role of quack in our age. As such he is both seducer and seduced, just as the propagandist, with whom he is so often allied, is almost always a propagandee as well.

One important difference between the futurologist and the old-time quack is that the modern futurologist is organized. The old-time quack tended to be more of a loner. Of course, he also clustered around universities in the Middle Ages, and Erasmus of Rotterdam's biting little book *In Praise of Folly,* written in 1511, shows us how closely connected quackery and university were even then. But the contemporary futurologist has his work really organized, thanks to better communications, more money, the greater popular interest in the future, the widespread absence of religion, and the by now ingrained belief that the future can be constructed with charts and computers. The contemporary futurologist has well-advertised organizations that grind out floods of words and figures, usually signifying nothing as far as life in this country or the world is concerned. Yet the foundations pay him and so does the government and so, indirectly, does the fool, who is fascinated by the whole process. Futurology has thus become a *racket* (a strange yet telling word that describes so many contemporary activities so well).

To think hard about the future, to spend time and effort and money thinking about and preparing for the future, is of course a legitimate concern, and in fact most people engage in it almost constantly in their personal lives and in their professions. But the futurologist qua futurologist, as a person with his own separate craft—organized and institutionalized scientific forecasting—is essentially a fellow who knows how to obtain large sums of money in return for which he says much but offers little that is useful and much that is not and that may actually be harmful. His predictions, whether he is a technologist, a Kremlinologist, a military strategist, a social scientist, have so far all tended to be wrong: he cannot point with pride to a single important prediction that he has ever made.

It is important at this point to distinguish clearly between discoveries and predictions. Physical scientists have made many important discoveries, but futurologists are in the prediction business—their domain is the future, which they can no more know than anyone else. For what the futurologist either does not know or fails to say, and what the fool, in his eagerness to be royally entertained with the things to come, conveniently overlooks, is that the future is unpredictable. This is not because of the limitation of the human mind or the inadequacy of the scientific tools used to predict the future or build a reliable model of it, but because the future simply does not exist. Many people seem not to believe that. When they listen to the gypsy woman or the futurologist, they give evidence of their belief that the future is somehow predetermined. The trick, they think, is to know it. But the future is not predetermined. It does not exist. It *isn't.* It *will be*—the result of the interplay of forces whose outcome is unpredictable.

Some predictions can, of course, be made with confidence. If you step into the ring with Joe Frazier, I predict he will beat you. But that is not a very interesting prediction because what I forecast, though very likely to occur, is obvious. There is a law that works to the detriment of the futurologist: Anything that is relatively easy or safe to predict tends to be obvious or trivial, while anything that is neither obvious nor trivial is impossible to predict. In other words, what we would like to know most we can least predict. In the real world there are always too many forces, and their strength and dynamism and growth or ebb create so many variables—a favorite term of the futurologists—that the outcome in all important areas of life simply is "in doubt." For that reason alone we cannot know what will happen. Some people will disagree and insist that the future, though perhaps unknowable, is "there," in the sense that it has been preset by God or the Devil or Fate or Something: it is already "in the cards" that you or I must die on a certain day and therefore, perhaps, ways can be found reliably to foresee things. But I do not think so.

The clever futurologist occasionally warns the fool that the future really is unknowable. Such veteran prophets as Herman Kahn and Anthony Wiener even have said, "Nothing would be more surprising than a future that brings no surprises." But the fool tends to give the futurologists even more credit than they claim for themselves. Apparently the fool imagines that, say, the year 2000 somehow already exists, that he or his son are destined to copter from some point to another in a spacesuit, that he will or will not be able to recycle his mother-in-law or to dial-a-vote, and that the curtain needs only to be drawn for all to see it; the train of life is running along iron rails, and all we need is a telescope fine enough to see what is ahead. The futurologist on the whole does not disabuse the fool of this notion—in fact, he seems to share it.

But what does the futurologist predict? First of all, he predicts "progress." Like the medieval quack who predicted that the patient would get well or the religious quack who promises the fool that he will go to heaven, the futurologist foresees nothing but progress, except as already stated: of late he also sees some dangers. And the futurologist, perhaps to please and attract the fool, perhaps for reasons of personal inclination, anticipates such progress primarily in the physical or technological realm. As Alvin Toffler (a comparatively white sheep among futurologists) puts it well in *Future Shock*: "Much has been written about the future, yet, for the most part, books about the world to come have a harsh metallic sound." [1] True. One reason for this is that it is easy to prattle about automated sidewalks, rocket travel, towns on the moon, or a relaxing game of pinochle ten thousand leagues under the sea. To some extent such expectations may even be realized: the self-sealing tire and the self-cleaning stove (though they would have been considered impossible by most people fifty years ago) do exist. For all we know we may soon all be living, technologically, in clover. But that is not very interesting, nor is it certain. We may technologically regress too. Just as today's warmakers have exchanged nuclear weapons for rifle and knife, and just as some exasperated motorists have reverted to being pedestrians or bicyclists, the society of the year 2000 may not be all that progressed technologically. But it will surely be very different sociologically, to use a silly term for the style of life that will prevail.

Much futurology, of course, deals with what it revealingly calls "software"—that is, human beings. But even here it tends to run in strangely ahuman channels. For example, a great many futurological inquiries are economic, reflecting the unfortunate rise of economists over the past quarter century into positions of strong influence in all areas of life. The economists, who despite their professed dislike of Communism are also essentially statisticians with a strong materialist and collectivist orientation, seem to see the entire human race as an appendage to various GNPs, the Gross National Product of Nations. The GNP is their lodestar and stabilizing fin, and around it they spin their futurological lore; but the GNP is only a meaningless figment of their sliderules. Yet to the contemporary economist, the human individual seems to have no mission on earth but to contribute his ridiculously insignificant bit to the GNP.

GNPs aside, the futurologist and the fool love *figures.* Futurology's infatuation with abundant figures is to some extent the outcome of our longtime domestic propaganda that figures are facts, that they reflect precision, knowledge, objectivity. Most of us apparently fail to see that excessive reliance on figures simply reflects a deep-seated fear of and aversion to human life with all its imponderables and imprecisions. It also reflects a discounting of personal views, judgments, and impressions that ultimately come into play in any event; for it is always personal judgment that determines which facts and figures will be used. Finally, excessive reliance on figures reflects disrespect for the individual. The economist-futurologist, like his shadow the social planner, see only categories of people—such as workers, farmers, students, drug addicts, good guys, bad guys, at home and abroad—that can and must be manipulated; they never see the individual persons.

The futurologist is above all a chartist, a trendist. He "identifies" trends that can be expressed in *figures* (and are for that reason alone not likely to be humankind's outstanding traits or concerns), examines types and rates of development in technology, medicine, communications; and extrapolates from all the variables (independent, dependent, intervening) a "model" of things to come. He builds into this model only what he considers relevant, and, despite the computer, there is a very serious limit on how many factors can be built into his equations. He then animates his construct with his assumptions as to what might develop and "tests" this against his model, which, unbeknown to the fool, is itself merely a figment of the futurologist's imagination.

Believing that life can be expressed in figures, the fool therefore is also convinced that the computer "knows" more than the man, because the computer can calculate more quickly and correlate more data than the human brain. Naturally, the computer can predict how many cars there will be in America in 1989 if it has been programmed with information on car production, sales, registrations, population figures, economic factors, and so on. If one pushes the button, the computer will then say: 99,875,783 cars. But this is still an entirely arbitrary figure, for wars, depressions, or some new inventions can make such figures much too high; or other new inventions, prosperity, and a rise in population can make the figure much too low. The computer no more "knows" how many cars there will be in 1999 than does any man. And about the things that matter most—what the quality of life will be, how people will work and live and love and interact; the things, in other words, that cannot be expressed in figures no matter how most behaviorists or psychometricians insist that all life can be forced upon the Procrustean bed of figures—the computer can tell us nothing at all.

The computer has given us merely the ability to make much more complicated calculations much more quickly. These calculations can help lead to new knowledge in many areas, though not of the future. And even that new knowledge still has to be produced by a person, and as always can be knowledge only of the causes or nature of some phenomenon, or knowledge of how to *do* something like sending a rocket to the moon. It can never be knowledge of the future. Probability figures that the computer puts out are based on what man puts in. If man puts in nonsense, the computer prints out nonsense; this is known to all computer users as the "G.I. in–G.I. out principle"—Garbage In, Garbage Out. But no matter what we feed into the computer, the computer still cannot tell the future. Much though the fool balks at this, the computer knows nothing about the future. Absolutely nothing. The computer only knows, like a fantastic superpupil, all it ever has been told, and it can keep it all in mind at the same time so that it cannot contradict itself. But it cannot think. And even if it could, it still could no more foretell the future than man, who does have the ability to think.

The futurologist, like most stockbrokers, is a chart-maker and -watcher, an extrapolator of trends. But trends are reliable indicators only of the past; at any given moment they may change rate or direction or reverse themselves. If General Motors sold at 80 the day before yesterday and at 81 yesterday and is selling at 82 today, we know nothing about what it will sell at tomorrow. Stockbrokers or futurologists, the fool is convinced that both have "inside knowledge," that the stockbroker already knows at least roughly what a certain security will sell at a month from now, and that the futurologist already knows what type of vehicle he, the fool, will drive ten years from now. Expectations about future motor vehicles are a good example of how predictors are tripped up by important variables that were not around when they made their predictions. Nobody foresaw as little as ten years ago that the ecological variable would some day exercise the greatest pressure on the gasoline engine.

One serious matter that makes the professional futurologist even less trustworthy than he already appears is his bias in favor of *change.* What is there to predict in the whole world except change? To conjure up disaster is just as interesting as to conjure up the Garden of Eden, or a strange new world, as long as it represents change. But there would be little profit or publicity for those reaching the conclusion that by the year 2000 the Soviet and the Chinese systems will still be about the same, or that we still will have roughly the same diseases, or that the cities will be big and dirty but basically unchanged, or that the human race will not populate itself out of existence. What would the fool do with such information? The fool as Malthusian, the fool as space traveler, the fool as cunning strategist, the fool as "one-world" citizen is in paradise. But the same old thing? The fool would be bored. He *wants* change, wants it badly, in fact, for he is not particularly happy with the Great American Dream as he is now living it: the boob before his tube—with his sixpack of Michelob and his two endlessly repair-needy cars in his suburban carport—is bored. Depending on his inclinations, he wants to be told of a world without war—or with plenty of action to keep those Reds in line; of a world replete with gadgets—or pastoral scenes in mid-Manhattan and communal dining at the Caravelle restaurant; or of a world with new mores in which he can have sex with everybody without those time-consuming and exhausting, not to mention expensive, social preliminaries. So the futurologist must foresee *change* in abundance, lest he lose his clients.

But the fool who craves change is not the only source of pressure on the contemporary prophet to forecast such change. If the futurologist did not predict great changes, for the better or the worse, his resources would dry up. To forecast an unmanageable population explosion is better business than to predict a sinking birthrate. Was that why not a single one of our futurologists predicted what has actually come to pass—a decline in the growth of the birthrate in the United States? Earlier predictions of its explosive rise have spawned entire new institutes to study it, attracted many millions of dollars in grants from foundations, furnished millions of words of news and tons of publicity, and made attractive material for thoughtful books and magazine pieces. A birthrate out of control is a hot political issue; it allows—if viewed internationally—the meddling in other nations' business; it commands interesting trips to India and Africa for comparative purposes. It is also infinitely intriguing, grisly, hair-raising.

But a mild *decline* in the birthrate, or any other situation of little or no change? That's blah . . . and the futurologist, always the seasoned grants-man, knows it. Are we accusing him of swindle, of sensationalism? Not totally. But the futurologist is the contemporary quack, and like every quack, he meanders between truth and fiction, cynicism and fervent belief. And he is operating a racket even though he himself thinks highly of it. (Capone is quoted as having said, "What do they want from me? I give the people good beer. I'm really performing a public service.") This is not to suggest that the futurologist is ready to stage a St. Valentine's Day Massacre at the Ford Foundation if other grant-seekers were to muscle in on him. It is only to say that he knows his bread is buttered on the side of predicting change, whether he appears as cornucopian or disasterologist, with the latter specialty now having become his fastest seller.

Futurology is not necessary. It takes no prophet to foretell that those believing in force will be involved in war, or that those who idolize production or consumption will generate pollution and poverty, or that those who live by elitism will intensify racial strife. The future, after all, grows out of current situations and the values to which people adhere. It grows out of the present. Anyone trying to predict the future should thus practice better presentology than do our social scientists. And that is the purpose of this book: to discern what some of the real forces are that now animate society and what some of the real conflicts are, and what their likely outcome. A decisive force has been discerned to be at work—*Woman Power*—that will make fools out of most contemporary futurologists. In many ways the 1980s will not be what the medicine men and their computers say—far from it.

2

THE BOOK—METHOD AND CONTENT

WHAT is this book predicting and what method has been used? Most futurologists and many of their clients have been severely criticized. How will *I* proceed?

This book, first of all, does not look as far ahead as most futurologies do; it looks only at the next decade and thus looks into what one might colloquially, but aptly, call the "foreseeable" future. Not that the foreseeable future cannot be easily misread, and often is. But if one uses a promising method, predictions concerning the near future have at least some chance of being accurate, which makes such forecasts more relevant. Despite all the propaganda on "long-range planning," the next century is just too far away to engage anything except our idle curiosity, for we can know or do very little about it. Finally, it is much more interesting and challenging to consider a society one is likely soon to experience oneself.

But perhaps an even more important difference between these predictions and those of others is that there has been an attempt to do what few forecasters promise and even fewer deliver: to look at the "software," the human situation, the quality of life and human interaction. This cannot be done by counting noses and predicting that the country will have so many inhabitants or so many congresswomen. While such parameters are important, they reveal little by themselves about what life will be like. What *kind* of women will be in Congress? Will people be reasonably happy? Reasonably free? Will they feel reasonably fulfilled? Or will our runaway technology—which the splendid French political philosopher Jacques Ellul warns may come to control rather than serve the human race—really become our master? [1] Will people live even more frantic and anxious lives than they do now, with the new gadgets they probably will have in abundance? Will they be even more misinformed? Superstitious? Hateful? Will they feel more frightened, or less so, by enemies foreign and domestic? Of war? Will they feel more frustrated politically? Will they get along with each other or be bitterly divided into classes, parties, sexes? This is not, in short, an attempt to foretell whether upon arising in the morning (and people will probably still arise, waterbeds or not) the citizens of this nation (and there will probably still be a nation and citizens) will have their clothes electronically (and perhaps centrally) preselected or even painted on, but what kind of a day they will face in terms of actual life.

Not unlike other futurologists (for once!), I will make a search for *change* and an attempt to forecast its shape and dimensions. But other kinds of change will be sought, the findings rarely expressed in figures, and a different method of prediction employed. The attempt will be to look at "life itself," not at its harsh metallic paraphernalia. "Life itself," however, requires some definition. Clearly, those who look, say, at the "multimouse"—the artificial composite of genes bred from more than two parents—also look at "life." This multimouse—of which so far over a thousand have been, shall we say, *manu-factured* and who have in turn produced in natural ways a large offspring of multimice—has made scientists ask whether multiman can be far behind; whether, to return to the beginning of this book, Einsteins or Freuds or Mickey Mantles can be produced at will on the conveyor belt, or, really, whether a multigal or a multiboy can be produced who plays tennis like Althea Gibson, dances like Astaire, thinks like Einstein, and works wonders like Florence Nightingale on the "fully automated battlefield" so joyously predicted by General Westmoreland.

All this may be possible. But it has not been included in the "life" we are looking at, partly because such developments are not foreseen for our target era, that is, the coming decade; partly because these bizarre prospects, despite their irresistible appeal for the "fool" as rather gruesome mental toys, are not the most important matters for our generation to weigh; and partly, finally, because there is no way to predict what the human race will do with such newly acquired capabilities until it is a little clearer which forks in the road, socially, ideologically, ethically, and politically, it will pick for its journey into the future. And that will probably become somewhat more apparent in the next decade. Thus, indirectly, these far-out things are also being dealt with in the sketching out of some of the basic characteristics of that future society that for better or worse will—perhaps, perhaps not—have at its disposal such fantastic new inventions as genetic control.

But it can be said that as far as the emerging human condition in the time beyond that envisioned in this forecast is concerned, when new capabilities may exist that practically unhinge the already quite unstable contemporary mind, all will depend on whether the human race, for the first time in its history, will be able to *deny* itself the use of some of its capabilities. Practically all history has been a story of mankind's inadequate capabilities to fashion a "good life" for more than a few. This was followed by a period of the new technology and the wanton use of all its new capabilities in war and peace, particularly in war. This in turn was followed by a period of some self-denial of capabilities, such as the use of nuclear weapons, though one must suspect only out of fear. A more reliable self-denial of capabilities that will soon be a necessity would be a sign of a new morality (please, esteemed reader, do not cringe) and a higher degree of maturity. Whether or how such maturity might be obtained in the intermediate future is of course at the core of this book, which thus points beyond itself and the time span it contemplates.

The actual method of forecasting will be the one that seems to have greatest merit: to take a fresh and penetrating look at the present; to try to discern the realities that exist; to try to assess the dynamism of the forces that push for change and vie with each other for domination; finally, to express some views as to which of the various forces are likely to prevail over the others. Ninety percent of all good prognosis is good diagnosis. To make a diagnosis of the human situation at any given time requires many personal judgments—the very thing that most futurologists so desperately try to "factor out" with the computer but that can never be factored out as long as human minds select the questions to be asked or the data with which to work. On the basis of a thousand ponderables and a myriad imponderables the social diagnostician and prognosticator must first form some judgment as to which are the really significant forces at work, the ones he must look at. He must constantly assess. If he assesses the weaknesses of the current system and the strength of woman power in one way, he will predict certain things for the United States that he would not predict if he assessed them another way.

One of this book's principal judgments and conclusions concerning the contemporary scene must be stated at this point, though it may seem like putting horse before cart. Of the various forces currently pressing for change, by far the most important and potent is, in my view, the women's movement. Not the Women's Liberation Movement in or by itself, but the aggregate of all women directly or indirectly affected by it, the changing approach by women to our individual and national existence. At this particular time women—all women—are in the process of altering their lives in society, in the family, and in their own consciousness, and thereby are altering society. Women are on the move, and the world will never be the same again. If a recent Hooper Poll showed that only one woman in four supports women's lib and three in four oppose it, four in four are nevertheless obviously somehow involved, somehow affected, must somehow come to terms with the upsurge of women in society. And so, of course, must all men. The most significant "accelerating change" today (and in the coming decade) will be produced by women, not by technology. In a peculiar way, however, and much against the will or expectations of those promoting technology, it seems to be precisely our technology that *sparked* the women's movement—not because technology was so successful in improving our lot on earth, but because it was so unsuccessful.

Technology has promised much but done little. The externals of life have been changed and as a result there are the jet planes, the computers, the bombs, the communications (and in their wake such things as all-pervading propaganda); but life—contrary to most early forecasts—has largely remained the same. In the quality of human life the changes for the *better* wrought by technology have been minor; more significant still, they appear destined to remain minor, at least if no other concomitant social changes occur. In fact, so minor have been the actual and anticipated changes for the better, so small the profit for most of us from unfolding technology, that *this* was probably the principal impetus for the birth of the women's movement. Most women, like most men, never had an easy time in our world; and women, like men, seem to have expected for decades that the new technology, if applied in the accustomed social setting, would automatically make life easier and better, more reasonable and dignified for everybody. But women began to realize at some point that this was by no means the case, that the promise of a better life as a result of more new technology in the unchanged social setting with its unchanged values was a phony one, a piece of superpropaganda, a swindle; and that they had nothing good or even exciting to expect from a further perfection of electronics, cryogenics, emission-free automobiles, laser-beam surgery, or genetic manipulation.

It reflects very favorably indeed on the collective intelligence and instinct and realism of women that they were able and daring enough to look through the impertinent public-relations screen shrouding the dismal current and probable future inability of our accelerating technology to change life for the better. Men generally have not yet understood that; and if they fight the women's movement, it is not just because they try to cling, cynically or not, to their predominant position in society, but because as dominant originators of and participants in the new technology they cling obstinately to the belief that things are on the right track, that technology will solve all problems, that their basic postures and practices (which have created so much physical and social damage throughout history and, if anything, are rapidly accelerating damage today) are the right approaches and will now finally be vindicated and crowned with success. Whether they are your friends at Chase Manhattan or the union leaders or the scientists or the government bureaucrats, they believe they have some mechanized more-than-ever male-dominated and male-operated paradise by the tail and will bring it home, if only they will be allowed to. But women will not allow it. This new insight on the part of women and the dynamic opposition to the actual male world is the most important element in this diagnosis of our time.

How did women come to see through all the error and deception, even though they were bombarded, by men (and some women), with the most intense polyandric propaganda barrage? Just as drug addicts can eventually become too habituated to respond even to increased dosages, women probably finally reached some point of saturation by the organized propaganda unleashed against them to the effect that more automation would bring more happiness. The entire system, and in particular the media, such as women's magazines, kept conjuring up before women's eyes the beautiful, soft, gentle, just, exciting, lovable world of today and tomorrow. The hallmark of that propaganda, containing like all propaganda a hidden threat, was the implication that if your life is not all it is promised to be, it is your fault. You either do not use the right diet, or buy the right cologne, or wear the right clothes, or fail to buy in the right store, or fail to worship with Billy Graham, or simply do not exercise enough; anyway, it's your fault if you are not happy. Society is perfect (American society, of course) or, where it is not, is in the process of improving itself just as fast as possible. If you in the least blame society for anything that ails you, you are therefore a fool. In fact, you are a subversive element.

This type of propaganda, which the psychological warfare specialists call "integration propaganda" (as distinguished from the much more strident but generally less effective "opposition propaganda"), insists that everything is perfect and you are to blame (while opposition propaganda usually insists that you are perfect and everything else is to blame). It is, however, far removed from reality. In reality the fault for your failures is distributed between you and society. This is so evident that America's women must somehow have become overfed with integration propaganda and its central theme, the great future blessings of new technologies. (And the indications are that women in other countries with other ideologies, who are bombarded by the same fervent integration propaganda, are also rebelling.) Another probable reason women no longer buy all the propaganda thrown at them is that they were only limited participants in the scheme of things; and though outsiders may often be slow to see the light, the insiders and powerholders, because of their more active and profitable involvement, are even slower to see it; thus the women began to see it first.

Whatever the reasons may have been, women in America, perhaps already the majority of them, finally dared to look around and say, "No, things are not as advertised. Nor will they ever be —at least not this way." The liberation from old intellectual fetters and baggage is progressing. Women now reject the old integration propaganda in the schools, in the magazines, from their political leaders, or in the movies (the country's greatest integration propaganda mill was once Hollywood); they are sensitized to the message and say, "Wait a minute!" As James Thurber concluded in the moral to his updated version of "Little Red Riding Hood," "It ain't as easy to fool little girls as it used to be." Which, incidentally, turned out to be a better prediction than all futurology of the past thirty years has produced.

Thus, it seems to have been technology, when obviously not fulfilling its major promises and in fact adding immeasurably to death and pain on earth, that really produced, as one of its principal (though unwanted and unexpected) consequences, the awakening of women to some of the radical wrongs in our society and their role in it. This awakening on the part of women to the truth that men were screwing up the works, not only abroad but also at home, not only in man-woman relations but also in race relations, *and* in urban planning, drug addiction, penology, and so on, now can no longer be undone. Regardless of what one may think of some of the plans and intentions of the women who are on the attack, it is crucial that their eyes have been opened, that they seek to bring about fundamental changes in society—that is, in the quality of life—*and that they will.* This is the center of the diagnosis on which this book's prognosis of a great variety of things to come is based.

To return to the different elements of the forecasting method, while a good diagnosis is essential for a good prognosis, it is not enough. If the diagnosis is that little Ernie is as bright as a button on the basis of some IQ test and that he has a flair for the law, the prognosis cannot be made that he will be a brilliant lawyer. In the negative this is different: if he is *not* smart and has *no* flair for the law, it can be predicted with confidence that he is *not* going to be a brilliant lawyer. But whether little Ernie will be the brilliant lawyer if he *is* smart and talented will depend on a great deal more than his basic intellectual qualities: his father's finances, his own character and mental health, the state of the profession, and all those other factors that the statisticians and quantitative analysts call variables. This really is only another way of saying that, to make sense, one's analysis and prediction must be *conditional: if* such and such does (or does not) occur, such and such will (or is at least likely to) happen.

However, to fashion a reasonably interesting or useful prediction, conditions, "ifs," must have some measure of reality. To say that if all the other runners stumble I, the slowest of the lot, will come in first, is not a sensible prediction even though it is conditional. The "ifs" themselves must be grounded in reality, must be real possibilities, otherwise we are only turning in circles and producing tautologies. And again, even in the search for the significant ifs, the significant variables, judgments must be made. In trying to predict the future, everything forces us to examine the present that will spawn it, to try to discover in the present the genes of that future.

If it is true that the essence of all good prognosis is good diagnosis, why is prediction so difficult? Is it not relatively easy to see what is going on right this minute, to see and assess the present? It is by no means easy, of course, and even about the present, as about the future, we can actually only make guesses and form judgments based on a few elements that seem important. Why is it so hard to assess a situation, its basics and its ifs (that is, its potentials)? And why is it so hard for people to agree on what they see? Four principal reasons make the analysis of the present so difficult and controversial.

The first is that observers tend to differ on what is truly revealing about a phenomenon. Technically speaking, one would say they differ as to what are the relevant *indicators.* Some will consider it an indicator of health (and therefore long life—the forecast) if a person's cheeks are a healthy red; others will say this proves nothing; others may consider this an indicator of imminent apoplexy. Some will consider it a significant indicator of strength in a movement if it is animated by a radical doctrine; others will consider this an indicator of weakness. The selection of false indicators leads to a false diagnosis.

The second source of controversy in gauging a situation usually arises over which type of *analogy* a phenomenon deserves. Analogy is a frequent forecasting tool; it forecasts even if the analogist does not mean to forecast. If I look at a mob of angry students breaking windows at a university and say, as does S. I. Hayakawa, President of San Francisco State College, "Just like Hitler's storm troopers," I am making a prediction, for Hitler's storm troopers, after all, took over the country. But Hayakawa's analogy is wrong because Hitler's storm troopers did not battle the German establishment but were paid and supported by it in the battle against Academia. Thus the prediction implicit in the analogy is also wrong.

To draw an analogy with something that occurred earlier is to make at least an *inferred* prediction; the analogist suggests, explicitly or implicitly, that the phenomenon now under observation will come to the same end as the phenomenon he compares it to. If I make an analogy between Columbus' trip to America and Armstrong's trip to the moon, I am predicting that space travel will radically alter and expand the living space of the human race. But that may not be the case at all. Analogies are good forecasting aids only if we pick the right phenomenon for comparison.

A third source of error or controversy affecting a prediction of "outcomes" is the observer's personal persuasions and attitudes. People not only diverge widely in liking or disliking something when looking at the current scene; they also differ widely in what they fear or hope will happen. The optimists see more good apples in the barrel than rotten ones; the pessimists more rotten apples than good ones. Moreover, people are not agreed on which are the good apples and which the bad ones.

The fourth element in misdiagnosing a phenomenon is in

misjudging the surrounding conditions, that "other side of the coin." A person may have looked at the Russian revolutionaries in 1918 and concluded that they were very weak. But the social fabric in which they operated was even weaker. It is often pointed out with wonderment that the Communists, when they took over Russia in 1918, numbered only fifty thousand. They should have been ineffective—and probably would have been, had the political system not been in a state of disintegration and the people *susceptible* to the Communists' appeal or methods. Which, incidentally, is one more warning to the prognosticator to be most careful in basing anything on figures (and therefore the computer). An observer can easily be led astray by judging a new movement, such as the women's movement, by old standards. If a person were to reach the conclusion that the women's movement is weak merely because it is not organized, not homogeneous, nonviolent, nonconspiratorial, and without the other revolutionary accoutrements of past successful revolutionary movements, he might merely misjudge our present times in which a truly revolutionary movement of the old type would surely *not* succeed, while an amorphous movement, such as the women's movement, might succeed all the better.

My prediction that the women's movement will be of decisive influence on our society, that it will have this decisive effect on our society in the coming decade, and that the effect will be highly beneficial for most concerned is precisely based on my diagnosis of our society as a whole, which I regard as highly susceptible to becoming the victim or beneficiary (depending on one's perspective) of the women's movement. For while that society is perfectly capable of mobilizing a million Keystone Kops, tapping every wire and bugging every house in the country, and thus has become able, fifty years too late, to cope with organized and conspiratorial revolution, it may not be able to cope with the women's movement just *because* the latter is unorganized, nonconspiratorial, nonviolent.

Have I looked at the present situation only through my own eyes and with my own method, rejecting all scientific counsel? Almost, but not quite. I have rejected many disciplines that claim to yield insights into present and future worlds, such as economics, econometrics, psychometrics, probabilism, behaviorism.* But I have taken into account the findings of anthropology. Anthropology, the study of the human being, of "man," of anthropos, of *homo* not all that *sapiens,* is one discipline not sidetracked from the outset by the blind prejudices and narrow assumptions of the other disciplines parading as "social science" in our day.†

Anthropology dares—to use that sick and sickening phrase that reflects our desperate desire for something "real"—to "tell it like it is," taking a dispassionate look at human history. It does not share mankind's foolish pretensions, its fatuous protestations, its absurd self-propaganda, its anxious claim to be "Godlike" that often comes into collision with humankind's true nature, thereby creating disaster. Not that the human race has not attained a remarkable degree of civilization—considering the basic ingredients it has to work with—or been able to make much of its good qualities. But it is still skating on very thin ice that is easily melted by passions boiling up from below. And anthropology looks at the origins of the human race and its essentially dismal record, particularly in this century. Anthropology does not agree that people or

* B. F. Skinner, perhaps the country's best-known behaviorist and author of the highly controversial book *Beyond Freedom and Dignity*, must be taken quite seriously mainly because he is a man who entrusts the task of thinking to his own mind rather than to the computer. I tend to share some of his depressing conclusions as to how conditioned the present-day human being really is, and how little aware of this he or she is, mistaking a host of his or her conditioned reflexes for the results of free choice based on individual conscience or other individual motivations. But I do not share Skinner's truly disastrous pessimism as to how the human being must therefore be treated, nor his curious confidence as to how easily the human being can be trained to behave in certain ways.

† There appears to be a great future for anthropology in the coming decade as a field of study and a means for humanity to regain—or gain—at least some measure of insight into itself and, therefore, a measure of sanity.

their leaders are "peace-loving" here, there, or anywhere; or that they are predominantly good, or civilized, or well-meaning, or honest, or capable of speaking or understanding the truth. It does not believe, as even our common language does, that to be "human" means to be generous, lenient, forgiving, understanding. Yet it does not believe, on the other hand, as do Christian religionists, that we are all "sinners." Anthropology has no such strange prejudices. Nor does it have, like some social critics, contempt for the human race.

Anthropology merely looks, without adulation or aversion, at the "Naked Ape," at its past history, its physical and mental attributes, its efforts and failures. It does not laugh at the haughty or romantic assertions and assumptions on which the average American's—but also the average Russian's or Brazilian's—creed is based; it disregards them as pure fantasy. It is neither angry with nor proud of the human race. It sees *aggression* as the most colossal danger and impediment to the good life in our day—not Russian or Chinese or North Vietnamese or Communist aggression against that sweet and innocent angel of our time, the democratic citizen, but *male* aggression, plain, atavistic male aggression, driven partly underground, but rendered only more virulent as a result. That view seems to make sense. Anthropology can help produce the realistic diagnosis that can in turn lead to a realistic prognosis.

Some anthropologists, looking at the human race as a whole, have reached some interesting conclusions and suggest that the unreconstructed male aggression rampant in our society, so obsolete in contemporary life and therefore so destructive, must and can be curbed only by women's taking a much bigger part in human affairs; that women can and must come to the rescue of our sick society. These anthropologists feel that unless women do come to the rescue, the human animal will become more and more the victim of the problems it has created and which will remain insoluble if solutions are attempted with the same basic postures and methods that have created them in the first place.[2] This seems a sensible and realistic diagnosis.

A considerable number of people, mainly young women but others as well, were interviewed on the subjects with which this book deals.* The reader will find that the conclusions in this book are, on balance, more optimistic than the interviews appear to warrant. The reason is that the interviews were only one source; more important, it was precisely the spirit of serious effort and concern they reflected that provided a basis for optimism.

There will occasionally be discussion of the possibility of a backlash that might end the rise of woman power and lead to a general repression of it and of progressive developments in general. Will such a backlash occur? Is this a hedging of bets? A fear of commitment? A retraction of what is predicted elsewhere?

As stated earlier, any sensible and responsible prediction must be conditional, for no one has the gift of prophecy. There are always forks in the road. To deny that, as so many futurologists do, is precisely the reason most of them fail.

There are formidable forces that would like nothing better than to ride the wave of a violent backlash. Unless this danger is constantly kept in mind and acted on by those trying to carry social developments forward, these forces will grow stronger. But even then they are not likely to win out; and because the danger of backlash is likely to be kept very much in mind by women active on the social and political scene, it is doubly unlikely to occur. It thus does *not* seem likely to come about and devour us all. The cloud is there, but it can be predicted, on the basis of all the factors considered, that there will be no deluge. Woman power, among many other good things, will also turn out to be good backlash insurance.

* Interviewees are quoted briefly throughout the text, and longer excerpts from several interviews can be found in the Appendix (pp. 263–352).

3

MAN IN THE PRESSURE COOKER

How can the American male stand it for another minute? Why does he not finally wipe that insipid smile off his face, rip that "Have a Nice Day" sticker from the bumper of his car, throw all the "reading matter" on his desk into the fire, tell all his bosses or customers to shove it once and for all, and stomp out from behind that desk at which he has sat longer than even a chimpanzee could ever be trained to sit? Whether he is a jobholder, executive, dentist, subway conductor, truck driver, publisher—how can he stand it? Is it the money? Of course, but it is something else: he has sold himself a remarkable bill of goods. He never counts his unblessings, as any man should, never faces them; for the purveyors of integration propaganda all around him have warned him that he must count only his blessings. So he never permits himself to realize how ludicrously the dice are loaded against him: even if he were to shoot craps with Meyer Lansky, his chances of coming out ahead would be better than they are in the life game he plays any day of the week. He keeps going mainly because he has learned the disastrous habit of drawing up balance sheets that omit liabilities.

Wildly accelerating technology has brought many frustrations, problems, irritations, and dangers to most people. But it does not seem to be understood that man has on the whole been hit far harder than woman. The reason is that what has been man's traditional habitat—the world of physical exertion, physical labors, physical accomplishments—has changed much more than woman's. Whether man was intended by God or genetics to toil hard and creatively or whether he merely conditioned himself that way over the millennia, man worked with his body, by the "sweat of the brow," hunting or warring or exploring, but also shoemaking, tailoring, carpentering. All these channels for man's exertions, aggressions, sublimations, satisfactions—indeed physical and mental hygiene—have been taken away from him. Ironically, now only the rich can afford to make furniture in the basements of their villas, or ride horses, or prune their fruit trees. With all his restless physical vigor and creative hands, man has no place to go. He can work off his physical energies in sports, after a fashion, but the emotional and economic limitations on that meager substitute are obvious. Moreover, man's enforced physical passivity has been further increased by his becoming a sports fan rather than a sportsman, by his sitting in front of the TV set that forces upon him a suffocating physical immobility.

Women, on the other hand, still have many more of the ancient outlets for their innate or acquired true capacities, such as bearing and raising children and doing the myriad household activities today regarded as "shitwork" by many (but not all) women. But while the women chafe under the continuation of much of their traditional world, man's traditional world has literally come to an end. The women's movement argues that this is precisely what reveals the enslavement and archaic situation of women in our society; that for women nothing basic has changed despite the runaway technology; that women have not been allowed to make as much progress as men. The true state of affairs seems to be, however, that whereas women have not reaped the (possible or at least expected) advantages of technology, men have paid a terrific price for that technology, having been deprived of innumerable sources of satisfaction, pride, or feelings of inner security and channels of personal creativity. They even have lost, by losing opportunities for creative physical labor, their chance of expressing their individuality, of maintaining their intellectual independence. Modern man's greatest physical exertion seems to be to move his lips and say "yes, sir" in one of the thousand disguises he has found in which to shroud these disagreeable words.

Lacking physical activities, man has become both tense and physically debilitated and therefore more belligerent than ever. The old soldier of yore, and the knight too, could at least enjoy a little relaxation between battles, and the farmer or cabinetmaker could pleasantly rest his weary bones at day's or week's end. But the modern bureaucrat in government or industry fights some paper battle with an—even to himself—insufferable nervous tension, seven days a week throughout his life, from his big or small office. He is under terrible pressure, not only from without, as shall be seen shortly, but from within as well. He is in the pressure cooker, but he is also an individual delayed-action bomb for all the stored-up emotions without outlet within his modern soul. As a result, though he must comport himself like a choirboy most of the time, he seethes with aggression. And his vocabulary reflects the fact that he regards aggression as the *summum bonum*: "tough," "shrewd," "hardheaded."*

Modern technology has not only robbed man of all the tranquilizing satisfactions of using his body and physical skills in his work, depriving him of that pleasant fatigue that comes in the wake of purposeful physical exertion. (This is not an attempt to glamorize the past: man being man always did his best to exploit

* It is interesting that "hardheaded" has now been superseded by "hard-nosed," perhaps in an unconscious attempt to eliminate the mind altogether and create the image of a brute animal pushing relentlessly ahead without rhyme or reason, just for the sake of pushing, crushing, destroying, attacking.

his fellow man mercilessly and forced him to work until he dropped. That does not preclude, however, that those fortunate enough to be able to work sensibly derived many benefits from their physical labors.) Modern technology has also forced man into a little room where he must sit all day, or into a factory where he must stand all day, while on his way to and from work he must sit or stand again, in cars, subways, or buses, immobilized inside a frequently immobilized vehicle, his nervous tension mounting in the face of all this physical paralysis. Too much has already been said about how unnatural in every respect, how unhealthy and maddening, the ordinary man's life style is in the technological age. But it has perhaps not been pointed out that no matter how unnatural and exhausting some of *women's* activities also have become, such as forever chauffeuring the kids, man's activities in our day are still much less suited to the needs of his body and soul than woman's are to hers. And man's satisfactions in his work are far fewer. The "housewife," hard and unjust though her fate may be in many ways, and ungrateful and domineering though her "male chauvinist pig" husband may be, at least does things that really need doing; she works to some extent for herself, her children. The man works for his boss, or his organization, or his clients, and even if he is an "independent" merchant or professional man, he works for a variety of hidden bosses, all of whom oppress him *and* are ready to drop him at any time. And the outstanding and disconcerting effect of the frenzied competition in our society is that no man is really necessary; on the contrary, should he vanish today, the gap would be closed immediately. Every man, no matter on what level, is essentially superfluous, expendable, and his awareness of this tends to destroy his self-esteem and add to his insecurity and frustration. In addition, he must labor under the most abnormal psychological conditions. The American family, as women claim, may be maddeningly patriarchal, but all business, including all bureaucracy, is much more so. The employee has a filial, subordinate relationship to his boss, requiring unconditional and blind obedience, even if he is a senior vice-president of a major corporation. A hundred million American men are thus reduced to the status of physically caged, disenfranchised neuters. But so grim is their fate that they internalize all these calamities and necessities until they convince themselves that they are free. Free! Small wonder they are on the whole an aggressive, repressive, and falsely smiling lot by way of compensation.

There is generally no way in which man can get close to the result of his work. Contrary to woman, he deals with maddening abstractions. For a thousand years, throughout the Middle Ages, artisans, architects, artists, and others would affix their proud "*fecit*" and name to their work; "he had made" this, fashioned that. The consequence of the impersonal nature of work in the technological-bureaucratic age is that most men in our society—except for a tiny minority—are incapable of producing anything except *money*, and never enough of that. As a result, they have become chronically harassed, depressed human beings. The abstractness of their labors has also robbed them, not only of the ability to express their individuality, but also of their financial security: their work can just as easily be done by someone else; all men on the same level are now interchangeable and therefore expendable. Perhaps *that* makes them so unattractive, and perhaps that unattractiveness has doubly moved women no longer to serve them. Man has become a Milquetoast though he may be seething with rage or dreams of glory; for that reason alone he deserves to do the dishes.

Of course he can make money—can't he? The system seems to permit it. But as though guided by an invisible hand, the system also seems to work in such a fashion that unless he is one of the chosen few who have inherited wealth or are endowed with that ultrarare capacity for being able to acquire money in large quantities, he never has what he needs. In some mysterious fashion his most basic needs, even if he compromises his true tastes, eat up all and more than he can make throughout his life. And throughout life he is the victim of chronic inflation, that Siamese twin of technology. (To be sure, our society's perpetual warmaking and arms-building also contribute to inflation, but perhaps not as much as runaway technology.) Finally, there are the taxes, which also prevent him from attaining any level of security.

Man must also suffer pressures from having to curb his natural aggressiveness in almost all situations. Engaged in a constant life-and-death struggle with all his competitors and "colleagues," he must smile at everybody, have lunch with those who wish to knife him (or whom he wishes to knife), be "cool" in all situations. He is supposed never to blow up, argue, complain. If he does, he is immediately tagged by icy little men from the personnel office as a fellow with a personality problem; if he complains about the system, he is counted disloyal, if not to the country, at least to the company, or boss, or group. So strong are the pressures on him all day that when he gets home at night, he is literally in shock, not future shock, but culture shock, the victim of the contemporary way of life. He then either drinks too much, or complains about the day, or is impotent, or all three, and his wife does not like it.

As for money, the word alone enrages him. He never has enough. Does he overspend? For years he has been accused by superficial social observers of wasting money in order to keep up with the Joneses. But on any of the thousand existing social levels in our not all that democratic society he must keep up to a certain extent, for the Joneses and many others demand it of him in many subtle ways. And he really does need the things he buys, even if the Joneses need and buy them too. Contemporary man is not really a wastrel at all; rather, he is quite poor, a fact he cannot accept for himself or his society, which, as John Kenneth Galbraith assures him, is "affluent." But money has always troubled him, and the psychic tortures deriving from it have recently been multiplied by easy credit. Finally, with no lodestar for his imagination except the living of the American Dream, he must acquire at least the basic symbols of that dream—that is, he must keep up, not only with the Joneses, but with his self-image, or else go to pieces. Thus he generates great pressures on himself. A Gallup Poll found, ten years ago, that people with an annual income range of $5000 to $50,000, when asked how much they would need to live comfortably, almost all gave the same answer: about 10 per cent more. This indicates that in our society a spiral type of pressure is at work, constantly pushing people on all levels into new realms of financial insufficiency.

Increasingly the bureaucracy or corporation helps man defray the most disastrous expenses should they occur. Fringe benefits are often impressive. Bills to doctors and hospitals that he would never be able to pay are paid for him, and so are his life insurance and retirement fund premiums. He has fought for those benefits. But he has also sold a big piece of his soul for them: like a little boy by his family, he must now be taken care of by the machine if something really bad happens to him, which makes him all the more dependent on the patriarchy and ever less of a "real" man. It also chains him to his place of work as the company town once did.

Yet perhaps the American male's greatest curse, which of necessity he sees as his greatest blessing, is that he has *a job and a boss.* Most men are employees for most of their lives—that is, slaves to others who judge a man's work by their standards, not the jobholder's. No matter on what level he works, he is told what to do and he does it, and there is no recourse against others' judgment of his performance. On the slightly higher levels he is, moreover, hopelessly involved in the sterile but deadly "game" of all-against-all that is rampant in most organizations, a game he is forced to play at every step; and he must burrow upward blindly, like a mole, if he is not to be pushed down.

To do this effectively, he must, curiously enough, be simultaneously self-centered and self-abnegating, often to the point of emotional self-destruction. Whether he is Indian or Chief (and in the colossal hierarchies of which our society consists most Chiefs are also Indians), he must be absolutely loyal to his boss and his group, participate in their futile battles, and place his identity entirely at their disposal, like a soldier. He may be permitted—as long as the boss has not yet made his own decision—to argue vigorously at some meeting for or against the production of a shorter kind of pencil, but that does not obscure the fact that he must surrender, indeed extinguish his identity. If he did not extinguish it, it would not just trip him up eventually in his job; it would actually suffocate him. Whether he likes it or not, he is a member of a tribe with ancient unconscious urges that, as Antony Jay said in *Corporation Man*, "appear ill suited to the demands of the day." [1] But the physical and emotional pressures of the job, the emasculating aspects of almost any job, are not exhausted by that. In every respect the jobholder is a man under intolerable pressure, no matter how little he accomplishes or how unproductive his work. In fact, the less he accomplishes, the greater the pressure.

Our man, our jobholder, must also be a *concerned citizen,* he must care deeply about the "issues," such as pollution, the death of the oceans, Operation Headstart, day-care centers, the population explosion, traffic congestion, the penal system, and so on. These things tend to bear down on him rather than be in the least under his control. Though he is in no position to do anything about any of them, these issues are screamed at him by self-seeking individuals (or abrasive zealots) via all the media, and he feels like a clod if he does not keep up, participate, help, sacrifice. He is plagued by smog, not just physically, but also by the silent accusation smog represents to him, the citizen of the democracy, the man who is responsible for his own surroundings, the person who feels he must do something about it.

Since World War II especially, the American man has been condemned to be an active and passive *culture person.* His woman will turn on Brahms at the very moment he has something quite different on his mind, or even launch into a lively conversation about that incomparable composer. He must go to museums, attend music festivals, read Genet or Camus, view surrealist art, dig Lichtenstein and Rothko, and attend extension courses on art appreciation where schoolteachers demand of him that he immerse himself in a sculpture by Praxiteles. He must not only drink fine wines but know them by vintage and even be able to order them in the face of sneering headwaiters who expect him to mispronounce Château d'Estournel or Schloss Vollrad's Spaetlese (and he does misprounce them). He is expected to dress according to the latest fashion, learn dozens of new words and notions, see esoteric films by Bergman and discourse fluently about them. This new culture wave imposes great burdens on him, and deprives him, besides, of former welcome sources of relief and relaxation: no more Laurel and Hardy or Buster Keaton or John Wayne for him. He must bear all this culture without grinning, even occasionally.

No matter how great the pressures on him, as an American he has the heavy duty, the social obligation, to be *happy.* Americans are happy, they laugh all the time. The "famous Eisenhower laugh," a mile wide, graced a million front pages for eight years, much to the surprise and even consternation of the rest of the world. In photographs most American statesmen, when not disporting themselves grimfaced in response to some crisis they have just created, are laughing out loud, mouths wide open, presumably because they are happy. In social behavior the show of happiness, fortunately, has abated somewhat: people no longer slap each other on the back quite as much as they did in the 1930s, or shout, when asked how they are, that they "couldn't be better"—an idiotic reply, not utterable in any other language. Still, the pressure to be happy, to have a happy romance, a happy marriage, a happy family relationship, and, conversely, the shame of not being happy, gnaws at many a man's vitals, often secretly.

Another terrible source of pressure on the contemporary American man is the need to be *well informed,* not just about the world, but about his own business. Yet so fantastic is the modern information hydra, so formidable the flood of "literature" raining down upon his head, that no man can master it even in his own field. The computer, of course, can store a great deal of that information, but that is not the same as carrying it in one's head. The pressure of absorbing what needs to be absorbed in order to follow one's profession well is prodigious. And the pressure to read all the drivel in *Time* and *Newsweek*, to live up to the image and self-image of the "well-informed citizen," is no less appalling.

Yet another source of pressure on the contemporary American male is his *sexual frustration*. It is not easy to say why he is continually in a state of red alert, often in such curious contrast to his general exhaustion and debilitation. But sex does pressure him mercilessly, and unless he is very young or very rich or as irresistible as Charles Manson, there is little relief from that pressure. And wherever he goes there is a copy of *Playboy*, which stimulates him further by showing him pretty girls undressed and suggests to him that he does not live right, that he is wasting his time, that he is not with it, that he ought to get in on the action. *Playboy* pressures him to participate; it wants him at the very least to buy *Playboy* cufflinks, from which purchase on, it is suggested to him, there is no way of telling how far or fast his own metamorphosis into practicing hedonist will proceed. But alas, the metamorphosis may fail to occur altogether.

Not only is his job *unstable,* which is one major source of pressure on the contemporary male, but so is his place of habitation. Contemporary man moves frequently, which is the source of great wear and tear, not just on his property but on himself. In *Future Shock* Alvin Toffler tells us that "of 885,000 listings in the Washington, D.C., telephone book in 1969 over half were different from the year before." [2] Men do not seem to understand how traumatic it is to move from one place to another. Americans think nothing of pulling up stakes and moving across the country for a 10-per cent increase in salary, thereby putting themselves under additional pressure.

As to sickness and death, there is a vicious cycle at work: the American Way of Life is conducive to the worst sicknesses, such as heart disease, high blood pressure, and ulcers; yet when such illness occurs, the victim is left in terrible straits. He may be insured by his corporation, but once he is sick he will have it brought home to him as never before that money is not everything, even if he should have some. Unless he is a millionaire, no doctor will visit him at home. His job will be in jeopardy, his treatment in the hospital bad at $100 a day, his surgeon a hyperactive entrepreneur. And when it comes to dying, things are far worse still. For most men it is hard to live decently; but it is even harder for them to die decently. Yet man is constantly reminded of his nervewracking mortality: no sooner has he settled in front of the TV to view a football game, than the disaster industries, such as insurance companies and now even the cemeteries, break in with their ads, telling him very frankly that he may "predecease" just about everybody.

Great though the pressures exerted on the contemporary American man by the race situation are, the pressures brought to bear on him by his *children* are still more fierce. There has always been conflict, but not the same form of pressure. More will be said later about the conflict between the generations. Here the reader will simply be reminded that fathers, whose authority in modern life is already so thin and shaky, are further seriously challenged by their young. "Men are really exasperated about this," says Jacques Ellul in *The Political Illusion.* "When they were young their elders would not listen to them, now that they are older the youngsters will not listen to them." [3] Instead, the young pressure them mercilessly, and often they must yield to that pressure. It is known that generals and senators, and even defense secretaries have had serious pressure applied to them by their sons and daughters on very important issues. Can anyone imagine that such pressure could have been brought to bear on Secretary of War Stimson or the elder J. P. Morgan? Adult man is indeed besieged in our day, and his realm of certainty and authority is narrowing. And he is saddened and bewildered by the fact that his children as often as not hold all his values—and even him—in contempt as he never did his own parents or their values.

But by far the greatest challenge and pressure directed at contemporary man comes from *women.* So great and all-encompassing is that challenge, in fact, that man does not yet seem to realize its full extent. He probably underestimates how many women are involved. Even more important, he fails to understand the depth of feelings of the militants or the dimensions of the change they are seeking. He thinks, mostly, that they want jobs and, if they get the jobs, the same wages as men. He is scared enough even by that prospect, precisely because he knows that women can perform, not "almost every" job, but *every* job he can. If he ensconces himself behind the argument that women, after all, cannot do jobs requiring heavy physical labor, he is hard pressed to name *any* job that today requires such labor. Man's ingenuity and his technology, after all, have made most jobs, from truck driving to house building to farming, from meat packing to railroading, physically easy. And all the better-paid and more important jobs, from running corporations to launching missiles, require no physical prowess at all. But he senses, of course, that the competition for jobs is only the tip of the iceberg, even if he is not fully aware of what the women's movement is all about. He feels that it is out to deprive him of what he thinks of as his very manhood, even though in reality the women's movement may want only to liberate him too from what is mostly a sham. But he feels the pressure.*

It thus emerges that man is under much greater pressure today

* Paradoxically, while he is pressured generally by the women's movement, he is often pressured by an unliberated wife's excessive mundane demands.

than ever before, from outside and from his own frustrated individuality. Much more than woman, whether or not she likes the contemporary waters in which she swims, man is literally a fish *out* of water. Then, striking "the virile pose" on every occasion for purposes of compensation, he really has no place to go. He cannot release his physical gifts and energies, and his resulting constant agitation and frustration are intensified by the fact that the professions all place a premium on the display of calm serenity and relaxed control—the hardest thing for him to muster under the circumstances.

One wonders how man has been able to keep his sanity under these multitudinous pressures. The answer is that he *hasn't.* Modern man has not retained his sanity. The sophist will cry out at this point that "nobody knows what sanity is." But while *he* may not know it, it is knowable up to a point, regardless of obscurantist "science."

In the 1930s many psychiatrists, disregarding Freud though paying lip service to him, saw sanity mainly as conformity; therefore their key word was "adjustment." A person not adjusted was a person not sane, and therefore he had to be made to adjust happily or at least effectively. It seems never to have occurred to these psychiatrists that absence of individual adjustment can be sanity, just as there can be at least temporary collective insanity in a nation at the very time when everyone is adjusted and in fact the sickest people are the best adjusted. It is all the more remarkable that psychiatrists in the 1930s never acknowledged this, precisely at the time when the entire German nation under Hitler gave unmistakable signs of collective insanity. For what the Nazis did was not merely criminal and barbarous, it was insane—as even most Germans have belatedly recognized. And in the Soviet Union sane men are now being placed in institutions, exactly as George Orwell foresaw it. The Soviets are apparently collectively quite mad.

Similarly, and perhaps almost to the same degree, American

man as a whole may be regarded as having responded with considerable mental derangement to the steadily growing pressures on him.* Indeed, the American male, collectively, reveals all the traits of mental illness: great nervousness, counterproductive activity, chronic haste, excessive verbosity or reticence, violent mood changes, pathological trust in leaders and their doings, many types and varieties of hatred of others, brutality, futility, alcoholism, and endless prevarication. These, after all, *are* symptoms of mental illness. He also displays, collectively, the greatest telltale symptom of mental illness: an inability to get moving, to get things done, to fish or cut bait; instead he lets everything that plagues him accumulate and grow, and tries to wash it away with cascades of promises and resolutions.

The men are paralyzed by their own indecision and the fantastic intricacies of the social and economic machine they have created. They are also immobilized by archaic notions of success and an insatiable appetite for power and prestige. They cannot get out of Vietnam, they cannot replace the gasoline engine (yet cannot make peace with it), they cannot desegregate (yet cannot maintain segregation). They cannot make a dent in the arms race, poverty, pollution, crime, drug addiction. Yet they talk about these things all the time, idly; they listen to the modern barkers—the machine politicians and the machine scientists (the experts)—but do not find solutions.

The men show other symptoms of mental illness: the enormous deviousness and intricateness in all their affairs, with everything from government to business to labor to the churches being something other than what they seem or claim to be; and a universal persecution and hunting mania, expressing itself in compulsive bugging, wiretapping, surveillance. There are other traits of

* This does not mean that American woman is sane; on the whole, though, she appears saner than the male. Ashley Montagu has stated that "Males suffer from hysteria and hysteria-born mental diseases by a ratio of seven to one over females." [4]

collective mental illness as well, but those enumerated should suffice to make the point.

Clearly, the pressures have been too much for man. His only organized response to them has so far been that he sticks obstinately to his guns (quite literally, unfortunately) in order to defend his citadel of disorder and disarray and waste and injustice. His principal though ineffective effort will soon be to keep woman out of the inner sancta of that citadel—out of his hair, so to speak—on the instinctive assumption that once woman really penetrates the façade of his power structures, his power may evaporate. Men are afraid women will see the true nature of the whole madly spinning, yet stalled Rube Goldberg machinery.

Therefore men insist, as never before, not just vis-à-vis women, but vis-à-vis the "masses" (that is, themselves), that nothing much is wrong, that all that is needed to cure whatever does ail us is the same and more of the same, that things are in good shape, that great progress is around the corner, that we are on the road to a technological paradise, that there is "light at the end of the tunnel." Richard Nixon even went so far in one of his speeches as to say that we live in "great" times, but he said it rather furtively and did not press the issue when there was no response (encouragingly so—people are at least still sane enough for that). Yet perhaps we do live in great times, after all, not because of what our leaders do, but because of what is shaping up in our society without their doing, in the form and as a result of the women's movement.

Probably women will from now on put formidable pressure on man's establishment, not with guns and bayonets or conspiracies against which he has learned to defend himself quite effectively, but by other means. He can, perhaps, with the help of many Aunt Toms, launch some male backlash against growing woman power; but he may then also find among his own ranks a great number of "quislings" (that is, feminists) who will neutralize what he will gain with the Aunt Toms. In fact, there already seem to be a good many male quislings in man's ranks. Quite a few men have already come out into the open and publicly embraced a new social attitude by forming and joining men's liberation groups, of which there now seem to be hundreds around the country. *Life* magazine reported on these male groups: "What most members say is perhaps most succinctly expressed by a member of the Berkeley group: 'With women, there is an oppressor. But our enemy isn't women, it's the role we are forced to play. We are oppressed by limitations on our sensuality and compassion.' " *Life* went on: "And others, too, complain about the inhibitions against expressing feelings, the demands of 'compulsive masculinity,' the terrors of the he-man." [5] This shows quite clearly that men—no one knows how many—are tiring of having to live and behave by the antiquated, laughable, and destructive code that not only oppresses them and robs them of avenues of expressing some of their true feelings, but is obviously pernicious for society as well. It is interesting that the above-quoted member of the men's lib group singled out compassion as one of the drives stifled by the contemporary masculine code. On all levels of government, industry, labor, religion, and other organizational pyramids as well, compassion is feared, ridiculed, detested, and suspected more than any other quality. Depending on the level of vulgarity of the apparatchik talking, a man showing the slightest amount of compassion toward friend or foe is labeled either a "bleeding heart" or a "bleeding ass." Compassion, which the world needs most, is regarded as contemptible and shortsighted, as *effeminate* by the "hardnosed." (But the effeminate are usually self-centered, not compassionate.) Compassion is a healthy quality that women are free to express; yet many men also feel it and many more would if they were free to do so.

A female reader of this chapter, when it was still in draft form, took its content to be a plea that men should be forgiven their oppressive ways against women; she thought that the enumeration of all the pressures on contemporary man were intended to explain and condone his ways at home and elsewhere. Nothing could have been further from my mind. The intent was merely to try to analyze modern man's situation in the society as it is, and the conclusion was that man, as a whole, was way off the track, having an increasingly hard time keeping the (male) establishment going and keeping up appearances, and would therefore be a comparatively easy mark for woman power trying to remold the establishment. The female reader also stated that, after all, many men greatly enjoy the tyranny and oppression they are able to exercise over others in the male world. This is undoubtedly true. But that pleasure is generally more than neutralized by the fact that, in the pecking order, the oppressing males are in turn generally oppressed by their superiors, at least nine out of ten. It is my impression that most males—in the pecking order in which all oppress all, and in a society that exercises so many pressures on the male in addition to those directly exercised on him by his job or profession—come out way behind on the balance sheet of oppression inside the male order.

Thus it is likely that man in the pressure cooker will ultimately be forced to submit to the demands of compassion and other "feminine" qualities, in himself and in women, if he is to regain his sanity and improve our society.

4

FEMINIZATION: THE WAVE OF THE FUTURE

THE prediction of this text is that the coming decade will be characterized by *feminization*, by the infusion of the feminine element into our society, in two interconnected ways: by a rapidly growing percentage of women in all professions, positions, jobs, and roles; and by a change in the average male's attitudes, values, views, ambitions, and behavioral patterns in the direction of greater tolerance, placidity, gentleness, understanding, reasonableness, and individual creativity. The word "feminization," like almost all other words in our frenetically verbal society, leads us immediately into the general semantic bog in which most thoughts, once verbalized, become extinguished again: "feminization," not yet in the dictionary, will mean different things to different people.

In a curious book, *The Feminized Male,* Patricia Cayo Sexton[1] develops a theory according to which most of the ills of contemporary society can be traced to the aggression of males who were "feminized"; whose manhood was suppressed in their early years by mothers and schoolmistresses. That the school system in particular, says Mrs. Sexton, is dominated by women teachers places a premium on girl-like behavior in boys; it gives good grades and sends off to the best colleges and the most important careers boys who obey, keep their homework neat and up to date, and do not engage in rough stuff of any kind. The results are not always rewarding.

"Murders are generally committed," says Mrs. Sexton, "by quiet and gentle men, 'nice guys.' Sirhan and Oswald, both reared under the maternal shadow, grew to be quiet, controlled men and dutiful sons. . . . Such an assassin risks no contest. . . . His victim is caught defenseless by the sniper's bullet and is unable to strike any blows in self-defense." Contemplating the emotionally deformed male who turns to aggression, only murderers come to Mrs. Sexton's mind initially; later in the book she refers to the radical rabblerousers in our cities. But one can think of a great many other acts than murder or rabblerousing that are being committed by these "quiet and gentle men, nice guys, quiet, controlled men and dutiful sons," yet with the approval of rather than *against* the wishes of society.

In any event Mrs. Sexton offers the thesis that our current cultural and educational system *feminizes* boys. And she has her own definition of feminization. "Many schools and academies are dehumanizing and unmanly places. Boys who succeed in them do so by grossly violating manly codes of honor and the norms of boy culture." Her theory is that these feminized boys are often boiling inside, and later become a menace to society by assailing it. It seems never to occur to her that such emotionally deficient males may become an even greater menace to society by joining it and then exercising their vicious aggressions, consciously or not, within rather than against the system.

Mrs. Sexton sees the salvation of men, and society, in a return to the he-man. "The decline of college sports," she says sarcastically, "may not herald a total victory for mankind. . . . If sports are replaced by greater stress on sedentary and passive academic work, the masculine quality of our males [*our* males?], already weakened, may collapse." Mrs. Sexton argues for keeping "the stadium" going because "it satisfies many of the boy's needs—the need for heroes, the need to test his strength, to engage in simulated combat, to have something worth doing."

Mrs. Sexton sees the problem as a dichotomy, but it is faulty. Either, she thinks, a boy is feminized by a lot of women and turned into a sissy who then becomes either ineffectual or a dangerous maniac, or he becomes masculinized and thereby attains "the vigor and assertiveness with which a man conducts the affairs of his life" and who needs to "engage in simulated combat" as a boy because that is something "worth doing," presumably because it will help him later to do the unsimulated thing. In a word, Mrs. Sexton is afraid that we are going soft, and advocates rehemanization.

Apparently Mrs. Sexton cannot see that most men in American society are simultaneously *both* undermanly and overmanly, if by "manly" we mean the generally accepted stereotypes. The flat feet, the paunch, the hemorrhoids, the unmanly posture at home and in the office only too often go hand in hand with crude aggression in daily affairs and enthusiastic support of aggressive, destructive, and boisterous national leaders and policies. A man can be both hard and soft, and often is: in fact, most men in our society are hard where they should be soft, soft where they should be hard. They are assertive where they should give in, give in where they should assert themselves. They obey the manly code of honor where it would be better left unobeyed, and violate it where it cries out to be followed.

The first thing to consider is that feminization—a word to which not just any meaning can be given if we respect language—is not the creation of effeminate males or an effeminate society. Effeminate means weak, foppish, unvirile, deformed, deviant. When, however, it is said that feminization of men and society is necessary to avert the greatest dangers and bring life into some harmony with the current state of the world, and when, in fact, it is predicted that such feminization will take place in the coming decade in the United States and much of the Western world, it certainly does not mean that effeminacy will be on the increase or that it could become our salvation. It means, rather, that *feminine qualities* are needed—and should be used—to make life more tolerable, decent, agreeable, sensible, and bring it more into harmony with basic human needs and inclinations. It means that the potential fruits of the growing technology can be reaped, and its dangers curbed, only if a new and different, a feminized, way of looking at life guides the hands at the levers.

To explain what is meant, we must engage in a semantic exercise. Most social critics insist, first of all, that there is no such thing as a "feminine quality." They argue, quite vehemently, that all human qualities can be found in some men *and* some women, which is perfectly true and perfectly irrelevant. They insist that any human quality—intelligence, stupidity, cruelty, kindness, intuition—can be present in man or woman, which no sane person will deny. They clamor that no one knows whether certain qualities or traits are the result of genetics, conditioning, or whatever, and that in different conditions women and men could just as easily have turned out differently, which can be neither proven nor disproven and is also irrelevant. But they deduce, further, that there is no such thing as a male or female trait—and there they are wrong.

The point is that when a term like "feminine quality" is used, it produces a resonance in most people's minds, it *means* something, just as the words "male qualities" or "male traits" mean something, evoke something, communicate something in the context of our present culture. Those who claim that nothing means anything unless it can be defined to their satisfaction—that is, made absolutely precise—are guilty of logocide, which can only lead to intellectual sterility, despair and, if applied to society, political disaster. Most social scientists will not accept the fact that when we deal with what is most important—human beings, human affairs—"scientific" precision ceases and only approximations, linguistic shorthand, near-accuracies, remain as a tool of communication, and a perfectly adequate tool at that. To deny that there are such things as female qualities and male qualities, to deny that these terms serve a purpose in making clear to others what one is talking about, is sophistry worse than the intellectual acrobatics practiced by the medieval theologians, and will surely be laughed about just as much in future centuries.

The sophists are not alone in insisting that there are no identifiable male or female traits. The women's movement, on the whole, insists on the same thing, though for other reasons, part ideological, part strategic. The women who state, rightly, that they are being discriminated against and who insist, rightly, that they want to have the same rights and duties as men, feel their whole enterprise endangered by any distinction between them and males, other than the simple sexual distinction. They do not wish to have even good or positive qualities attributed specifically to them, for that would reopen the door to discriminatory thinking and practices. In that respect the women are much like such oppressed minority groups as blacks, Jews, or Italians. These groups rightly object to being called shiftless or crooked or criminal, but they also object when positive qualities are specifically attributed to them, such as sexual prowess or superior intelligence or fine singing voices. For their entire case rests on the claim that people are people, that everybody is the same in the sense that everybody may have—or lack—any quality, good or bad. "Don't tell me we are blessed with this, that, or the other thing," say the blacks, the Jews, the Italians; "we are just like everybody else. We're all individuals, good ones and bad ones." And so speak many women.

But it isn't quite true. There are some differences among races and between the sexes. Whatever their origins, they are discernible and meaningful. This book's entire line of argument rests on the fact (not the assumption) that there are significant differences between men and women, at least in the world as we find it now, when we look at its present and past; and that only with the growing interaction of male and female qualities—with the world of men and the men in it, becoming more feminized—will people become more "themselves" and will human society finally move into calmer, saner, and more pleasant waters than it has so far sailed. Fortunately, this text does not have to bear the burden of proof that there are differences between male and female traits. The militant women themselves, despite their general reluctance to acknowledge any differences, provide us with the evidence.

"I think," says Gloria Steinem, "all human beings have the same potential for hostility, aggression and violence. But," she continues, "for the next fifty or hundred years women are going to be very valuable in positions of power, because we haven't been brainwashed into thinking our identity depended on violence and controlling others." This is a great sentence, going directly to the heart of the difference between women and men, not the natural difference, perhaps, but as, more importantly, it exists here and now and presumably will continue to exist—though in declining measure—in the "next fifty or a hundred years." For to say that women "haven't been brainwashed into thinking our identity depended on violence and controlling others" is to say that *men have,* which is exactly right; and this is a vast, and vastly important, difference between men and women. There are others as well.

"I'd much prefer," Gloria Steinem continues, "to have Margaret Mead in the White House than Nixon or Johnson. At least she wouldn't be having to prove her masculinity in Indochina." This points again to one of the significant differences between men and women, regardless of its genesis and irrespective of its permanency or transiency. Gloria Steinem regards it specifically as a male need to prove masculinity by making war or at least not losing those man has inexcusably started.* If a woman—Margaret

* This does not mean that Margaret Mead, specifically, should be President of the United States; and Gloria Steinem probably also means this metaphorically.

Mead—were the leader, she would not feel that need; she would act differently, because, as a woman, she is different; different because women and men have different psychological needs. And their psychological needs are different, because while both sexes have been brainwashed, they have been brainwashed differently: the women to accept themselves as inferior creatures, the men to accept themselves as superior creatures and to regard force, used overtly or covertly, as the most effective instrument in any situation. Gloria Steinem's point is that Margaret Mead would act differently in the White House than Nixon or Johnson because, being a woman and as such having motivations different from a man's, she would be *free* to follow other aims and policies.

In another passage in the same interview Gloria Steinem says, "It's not that women are more moral or have natural rhythm or are closer to the earth or any of that, but culturally woman are less violent. They are less likely to feel they have to defeat people in order to prove themselves." Thus she believes, in the words of her interviewer, that "until both sex roles are equalized and humanized women in power would be very healthy for the country." Conversely, she describes men, or at least "too many" of them, as "restricted and dehumanized by foolish ideas of masculinity—masculinity seeming to mean making a lot of money, subjugating other people, beating each other up in bars, shooting small animals, suppressing emotions." This is not a portrait of just any person, male or female; it is meant to be the portrait of a male as distinguished from a female, to point to the generic differences between them. Thus, contrary to those who deny them, Gloria Steinem stresses the differences between contemporary men and women.

She attributes these differences to cultural causes. Others may

---

The passage was quoted mainly in order to demonstrate that its author acknowledges differences in qualities and traits of men and women. As for women like Golda Meir and Indira Gandhi, it could be said that they are not especially representative of their sex and also that their wars require separate analysis.

insist that the differences are more intrinsic, but that does not matter. What is important is that the differences are real, that they are discernible and can serve as the basis for visualizing and describing alternate worlds, that they can provide a "handle" for changing human society. Proceeding from Gloria Steinem's statement that there is a difference between men and women—first of all in the area of self-assertion, in that women, contrary to men, need not "defeat and control people in order to prove themselves"—some other differences will be outlined that can be said, always only *grosso modo,* to distinguish men from women in culturally, socially, and politically significant ways.

1. While women have been brainwashed into accepting certain roles for themselves, they have not been brainwashed, as Gloria Steinem says, into evaluating themselves only by the power they can assert individually or collectively and by the number of scalps they are collecting. In general, they have not been brainwashed, as men have, to jump instinctively to the defense of the (male) establishment whenever it comes—usually for good reason—under attack or is otherwise in danger of suffering or revealing some cracks in its armor. Men are conditioned to dissemble rather than correct, or even try to correct, any flaw in "their" society. Their loyalty tends to be to the machine, and if they have not been sufficiently conditioned to jump automatically to its defense and preservation, that reflex is reinforced by the danger of being fired or otherwise destroyed. Women do not react that way to the fortunes of the (male) establishment mainly because as females they are *outsiders.* The closing of ranks, the raging ire against all who dare even to raise a question, justified or not, is simply not their role, not their conditioned reflex; they have not been conditioned into it, they are not "interested parties" to the same mind-destroying extent. Thus, while the women, being outsiders, actually know much less about the (male) establishment than men, they have a more detached and therefore better view of it, simply because they neither share to the same extent in its spoils nor are

equally subject to its pressures. They cannot be motivated by "My corner of the establishment, right or wrong!" for they are not fully participating, physically or emotionally. That gives them certain advantages vis-à-vis the (male) establishment: they can permit themselves to see and judge it more clearly even if they do not know the workings of its inner mechanism.

2. Women are on the whole less brutal and callous than men. One outstanding trait of our society is its brutality and its callousness, with callousness dominating the scene at the higher levels and brutality dominating the scene further down. The prison guard is brutal, the warden (or the commissioner or the governor) callous. The soldier is brutal; the general is callous. The enforcer is brutal, the don callous. So is the policy-planner, the public-relations front man for business and government, the congressman, the judge. The higher up the man, the more soft-spoken, urbane, civilized, charming—and callous. The lower the man, the coarser, more benighted, uncivilized,—and brutal.

Women have not been conditioned that way, at least not yet, and, it is to be hoped, never will be. If anything, they have been conditioned to be the willing victims of callous and brutal treatment. In the interview Gloria Steinem says that "women have been trained to be masochists." That too makes them *different* from what so many men have been trained to be in the home, school, fraternity, army, everywhere—namely, sadists, or at least callous persons, condoning brutality everywhere, believing in the application of force, subordinating all humane impulses to the requirements of the (male) establishment and their place in it. It is primarily because of this institutionalized brutality and callousness on the part of men that so many needed reforms either never occur or are vitiated as soon as they do. It is the reason a male-made revolution can perhaps succeed in tearing down some structure, but can never succeed in realizing the lofty ideals on its banners. Czarism and Stalinism are the same, not because the Russians are Russians, but because men are men. Women are different.

Man does not mind it that woman is less callous and brutal, as long as she does not try to enter the (male) establishment. If she does, however, he insists that she be a "tough gal" who can fall in with him from the beginning. And many women have, and thus have become pretty tough people themselves. Most women do not understand what men expect from them, under current conditions, as the entrance fee to their male paradise. When men say, as they are wont to, that women can have any job they want, "provided they have the qualifications," they do not mean, as women are wont to think, that the new lady executive in the meat-packing concern must merely have the same facts and figures at her fingertips as her male colleagues, but that she must have the same *spirit,* the same *posture,* the same *value system;* that she must cooperate as smoothly with Mayor Daley as a man does. That, in other words, she really cease to be a woman.

Against this male prerequisite to female participation women have until recently been rather helpless because of the small number of them trying to enter the ranks of men. But the trickle is becoming a stream; and faced with females entering their domain, men will no longer be able to make their own rules as to what type of person the new entries will have to be. Women will be able not just to enter the (male) establishment but to enter it on their terms—that is, remaining women. And that is what will transform all of society for the better: many females will not merely do many more things, but they will be able to remain women doing them, putting their own stamp on them and at the same time on the men with whom they will be competing and cooperating.

3. Women, furthermore, are more compassionate than men. One need not go into the tedious discussion on whether this is so because they are mothers, givers of life, nurturers, more aware of

life's worth and the true nature of pain and suffering. What is important is that they are more compassionate, which is the obverse of being less brutal or callous than men. This compassion, which the world surely needs more than any other quality, not only is rare in the ranks of the (male) establishment on *all* levels, but is generally persecuted by that (male) establishment with great fervor. Compassion tends to be ridiculed, despised, fought. Men who display it tend to be fired, pitied, shunned.

What is meant by "compassion"? It is not simply a certain awareness of the people's needs nor is it passive pity. Compassion gives individual human needs and rights preference over the real or imagined interests of the establishment in case of a conflict between the two. Otherwise, what goes by the name of compassion is just a sop to one's conscience, a personal quirk, a public-relations stunt, a clever political move. Men might argue or misunderstand this point because they have had true compassion driven out of them so thoroughly that they no longer even know what it is. Men, especially young men, actually train themselves constantly in the art of not having compassion, of being "hard," "tough," "shrewd," "hardnosed." They know they cannot afford to be otherwise if they want the rewards of a good job and the satisfaction of their peers' or elders' approval. Of course, not all women are compassionate, and in fact some have done terrible things: the female guards in German concentration camps were notorious for their unbelievable viciousness—but these women were exceptions. In men lack of compassion is the norm.

That is why jails and concentration camps and state insane asylums and refugee centers and armed forces are the way they are: not because money is lacking or trained personnel are unavailable or reforms are slow in coming, but simply because all these things are man's work, and man, being essentially brutal or callous, only pays lip service to reform in order to mollify the "bleeding hearts" he really detests. Prisons (as they are at present) or concentration camps or wars, even if individual women did and do participate in these enterprises, are not likely to be the product of women's minds, women's designs, women's efforts. Women are too compassionate, and once women take their rightful share of power (without having had to become un-women in the process), these horrors are likely to be at least mitigated. More significantly, the aggression now permeating almost any social transaction, almost all activities and relationships in the (male) establishment, is likely to abate.

4. Women are also intellectually much freer than men in contemporary society. The reason is again because they are less brainwashed to act or think exclusively in terms of the defense of the (male) establishment than are the men who consequently are unable to form an independent and original mental picture of society and its true needs. In addition, since World War II, the free male intellects have largely been taken over by the government and the foundations. At any one time, we learn, one third of all professors are on airplanes either going to or leaving Washington. For the (male) establishment this buying-off of the male intellectuals was an excellent move: the thinkers were defused, integrated, pressed into service by the (male) establishment in return for greater financial rewards than they had ever dreamed possible in the previous fifty years and at least a heady whiff of establishment power, though not, as they had hoped, a real share in it. And the seduction of the thinkers was facilitated by the ideological trends of the times toward computerized social sciences that would provide the keys for the control and conditioning and regulation of large populations at home and abroad. Many behaviorists, the economists, the econometricians, the demographers—all the "machine scientists"—got to analyzing and interpreting all of society and trying to hand the (male) establishment the tools to run society as it saw fit. The pipedreams of "pacifying" unruly natives abroad or "fine-tuning" the economy at home based on such science were pernicious, antihuman, totalitarian *1984*-type dreams. In the hands of the operators and politicians the new tools

did not work too well, however, and the labors of the machine scientists in their service produced little but empty words for a quarter of a century.

Women, by contrast, have produced truly impressive work. Books like *The Feminine Mystique* by Betty Friedan or *The Politics of Sex* by Kate Millet, or works by Germaine Greer, Shulamith Firestone, and quite a few others, whatever their weaknesses or biases, are true breakthroughs in social analysis, full of original thought, and have thereby furnished stimulation for all of society about its next steps. Some of the books women have created are monumental contributions to our understanding of humanity that will be long remembered. Men have made few such contributions in a long time. In fact not since Freud, whom the women militants, and largely unjustly, dislike so fiercely, have men made basic contributions to the understanding of society except perhaps for some anthropologists. The contributions of the existentialists probably do not qualify as real breakthroughs and, moreover, are not of recent vintage. The Einsteins and Oppenheimers were great intellects, but they did not work in the area of humanity or human society. The reason for the discrepancy between what men and women have produced in the understanding of society and people today is mainly attributable to their *freer* intelligence (and perhaps to a lesser degree to the extra effort they were impelled to make by their position). Men too might attain or recover their intellectual freedom some day to see the human present more clearly and recognize the emperor's nakedness. But at the moment, chained to the establishment on the one side and to the computer on the other, blinded by methodological superstitions and muzzled by the hands that feed them, they can produce little that is truly original. Women, on the other hand, are free to let their imaginations soar.

Women produced such important and potentially revolutionary work, not just because their intellects were freer, but also because they had finally managed in our century to enter the places of higher learning.* And again, coming in from the outside, and being under less patriarchal pressure than many men, they were able to pick and choose instead of swallowing the proffered "education" whole. What they picked was mainly the chance to acquire a solid knowledge of the past—that is, history (for example, Germaine Greer)—and a rigorous discipline of the mind without which no truly innovative ideas can be conceived or effectively communicated. While male intellectuals were wasting their time and often other people's money, women acquired intellectual skills and produced ideas and works perhaps no less original and important than the works of Copernicus and Galileo.

It is interesting to contemplate, now that women have acquired the intellectual tools and made a big start in the area of intellectual creativity, where their intellectual journeys will take them next. Anaïs Nin has said, "[The psychiatrist] Otto Rank said that we do not really understand the psychology of women [because] women have not yet articulated their experience. Man invented soul, philosophy, religion. Women have perceptions that are difficult to describe, at least in intellectual terms." [3] Men, one might add, have also invented the nation state, political ideologies, social sciences. Liberated women may well produce other and perhaps more useful intellectual results.

5. Are women more realistic than men? That depends on what is in the focus of their attention. As Gloria Steinem points out, to her great merit, though both are brainwashed, men and women are brainwashed on different subjects and in different ways. Therefore, in the areas in which women are less brainwashed—that is, in the concerns and needs of the (male) establishment—women will naturally tend to be more realistic. For that reason they will also not have their minds beclouded by that ultimate

* The fact that fewer women are in universities now than in the 1930's is not in conflict with what is said here about the work of outstanding women.

glue with which, aside from the desire for profit, the (male) establishment is held together: nationalism. Increasingly, nationalism has come into conflict with true love of country and the people in it. Nationalism (not just American nationalism) has become an abstraction, a sort of politicoeconomic priapism, damaging to all, including the nation. Some recent foreign and domestic policies have been veritable orgies in unrealistic abstractions. Women seem more committed to concrete concerns, which is why the more strident tribalism, which immediately makes all sense impossible, is not a typically female trait. Women are less inclined to worship at the shrine of that bitch-goddess (or shall we say that cur-god?).

Women, being more realistic than men, are therefore also more concrete.* Men, partly because of chronic failure to make their technological schemes pay off in terms of happiness, have generally taken recourse to abstraction. Man's legislative activities, his strategic theories, his social schemes are really all vast abstractions—as is even his absolutely demented governmental spending, to the extent that it is not a deliberate and cunning political move by professionals.

Which brings us to one more difference between men and women: as currently conditioned, at least, women are not such *wasters* as men. They are not desperate enough, stumped enough, defeated enough to appropriate a billion dollars for just about anything at all. Perhaps they are more economical because their domestic role has trained them to be. Whatever the reason, they are likely to be more careful of money in government if and when they get their hands on the levers. They will know that an ailing society requires other things more than money.

* There is an old but splendid joke attesting to woman's more concrete concerns. Asked who made the decisions in the family, a woman said: "Well, I make the little decisions." "Such as?" "Such as where we live, what house to buy, what schools the kids go to." "And your husband?" "He makes the big decisions, such as whether we should disarm unilaterally, go to the moon, and so on."

It also is to be suspected that the spending of vast sums, far from being a necessity, is really a masculine perversion. Gloria Steinem thinks men feel they must express their masculinity by making a lot of money. It also seems that, perhaps especially, those who are unable to make it must also express their masculinity by spending it in huge amounts. To authorize the spending of three hundred million dollars for some project by the stroke of a pen is to lord it over ten million pikers, if only for a moment, and is probably a gigantic ejaculation substitute, of which women are not in need. In fact there is a certain male brutality and callousness in current ways of spending government money, which, after all, represents the work of people. A more feminized society will probably husband (*pace* reader!) its resources more carefully and treat the fruit of people's labor more gently.

The women, then, by their valiant intellectual efforts, have produced the true key to the alleviation—not the solution, a silly word in any event—of many crucial problems. That key, whether it is so defined or not, is the *feminization* of society, its penetration by women, and, beyond that, the penetration and the tempering of the male mode of thinking by feminine elements. Only this can alleviate the major problems now facing our society. For what are these problems? War, racial discrimination, sexual inequality, poverty, ecology, drugs. The key to alleviating *all* of them is a change in attitude—a change toward more humaneness, more compassion, less greed, force, roughness, and fear; not the sliderule-produced sets of figures proffered by machine scientists, the social statisticians, and the social planners.

6. Another difference between men and women—and this one like all others is connected with the basic difference that women are less violent—is that women are less inclined to be *gamblers*. Even though large numbers of women go to the racetrack, play bingo, and sit at roulette tables in Monte Carlo and Las Vegas, gambling has always been a predominatly male vice. And in view of the fact that reckless and compulsive gambling, though in dis-

guised form, is often a prime motivator of men in the conduct of foreign affairs, in courting war, in stating their open or concerned ultimata to each other across boundaries (brinkmanship), the relative absence of the gambling instinct in women assumes great significance when we contemplate their coming influence in the conduct of foreign policy. Women have more respect for life and treasure than the men in power, or even than most ordinary men, and will therefore be less inclined to gamble with them.

7. Women, being more realistic, are also less prone to become fanatical believers in leaders, systems, causes, countries. Without the fanatical belief in leaders and causes (which can carry a pseudorelaxed, pseudotolerant mien as it so often does in America) on the part of their supporters, the men in power (in all countries) could not exercise all the open and hidden acts of national and international cajolery in which they are constantly engaging. Once they participate more in policymaking, once they know more and bring their influence to bear more strongly, women will not be likely to support the leader to the self-defeating end in the name of some abstraction such as "honor" or "commitment"—terms that sometimes do not apply to the situation at hand—or, worse still, in a mere chase after rainbows. Women do not take as easily as men to ideologies that give carte blanche to their adherents to exercise any amount of violence and risk any danger.

8. Women, being more realistic, are also therefore more *skeptical.* (Cynicism, on the other hand, goes perfectly well hand in hand with leadership worship and other forms of satanic worship, and is again more a masculine quality.) Being more skeptical, women are more individualistic, and individualism has been nearly lost in the subdued, harassed, constantly competing American male. The political significance of this is that women are less likely than men to have themselves regimented like storm troopers, or to participate in or condone the regimentation of others. They are less likely to be intellectual cannon fodder, as most men are these days, before the big guns of the media.

9. A final important difference between men and women is that men, still caught in archaic, atavistic patterns, are hunters: they like to stalk their prey, to hunt it down, trap it, imprison it, strangle it, kill it—and their prey usually is other men, people, the "enemy." Some women may also hunt people, but usually in order to possess them, not to kill them or otherwise harm them. Spying, stalking, trapping are essentially male proclivities (Mata Hari was a woman, but she was in the service of men). Some activities must be curbed by society, and the invasion of some people's privacy is probably the only way to do it. But men, proceeding from this limited necessity, tend to abandon themselves with a passion to this hunting, voyeurism, vigilantism. They are not able and do not intend to draw the line between what is minimally necessary and what gives them kicks or other advantages, however unconstitutional they may be. Women, being less inclined to the hunt and also less voyeuristic, are therefore the more natural respecters of people's privacy and the general right of people to live unmolested by the state. A more feminized society is therefore likely to mark a return to greater respect for the privacy and integrity of the individual in this country.

One unexpected phenomenon of modern technology is that it has rendered old-fashioned man, with his toughness, his bellicosity, his reliance on force and cunning, as obsolete as the dinosaur. The virile pose he strikes daily, whether or not he has his name on the door and a Bigelow on the floor, would be *ridiculous* if it were not such a threat to all, including himself. Technology has done away with many of the simple physical hardships and dangers that in former times could be overcome only by hard men. The hard man of today is just a caricature of the hard man of yore. But he still holds all the power. Will he retain it?

In the first sentence of *Without Marx or Jesus,* Jean-François Revel says, "The revolution of the twentieth century will take place in the United States. It is only there that it can happen. And it has already begun." [4] This seems true. But "the revolution" will probably be the result of feminization and not of the growth rate, as Revel anticipates. And in all likelihood "the revolution" or, better, the great change will begin in America, because in America the women's movement is more dynamic and widespread than in other countries, even though it may be younger there than, for example, in France, where Simone de Beauvoir wrote those seminal classics *The Second Sex* and *The Mandarins* quite a few years before the American feminists even had begun to write. Yet since then, American women have labored harder than the women in any other country, and are therefore likely to be the first to see the fruit of their labors. That fruit will be a more humane and intelligent society brought about by a true feminization that will be quite different from what Mrs. Sexton fears it will be.

5

WOMAN POWER AND PEACE BETWEEN THE GENERATIONS

THE strife between the generations seems to be worse at present than ever before—even though two thousand years ago Aristotle complained of the "bad manners and morals of the young." Can peace be made? Such peace would be invaluable to all mankind; in fact, the benefits it might bring, looked at on the basis of present standards, would seem almost utopian. But peace between the generations does appear to be on the horizon as a real probability for the coming decade. And woman power seems destined to bring it about.

One of the major reasons life is so hard for so many, particularly women, is that relations are so bad between the generations, not just between middle-aged parents and teen-aged children, but also between young adults and *their* parents. To be sure, there are the traditional families, securely tucked away in various regions, in which the parent-children relationship is just as good as it can be. But most young mothers would rather miss their favorite concert or party or art class or bowling competition than have their mothers babysit. And which young woman would like to go about her job, leaving the children in the care of her mother or even live in the same house with her? With the two-generation family leading a precarious existence, the three-generation family is truly long gone! And in fact modern architecture for almost all levels of income no longer has any place for such an anachronism. The generations simply do not get along, because they do not share the same values or views, and because life has changed and keeps changing so rapidly.

One of the most vexing problems for the young woman who wants to do her own work, if that work cannot be done at home but entails a job in an office or elsewhere, is what to do with the children and the home. And as many young women know, day-care centers, even where they are available, are usually an unsatisfactory solution. The "natural" thing, clearly, would be that the young woman's parents (or her husband's parents), if they were retired and had the necessary physical and mental health, would take care of the children and chores during the woman's working day. But for most young women this is unthinkable, for her relations with her parents are possibly the worst that any intergeneration relations have ever been. She will tolerate her parents and in-laws and be more often than not—but also quite often not—a dutiful daughter, and the man a dutiful son or son-in-law. But the idea of integrating parents into the routine of life or entrusting them with the children or, worse yet, having them live in or sharing a house with them is for most intolerable.

It is not too surprising that a country with a culture heavily stamped with that "momism" castigated so sharply by Phillip Wylie a generation ago should eventually have entered a phase in which open alienation and hostility between the generations would become the rule. Naturally such alienation and noncooperation represents a big loss for both sides in every way, from the most material to the most intangible. Besides, it not only reinforces in the older generation that feeling of futility that is imposed on old people (with the so widely advertised opportunities for the elderly to "keep busy" being hardly more than a sop) but in the younger generation as well: by rejecting the older generation, the younger people contribute to (and cannot but feel uneasy about) a life style in which they too will be and feel unwanted and useless and rejected in turn by their children.

The deep-seated antagonism and noncooperation between the older and younger generations is not just the result of differing ideas and concepts of what life should be. Psychiatry has—in contrast to some of its more dubious findings in other areas—revealed the intense hostility (or at best ambivalence) toward parents even in relatively healthy people. This hostility has always existed, but was apparently kept in check emotionally and in its external manifestations by earlier attitudes toward aging, by religion, and perhaps by simple necessity. Still, we know that children have always wanted to be free of their parents, and today have collectively managed to become so to a remarkable degree. But real freedom from the older generation need not exclude close cooperation or even cohabitation, and that there is so little of this and that such great emphasis is placed on physical separateness suggests that real emotional freedom has *not* been attained.

Certain attitudes on the part of liberated women seem now to be emerging which suggest that relations between parents and children are likely to improve considerably, perhaps beyond any level of freedom-plus-friendship-and-love that they have ever seen.

The currently young and very young people—that is, those who will be the young and middle-aged parents of the 1980's—appear to be less repressive, less demanding, less rigid, and will therefore be less hatable to *their* offspring. This in turn is the result of changing values and a different outlook on life, a less authoritarian posture in both young males and females, and it is related to woman power. Those who are today the "older generation" really did torment their children with their demands, notions, expectations, and "standards"; worse yet, being a "tense generation," a generation overwhelmed by the unexpectedly severe demands of the technological age (from which everybody had vainly expected an easing of their lot!), they tended to make life hell for their children in many ways. All the standard middle-aged types of the present and recent past—the social or professional climber; the compulsive partier; the "hard-working, hard-playing" father; the dieting, hairdresser-addicted, to-a-million-causes-dedicated mother, with her frazzled nerves and sexual frustrations; the hardhat bigot dedicated to war and violence, angrily holding on to increasingly obsolete ideas—are all anxiety-ridden, anxiety-generating types. More often than not they inflicted lasting damage on their children of which the children may not even be aware. But whether they are aware or not, the damage inflicted on them drove them to ring down an iron curtain between themselves and their parents, for good emotional reasons of self-defense.

The disappearance of the current future-shocked generation of adults and the arrival of the new and less driven, hostile, and anxious successor generation will make it quite probable that the current generation of young people will get along much better with their children in every way than the current generations do. The frantic mother who poses in a microskirt next to her grown daughter in the same microskirt for some ad with the legend "We Are Always Being Taken for Sisters," will be a ridiculous relic of our own age. Once the future shock subsides—and one of the principal effects of that shock is that people no longer dare grow older—people will be free to be their age, so permissive will that new society be! And the person free to be his or her age, who need not always strain to be or to be taken for or look "ten years younger," will be a happier person and better companion, particularly to his or her children. And if and when, as a result of that change and of the resultant beneficial changes in the intrageneration relationship, he or she gains or regains a more desirable and secure place in a society that prides itself on prolonging life, he or she will be even more in harmony with their children. And the children will reap the benefits in emotional and physical freedom while maintaining a decent relationship with the parents. The present generation of youngsters will be, as parents a decade from now, less intolerable; and their children will favorably respond to that.

It may even be anticipated that because of closer interaction between nations in the future, Americans may learn and benefit from the fact that elsewhere in the world, such as Asia or Africa, where Americanization has, fortunately for them and us, been resisted in certain ways, the older generation has a better life and a better relationship with the younger generation than Americans have at home. To the compulsive tourist, whether he goes from Hilton to Hilton or Y to Y, this difference between cultures is not readily apparent, nor is it apparent to the career clerks in our overseas establishments. But it is a fact of much non-American life. And when Americans come to the realization, as many of the young already have, that America's destiny is not to teach "backward" natives in every country to think "progress" or worship flush toilets, but that, as a rather young and on the whole quite uncivilized country (despite those wild pursuits of "culture" by the middle class), they will learn a lot from the entire world and not just from the more "sophisticated" Europeans. They may even learn how to have better and (for all concerned) more profitable relations with their elders and their children.

It is particularly encouraging that among the young there is such a lively interest in how other peoples live, and not just other peoples, but also what life was like in other ages. Our own arrogant rejection of virtually everything that is not American also extends to everything that is not *contemporary*, particularly as regards thought and customs. This rejection of the past is understandable, for people, it seems, were not too happy or successful in the past either. Still, it is astonishing that we should put so much stock in our own modes of thought while so condescendingly dismissing those of all other ages as at least obsolete if not foolish. Is it not likely that people a hundred years from now will regard *our* modes of thinking as just as silly, stilted, and peculiar as we regard those of the fifth or tenth or eighteenth centuries? By disdaining all but contemporary thought, we not only insure ourselves of a distorted and limited range of vision, but squander what the human race has thought and felt before us. The young in large measure no longer feel that way, but seem to have a healthy respect for the opinions of mankind in other places and eras.* For this many brand them as kooks. But who can make a convincing case that Buddhism or Zoroastrianism or early Christianity cannot contribute as much or even more to such problems as arms control, race relations, or drug use than our "highly sophisticated" systems analysis and other forms of contemporary thinking? In a recent article on drugs a writer castigated the views of one of his antagonists as "sheer nineteenth-century thinking." What makes him so sure that twentieth-century thinking is so much better, and that even if it were, it would then not be dismissed soon as "sheer twentieth-century thinking"?

Susy P., a young sociology student at UCLA, says, "As a result of broader views and less faith in force—the two usually go together—the current young will be better parents. Then their own children will live in surroundings and in an emotional climate that will make it possible for them to treat their own children, that is, the next generation, differently, partly because of their own new outlook and reduced anxiety, partly because they will be the first to be able to have and enjoy the support of their own parents." But will those who are now in youthful rebellion against the system not settle down and become adjusted to the old system as they grow older? "Probably not. The chances are that those who see in the current protest wave of the young merely the same thing they did when they were young could not be more mistaken. We young people of today are not just rebelling

* Many of the rebellious young are appallingly ignorant about history and its meanings, among other things. Lamentable though this is, ignorance is not the same as disrespect and thus is easier to correct.

against our parents or certain individual values or constraints which they represent; we are rebelling against the world as we find it, as it has been fashioned by all the preceding generations. Sure, some will come to terms with society as it is, in order to make a living. But they can do that without embracing current values, and if they hang on to their new values, society will change."

The young are not so much rebelling against some aspects of society in the way that past generations might have objected to certain social injustices (and taken to "leftism"); they are simply rejecting it. This seems different from rebellions of the past. It is rarely considered that the most radical of the rebels of the past—the Communists—were and still are in many ways a very conservative, bourgeois bunch of people. They wanted far-reaching redistribution of goods and power, to be sure, and believed that force was the permissible, in fact the only way, of reshaping society in their image. But their vision of the world was not too different in essential respects from that of capitalists and democrats: humming factories everywhere, lots of housing, happy workers with one or several chickens in every pot, a million schools in which every little toddler could receive an "education" (that is, be taught the precepts of the prevailing mores and how to integrate himself and all his energies into society). And like their democratic counterparts, Communists also believed in having a group of leaders who were setting the aims, the style, the scale of values for the rest of the people.

The "workers," in the Communist view, must of course work happily all the time and enjoy a great deal of "cultural well-being" in their ample leisure time, but that was Henry Ford's credo too. It is no accident, though some doctrinaire Marxists claim it is, that the Soviet Union is today the most bourgeois, reactionary, and authoritarian nation in the world. The Soviet leaders, like their capitalist brethren in government and industry, really think of nothing but the Gross National Product, productivity, organization—all essentially anti-individualistic concepts, devised by *man.* "Man" is here used advisedly, for it tries the imagination to think that women could have invented them. Only the abstract, domineering, masculine mind could aim at chaining entire nations of living human beings to these meaningless and unprofitable notions—unprofitable, that is, for most individual citizens of any country. It is amazing how low the American, but also the Soviet machine technocrats really set their sights, with regard to the good life, the development and exercise of the human potential of the average person. Supertribalists by revealed knowledge and obstinate conviction, they have tried and still try to create a society, with the help of technology and propaganda, that fails to correspond to the most people's elementary needs. While it created magnificent military power and industrial efficiency, productivity, organization, it also created more unhappiness and exacerbated the strife between the generations. And the young are not buying, either here or there, and in particular woman power shows them a different road.

"The rejection by the young generation of the current world is quite different from the rejection of the capitalist system by rebels or radicals in the past," says Jim S., a student of economics. "Many of whom, incidentally, became violent renegades and fervently joined the system they had fought—a most unlikely development or course to take for any of today's young, who do not wish to play the game on the terms of their elders. We are now stepping out of the value system of our parents altogether, and for good." Considering how brainwashed most children were in the past, by their parents and society, whether they conformed or rebelled, this new posture is quite remarkable. And in fact, the true measure of the step the young have taken and the distance they have already traveled away from old mainly male values can perhaps be seen in their *lack of hatred.* The traditional hatred felt by past rebels, such as the Communists or the Nazis, against the groups and persons embodying and controlling the prevailing order, was always a form of reverse attachment, even of slavery: to go through life hating old J.P. Morgan is to wear the chains of attachment and involvement just as much as it would be to go through life loving and trying, hopelessly, to emulate him. This does not mean that some of the rebels in our day are not boiling with hatred. But among most of the white and a good many of the black young rejectors of the current society there is a conspicuous lack of hatred.

It is not easy to trace just why or how the young who reject the current situation so completely came to embrace their position. Probably it is not all their own doing. What happened, perhaps, is that they simply became "overloaded" by the threatening and beseeching stimuli around them. They may also have come to reject the prevailing system because for a growing *man* it simply takes too long ever in the conventional channels to assume his place and then exercise his faculties and natural aggressions there. Menial work or the crafts, at which a relatively young man could excel at an early stage of his eager manhood in the past, are dwindling though trying to make a comeback. And in the choice places for the application of intelligence and learning, in the professions or industry, too many years of drudgery and slavery are necessary before a man can come into his own.

Besides, as recent studies have shown, the average man at the top—if and when he ever reaches it—lasts a surprisingly short number of years, unlike the tycoon and entrepreneur of another era. If a man rises to the top today, he is likely to be at least in his forties and ready, if not for his first heart attack, to be retired soon, meanwhile being pursued and having his heels snapped at by eager, young, frustrated, and cruel men. That is, if he makes it. But the chances are more than 99 per cent that he does not make it or does not make it very far and, sick or exhausted, settles into a professional spot of limited glamour and reward, burdened with the unfulfilled dreams of his youth.

Suddenly at some point the young of both sexes began to see

that. They began to see what was really going on, even without having half as much specific knowledge of life as their elders, because they were not yet participating, not yet committed to the system. Only nonparticipating, noncommitted persons can see its terrors and errors. With their big or small stake in it and their constantly stimulated defensive mentality that alone makes it possible for them to stand their own participation in what they, with unconvincing humor, call the "rat race," the participants cannot see it, because people have a hard time seeing themselves individually or collectively when in action. But at some point the young and the liberated women began to perceive reality differently; as a result they created a new value system for themselves. This is at the root of the struggle between the generations, and has cost both sides dearly.

All this may seem a far way from the topic of the family and the coming peace between the generations, but it is at the very heart of it.

Paul S., a young sociology professor, says, "If the older generation had the courage to see things as they are and as they make them, they would not only have to turn around automatically with regard to many of their most cherished opinions and myths, but they would then see the pioneering role played by the young and the women in the necessary softening and, one hopes, gradual dissolution of an archaic, brutal, unrealistic, and destructive value system to which they in their majority adhered. They would then see that many of the young now regarded as subversive were in fact constructive, and they might then not only reconcile themselves with these young people ideologically and personally, but even grudgingly pay them some gratitude and respect. "The older people may even come to see, though this is asking a great deal, that in the intrageneration battle the young too have suffered a lot—more perhaps than their elders. It is the custom nowadays to commiserate with some gray-haired businessman or doctor or colonel about his long-haired draft-dodging son or hippie daughter, after 'all they have done for the kids.' Nobody seems to commiserate with the kids who are faced with an 'old man' who bellows out his crazy nonsense about the world at home and abroad to his adolescent children, or who are faced with a mother who simply does not understand. It is quite hard on a young boy or girl to find their father stuck in the current value system, just *because* they love and need him. It is not only parents who would like to love and be proud of their children, after all; the same holds true in reverse. Therefore, there is a lot of self-abnegation and quiet tragedy in kids placing their values over their love of and relationship with their parents, particularly their fathers."

It is important to note, when looking at the war between the generations and its implications for the family of the future, that the men of the older generation play a more dominant role in the battle than the women. Though mothers may be just as distressed as fathers about what their children do and how they live, the struggle by the young is against the older *men,* their views and values, their system. One often has the impression that despite conspicuous exceptions conservative women are to some extent on the sidelines in this struggle, not just because their role is less powerful in the scheme of things, but because their views endorsing the old order are less firm and abstract than those of their husbands.

On some of the matters that have had the most solid male support, from magnate to hard-hat, in the past decade—such as foreign-policy postures, defense spending, gun control, law and order, race problems and so on—women seem less dedicated to current approaches and therefore less in conflict with the young. This may be because as women they are less convinced that our essentially aggressive and materialistic approach to almost everything is the right one.* And as mothers they probably have more

* As Eugene McCarthy pointed out during his curious campaign in 1968, we *make war* on everything—not just on the Vietnamese, but on poverty, disease, drugs. This is the supermale way.

compassion for the travail of their young. Also, they may have more genuine love for their country than some males. Finally, and perhaps most importantly, to the extent that they are members of or sympathizers with the women's movement, they are themselves in opposition, not just to the men, but to the entire male-generated and male-run order and the values on which it rests. All of which indicates that the growing role of women and the growing influence of their thinking is likely to help heal the breach between the generations and benefit the family of the future.

A solid improvement of relations between the generations can be expected only when the current crop of youngsters takes the helm and then gets along better with *their* offspring. And though their offspring, as any other in history, will in all likelihood be rebellious in some ways, they are not likely to be as fundamentally alienated from and hostile to their elders as so many of the young are today. This new harmony between generations, which should be reality in a decade or so, will open avenues much more attractive to all than what is now, in the current transitional period, being done and contemplated in the form of day-care centers and other semicollectivist devices, where strangers, in strange surroundings, exercise their potentially undesirable influence on children. Instead, with a good measure of peace and harmony, and therefore cooperation between the generations, the two-generation family is likely to emerge stronger, and even the three-generation family, in some new form, is likely to make its reappearance. This will solve many problems, particularly for the young working wife of whom there will be more and more. It may seem outlandish as a prospect, but it really is not. And society will owe this coming peace between the generations in large measure to growing woman power, with liberated women pouring oil on the troubled waters, and helping a new and better value system to emerge around which all generations can more profitably gather. In fact, woman power's helping hand will determine whether the current young generation can fulfill its promise.

6

WOMAN POWER AND THE FUTURE OF HOME LIFE

WHAT interests many of us most, perhaps, is what the relationships between individuals will be in the near future, what the customs will be, and whether there will still be real family life of the kind that today seems to be rapidly disintegrating. What will families be like, and more interesting still, how will people feel about being members of families? Shulamith Firestone, in *The Dialectic of Sex,* advocates and predicts the end of the nuclear family in our day. Is that likely to occur? Barbara D., a social worker in the Bronx, says, "Of course, poor sexual relations often are a burden on family life. But the entire idea of the family is based, after all, on the assumption that people can live well with each other, and their children also, after the honeymoon is over. Yet this is where the real trouble starts. As soon as the sexual infatuation recedes, it turns out that husband and wife are essentially bored with each other, as most parents are also with their children, really, so that nothing else can take over and maintain the bond in this primary group and be a source of real satisfaction. Again and again, listening to the complaints, I wonder: Why are people so *bored* with each other? There can be only one answer: Because they are so bored with themselves. And, believe you me, people are bored to tears! Most of them think they simply can't stand to live with their spouses for the next twenty years. But what they really can't stand is to live the next twenty years with themselves! And, of course, being bored they also *are* boring, and the thing compounds itself." And Tom C., a well-known gerontologist, adds that "most men about to retire are simply petrified by the prospect of having to endure the boredom of spending long hours with their wives again."

Have Barbara or Tom ever wondered why people are so bored and boring, and what, if anything, might be done about it? Barbara says, "Yes, I have. It mainly is, as the liberated women nowadays point out, perhaps somewhat weirdly, because people have not reached a *higher level of consciousness*. Not a very high level, mind you, no Nirvana or Samadhi stuff, for God's sake. They don't need that. Just a little higher level of consciousness that would take them out of the great dullness of the most elementary material world. You remember J. D. Salinger describing the ultimate bore in his *Catcher in the Rye*? 'He was the kind of guy who always told you how many miles he was getting to the gallon.' Hell is nothing, I think, compared to living with a man who will tell you for twenty years how many miles he gets to the gallon, or living with a woman with similar interests. Now, a person with a little more feel for life—that of others or his or her own—would neither be so fascinated by the material trivia nor fail to sense that others may not care to hear about them.

"Then there are the sports. The average male—we will come to the female later—is such a bore to his wife because of his attitude to his favorite sport. More often than not he is a fan: football, baseball, basketball mainly. He knows all the players, all the scores, all the games. This in itself would not be so bad. But in his attitude toward these sports and to the particular heroes whom he worships, there is something irritating and boring. The intensity of his enthusiasm and adulation, which of course the marriage partner does not share, also tells us something about his boredom with his own life, his own low self-esteem, his hostility to those who do not share his infatuations and fantasies. The fan—and most people do not seem to realize that the word 'fan' is short for 'fanatic'—is sick in the head. But whether he is or not, he is an intense bore to any but another fan, and certainly to his wife, even when he does not view or speak about his favorite dreams of glory. In that sense his constant talk about sports is even more aggravating to his wife than her talk about clothes or food which he in turn disdains."

Perhaps still worse, according to Irene G., a practical nurse in Middlebury, Vermont, is the involvement with political affairs, or what passes for it. "My father would for years and years, day after day, spout this stuff about political things, candidates and so on, you wouldn't believe it. It would drive my mother absolutely up the wall. It wasn't that she disagreed with him—Lord, no, they were both square as can be. She just couldn't stand his drawing himself up, regurgitating all the stuff he had just read in his crazy newspaper! The worst was his interest in foreign affairs, the world, you know. Believe you me, he didn't know beans about it, but the Reds here and the Reds there and we got to watch out and do this and that and they're smart as hell. As though he had discovered this all by his little self and no one else was so shrewd and toughminded as he was. Or he'd hold forth about the blacks or Congress or something—it was awful. That just wasn't a person talking, just a record player. A person who had no feeling or thought of his own, that's what made him so boring. Just brainwashed as they come, an intellectual slave, a total bore. I felt so sorry for him, too, because I always felt there might be something else to him, some personal life, some personal reaction. But nothing, ever. And Ma, who was a bore in her own right, though she talked about other things than Pa did, was just bored to tears with him, and he with her, really."

This "same-think" or "group-think" is not imposed from without, as some social critics seem to believe, but is a deep inner necessity, a final result of, perhaps, the age-old compulsion to be like the rest of the tribe, which would act with hate and expulsion against any deviant member; the intellectual barrenness into which traditional religion has led people and in which it has left them marooned; the indoctrination of the young which in America as everywhere else goes by the proud name of education. There are many explanations for it, depending on whether one discusses the matter with a psychiatrist, an economist, a socialist, or a priest. Yet one reason for it, rarely mentioned until the women hit on it, is probably the extremely low level of consciousness on which most people live. Only "safe"—that is, nice—thoughts occur to them on that level. This does not mean they do not have absolutely wild sexual fantasies and constantly imagine a variety of "forbidden" activities that would have made Minsky blush. Nor do the victims of low consciousness fail to have other outrageous thoughts, such as killing the boss, the wife, the kids, or that most sacred of living beings, the dog, or even the neighbor's dog. But people's critical faculties rarely if ever turn against "society," the system, their own real fates. Most people's very souls abide by conventional values to such an extent that their minds never even contemplate a critical or noncooperative stance or a simple spontaneous reaction to anything that would make them a little more interesting.

The need for intellectual conformity accounts for the "party line" to which most people cling. The party line in turn makes them utterly predictable—that is, still more boring. This intellectual conformity is disastrous in many ways, but perhaps most so in the family circle, where the spouse, male or female, whose amatory preoccupation with the other half has declined, is chained to the other, emanating boredom. The fact that the partner, as Irene observed, is just as boring is no help: two bores are rarely interesting to each other for more than a very short while. And boring-ness cannot diminish unless people can manage to become more conscious of their real selves, and thereby more genuine, individual, original.

It is in this connection that there is much hope for the family. For the smugness that goes so clearly hand in hand with the low level of consciousness and the resulting active and passive boredom is apparently coming to an end under the impact of current events and woman power. And even though this may no longer benefit many now in middle or old age, it is likely to benefit those who will form the families of the 1980's. Their constantly growing nonacceptance of the world around them or of the role in "society" designated to them by it, their strong desire to "think for themselves" will make people more interesting to themselves and each other. This does not mean that mere involvement in events, activities, or people beyond one's personal affairs necessarily makes people more interesting; in fact, the zealot—man or woman—who forever believes in and espouses causes is also an immense bore, particularly to his or her spouse.

Rather, the effort at self-recognition, at least to the extent that it is possible, and beyond what is now regarded as possible, makes people more interesting, certainly to each other. Curiously, the contemporary young person, just because he or she is striving for a new consciousness, is more interesting and alive than his or her predecessor, and therefore appears to be more promising *family material,* despite his or her "morals" that appear "loose" by obsolete standards. In the extreme cases produced by the social travail of our time true monsters have emerged, like the Mansons and their adherents, their "family"; but they are rare exceptions.

Much though the current young—and even some liberated women—might laugh indulgently at this, they are potentially much better husbands and wives than past generations, simply because they are more conscious of themselves, of others, and of society, and therefore more responsive and stimulating company.

Some of the older generation also tried to raise their consciousness, but not too successfully. Psychiatry has been used a great deal as a "consciousness-raising" device in the past fifty years. The neurotic and more so the psychotic is largely or totally unconscious of what goes on without and within himself, and in fact the generally low consciousness in the nation is a form of collective mental illness against which the young and women's lib wage a mighty fight. Woman power seems destined to succeed where psychiatry has failed. With "co-counseling" and other devices to raise consciousness, people will become better family partners because they will be more interesting and more attuned to others' moods and needs.

The Selection of the Marriage Partner in the Eighties. In view of the fact that, thanks to woman power, both men and women will in fact be more liberated, socially and psychologically, than they have ever been, they will then be far better equipped to select the right partner for themselves. This, of course, will be a great boon to family life. As people's levels of consciousness are raised, they will become more *realistic* in the best sense, so that the now so frequent and unpromising marriage of puppet to puppet, symbol to symbol, body to body will largely cease. Until recently, and in much of the past, the "pretty girl" married the "handsome boy," and the handsome boy the pretty girl. Parents, but their often brainwashed offspring as well, looked for a "good match," which did not mean a matching personality, but a person of the other sex, impersonally desirable when measured against the values of the age: "family," ambition, charm, looks, wealth, success. People have tended to look for a marriage partner as they look for a car, which, impersonally, has certain desirable features, such as durability, comfort, looks, price.

It is really quite amazing that our good citizens have always liked to make fun of what they hear are the methods of selecting a marriage mate in, say, India, where parents arrange marriages for their offspring at an early age, not even giving them a choice. Mismatches, we insist, must be the result of such archaic procedures, and we are right—up to a point. What we do not consider is that we make our selections hardly in a very different or better way. Whereas in India the parents follow certain standards of selection, not looking deeply at the individual (and fully realizing that they don't), we also select mainly by certain standards, not looking deeply at the individual (but, unfortunately, not realizing that we don't).

Anyone who reads case studies of divorces or bad marriages cannot but be struck by the impersonal ways in which people make this most fateful choice a person can make. "Well, he was an up-and-coming young dentist. He also was very considerate." "We had been childhood sweethearts." "He excelled at sports and was a real outdoor type, you know. I always liked that. I spent much time outdoors too when I was a kid." "She was as pretty as a picture. Blond hair and a figure you wouldn't believe." "She seemed like a real good homemaker, always so sweet with the children on the block." "She said she would wait for me until I came back from the war. A faithful sort of girl." All these qualities are good, perhaps, but they are not justifications for marriage. They are internalized standards, relied upon by people brainwashed by their parents and society, people who select a mate for *themselves* as schematically as the people in India select one for their *children.* Given the American environment and the attitudes toward life, the marriage then does not work, and the family falls apart or becomes living hell.

Love and Romance. But don't people fall in love? After all, not every Jane marries her Jim just because he is a personable and rising young proctologist in Rubesville, and not every Jim marries his Jane just because she is pretty or from the right side of the tracks. Most people get married because they fall in love—don't they? If they fall out of love, well, that is unfortunate, but what better way, what freer and more personal choice, what more promising beginning can there be for a marriage than people falling in love? They certainly do fall in love, or at least they did. In fact, to fall in love has been, particularly in this "romance"-bent century, a national craze, a national habit, a national affliction. Romance—largely unknown in Asia and much of Africa—is the thing, and it is just un-American to question it as the source of ultimate bliss or the finest of guides.

It is assumed, of course, that to fall in love is very *spontaneous* and *personal;* that it is a unique, direct, and profound experience between two personalities and individualities; that the strong bond that suddenly springs up, the enchantment with the other person, the insatiable thirst for the other's company, the total acceptance of the other's virtues and vices, the lift provided by the reciprocation of the romantic feeling add up to the "real thing" and are the best harbingers for the creation of a solid family.

Nothing could be further from the truth. Every person who has ever been in love knows that the feeling generally fails to last, unimaginable though that may have seemed while it exercised its hold. Every person who has ever been in love is also likely to have had the extraordinary experience that the being-in-love state not only did come to an end, but was superseded by one or more such emotional episodes! Not only were the bonds created by one's inloveness thus loosened by the evanescence of that volatile feeling; the relationship was finally obliterated by the same mysterious inloveness occurring with someone else.

It can therefore be said that to be in love is *not* a good foundation on which to build a family. What, anyway, is being in love? David S., an Adlerian psychologist, says, "In no area of human emotions, perhaps, is our ability for self-deception as great as in the area of romance. Freud, of course, regarded infatuation actually as a pathological state, and much can be said for it that it is. Like an illness, or at least most illnesses, the change from the normal state is definitely a transient phenomenon. It also is definitely unnatural, like an illness, in that the responses of the victims are unnatural. While Eve's good looks and pleasant personality or Bill's decent character and fine achievements arouse a certain range of positive, but moderate, feelings in others, they lead Bill to blush and stammer when he sees Jane, and Jane to suffer increased heartbeat, sleeplessness, or even fainting when she thinks of Bill. Their responses, though pleasant to them, are clearly deranged.

"What is unnatural and, thank God, generally of a passing nature, except in more basically disturbed people, is the distressing emotional dependence of one upon the other. If Eve or Bill goes away, or falls out of love, the person left behind becomes morose, anxious, even desperate to the point of suicide, cannot enjoy either food or company or a game of tennis, neglects their tasks, their appearance, cannot concentrate, and so on. All this passes, generally, like most other afflictions. What psychiatrists have tried to promote—if one may use such a term—ever since they have come to the fore in our society, is love rather than romance, love from one individual for another, rather than infatuation, which—no matter how violently the infatuees might argue against this—is more often than not involvement with a personified image: it is a schema, a projection, a dream, superimposed upon a real person of flesh and blood but not real nevertheless. And practicing psychiatrists always find that there is a direct correlation between an insufficient sense of reality in general, a lack of true consciousness on the one hand, and a tendency to fall in love on the other, and to let oneself be engulfed by it and permit it to determine one's decision."

But haven't people always fallen in love, and if so, what function does this serve in the natural order of life? Bruce J., a midwestern university anthropologist, says, "Well, it really is very simple. For people to fall in love means for them to desire sex with each other, which is the way to propagate the race. Also, of course, for many people to be in love means not just that they desire sex with each other but that, consciously, they want that particular person of their emotional choice to be the father or mother of their children. But somehow this business of in-loveness and wanting procreation is really a manifestation of that side of man that is promiscuous rather than monogamous. It sounds paradoxical, for the person who is in love seems so strongly dedicated to monogamy at the moment. Yet in view of the unpalatable though inescapable truth that the person who falls in love is generally a *repeater,* his or her infatuation is a poor foundation for a family as we know it—that is, a family between one man and one woman, having several children. Love and romance seems to be a rather new feature in human affairs anyway. Presumably, people have at all times experienced some pangs of it, ever since they began to become distinctly different from other apes. But there is no indication that they made so much of it as in our day or culture." One might add that the struggle of the young and of women's lib for a higher level of consciousness *is* in some way a struggle against the blind tyranny of infatuation and romance.

If being in love is not a good foundation for a family to get started, nor the right cement to hold it together, two questions arise. First, what should a family be based on instead; when and under what circumstances should people join together to found a family? And second, what should people do who are in love? Should they deliberately refrain from founding a family? Should they make love and then part? Should they produce children?

No answer can be given here as to what people should do; the concern of this book is observation and prediction, not the positing of rules nor even the proffering of help to the perplexed, at least not in the form of advice. The point is that the paradox of people so violently desiring marriage with each other because they are "in love," and so often being condemned to failure because being in love so often presents poor preconditions for founding a family, is likely to *disappear* in the future. People will fall in love much less in the coming years than they have in the past, or at least in ways different from those to which they have been conditioned by their elders, their books, their films. Conditioned? Didn't we say that falling in love is the most spontaneous and personal, individual and direct emotional reaction a person can experience? We said no such thing; we said it *seemed* that way. More often than not, the victim of infatuation is a victim of conditioning, aside from being, usually, a victim of anxiety.

From earliest childhood people are taught that to fall in love is ecstasy, that it is approved of by everybody, that it makes otherwise sinful or sordid thoughts and activities pure or even holy, that it rates certain advantages ("Everybody loves a lover"), that it is a sign of maturity yet youth, and so on. As a result, people are forever *poised* to fall in love, not as a spontaneous act, but as a response to all the anterior conditioning that is so deeply imbedded in Western folklore, for whatever reason, but that now seems to be losing its hold. Until now, he or she, predisposed to fall in love, was like a powerful projector already loaded, merely waiting for the light to be turned on, bringing the machine to life, and—Eureka!—the glorious image appeared on the mental screen. Just as there is rarely anything lasting about falling in love, there is rarely anything really spontaneous about it. As this type of conditioning will decrease (and anxiety in our society with it) people will fall less in love, and this phenomenon will therefore represent less of a problem in the selection of a mate and the founding of family.

"But," says B. W., a Jungian analyst in N.Y., "perhaps an even more important aspect of falling in love than conditioning—a factor that makes falling in love clearly appear as even less natural or spontaneous—is that in our particular society and time falling in love is really very often a refuge. It is a refuge from the unreality, shabbiness, crudeness, and sordidness of what our generally accepted way of life really represents to an awful lot of people—a constant terrible battle for little visible gain, fought under great dangers and against great odds, under depressing conditions, with little hope of more than barely holding one's own against the onslaught of extensive demands, financial problems, personal hangups, declining health and strength. To fall in love is a refuge into another world, a fling, a magical escape. In that sense *infatuation* is the opium for people that religion was in Karl Marx's view but now obviously no longer is. It also appears, and this is of course the height in distortion, as something *real,* in a world in which everything—work, play, health, relations, fun—have become less and less real, in the sense that they have become less personal, less controllable, less profitable, enjoyable or simply one's own. Thus a romance seems real." But it usually is not. Woman power is fully aware of this. And its efforts at consciousness-raising *will* make others aware of it too.

Another New York psychiatrist, Dr. R. R., points out, "When we see a businessman falling in love with his secretary, it is generally not because his secretary is so attractive, but because his business is failing." Failure, of course, can take many forms and plagues people from an early age. Particularly in our excessively success-oriented society failure is easy to come by, in the sense that measured against our own extravagant expectations (and those of others) we fail only too easily and frequently, and then seek solace in something that will be both pleasurable and real. One can come to the (it seems perverse) conclusion that the unhappier and more disturbed and deranged and frustrated and ineffectual a society is, the more its members are likely to fall in love, generally with disastrous results.

At present it is sex rather than romance that is so avidly pursued as the consolation prize for failure. That is only because people have learned that "real" romance is hard to find. Romance remains their ultimate fantasy.

As people's level of consciousness is raised by woman power and other contemporary forces, in the way we expect it to be, and as people recognize each other better for what they really are, rather than, at the slightest provocation, matching dream with dream and yielding to their conditioning, something else will take over as motivator for marriage. That something else will be a drive closer to real and personal love. Then, living in a generally less destructive and tyrannical environment, less polluted with war, lies, and other nonsense, less poisoned by crazed competition, the family is likely to be much stronger and a source of much more satisfaction and security than it is now. And all this is likely to occur quite soon—in the 1980s or even earlier.

A further factor in strengthening the family in the 1980s is likely to be a change in *sexual mores* throughout society. It is apparent that the attitudes toward sex, and the practices resulting from them at present and in the recent past, were the least conducive imaginable to the stability or enjoyment of family life. Most people, as everyone knows, are both monogamously and polygamously inclined, and even in the best of circumstances are not entirely happy either way—it just is not in the human condition to be entirely happy in any event, and the proclivity to be both passive and active, slothful and industrious, to fight and to flee, to be aggressive and restrained are just as much part of people's ambivalence as the conflict between polygamy and monogamy.

This conflict was quite effectively taken care of during, for example, the Victorian Age. Men lived enthusiastically by the double standard, which was easy: sex could readily be found with the often very attractive and not unwilling lasses of the "lower classes," as we can read in novels of the period. And thanks to an absence of modern communications, the husband was under less effective surveillance by his spouse than he is today, when she can keep a sort of electronic eye and ear on him wherever he goes. Undoubtedly, the comparative ease with which men in earlier days could find sexual diversion from time to time *was* in a way effective cement for many a marriage. Just what the women did for sexual diversion is not well known. Were they, to a significant extent, Madame Bovarys?

What has perhaps been very detrimental to contemporary marriage, in addition to all the other stresses that tear it apart, is the rapidly shrinking opportunity for the ordinary middle-class person—that is: about 90 per cent of the population—to have clandestine extramarital relations at least at some time. "It is," said H. L. Mencken, "to the everlasting shame of the American husband that he has no mistress." Mencken attributed this sad situation to lack of time, lack of money, and lack of vigor. What riled Mencken, no doubt, was that when he was writing, husbands in other Western countries still did have mistresses. But it was in the trend of the times that, except for the very rich, who could ride in their Isotta Fraschinis and maintain oceangoing yachts, men were less and less able to have the mistresses they needed for relaxation from their arduous lives, as even Moses had his "cinnamon-colored" concubine for the relaxation he needed.

Deprived of opportunities for sexual diversion, a sexually unsatisfied yet enterprising husband often has only one choice: an illicit romance spiced with "real" love. If he is "madly in love" and at least verbally ready to cast away his family, he becomes a tentatively acceptable suitor for single females, who have been conditioned to shun married men. This is then often the end of his family.

The "predatory" female, taking advantage of the man's frustration, will often demand genuine romance as the price for her favors. In earlier days he had to bring a gift; now he must bring love and a determination to shed a wife who does not, as the cliché goes, understand him. And the predatory female even tends to make an official credo of this: Helen Gurley Brown, in *Sex and the Single Girl,* recommends that the husband-hunting girl include married men as suitors, but only for the ultimate purpose of weaning one of them away from his family and marrying him. The resulting new marriage—and many marriages result from the restive husband's obligation to romance the new partner seriously if he wants to succeed—does not, on the whole, seem to work out well. The children are in the way, the husband feels guilty, he tends to be ruined financially even if he earns fifty thousand a year, he is too old, his new wife demands children, and by that time he has fallen out of love again. This unfortunate sequence is one of the most prevalent in the country today; and it is hardly conducive to a stable family life. Curiously, this form of adultery appears to be sanctioned even by the most conservative segments of society. To be married two or three times—and usually only the first marriage is not the result of long and intensive adultery—is acceptable, despite the social and psychological havoc it creates, particularly for the children. In a more sensible future society with freer relations between the sexes the marriage-divorce-remarriage cycle is likely to vanish as a form of human torture or threat to the family.

Community Living. Some aid to the beleaguered institution of the family is likely to come from an unexpected quarter: disillusionment with other forms of "family" life. It is often hard to know how good or bad one situation is unless one has tried another. To many of those who were smarting in the conventional bonds of the family, communal living seemed to be the answer. But some of the returns now in from those who have tried it reveal that they were somewhat less than satisfied with the new arrangement. Vivian Estellachild of Berkeley had this to report in *Women, A Journal of Liberation*:

"Gluttony, drunken brawls three to five nights a week, constant high key frenetic living as well as the sexual frenzy, lack of any creative activity, reading, writing, discussions, religious or revolutionary activity contributed to my misery. . . . Another was the rapid turnover of people and transients. . . . I left and so did a few other women. The next time I saw the men [from the commune] they were in town looking for 'some ass,' and only four women were left on the farm." The male brutes, in fact, would become very "uptight" when talked to about women's liberation and laugh at anything else under discussion. All they really cared for, it appears, was "ass," and life was hell for the women. "Mostly they [the women] were warm, loving, generous people. They were being used. Instead of suffering the miseries of shitwork and alcoholic husbands alone in a house in the suburbs, they were together doing the shitwork as a group. The children and the constant hysteria of the men caused the babies to be in constant tears." [1]

This is the kind of testimonial that can only help the family in the coming decade to be looked upon as more of a blessing than it was during all the years it was taken for granted and often much maligned. It will help the family, one should think, to become stronger than it has been in the two or three most recent decades, which really were the decades of its increasing disintegration. The current high rate of failure to attain satisfaction, let alone happiness, in communes *or* conventional families will render it clear that it is not so much the mechanics of symbiosis, or the arithmetic of it, as the general atmosphere in society on the one hand and the type of individual on the other, and indeed the "level of consciousness," that makes family life possible or not possible.

The Old. The possible reestablishment of the three-generation family, not in its ancient form, perhaps, but in some new forms better adapted to current needs and capabilities has been mentioned. That, as any other improvement in family relations, can occur only if our current monstrous and dismal attitude toward the aging is finally buried. "The deeper cultural reality," says Coleman McCarthy, "that allows the old to be the nation's resident castoffs is that American values have been largely shaped by both the Calvinists' mystique of achievement and the American frontier notion of self-reliant individualism. These two creeds naturally exclude the elderly because old men and women are seen as no longer achieving and no longer self-reliant. . . . Some of the elderly's sufferings are inevitable, the results of sickness and family scattering. But many are not; they are caused by a value system that plays down filial respect while playing up much that is passing and cheap." [2]

Despite its "reactionary" ending, this passage expresses very well why the old are in such a plight and with them the nation.

For people can be certain only that unless they die young, they will be old soon enough, as a result of which their own miserable treatment of the old—rooted primarily in the achievement-orientation for themselves and all others—will come home to roost on *them.* Thus neither they nor the old are fit to be lived with, really, as long as the current value system prevails. Should that system be adjusted to the true needs of people by becoming permeated with feminization, by becoming gentler and less competitive, attitudes toward the old will change for the better. People will then no longer be terrified of becoming old. That will also reduce their youthful frenzy for swinging, regardless of cost, which is also detrimental to a good family life. It will help younger people not to be ashamed of being socially involved with older people, an emotion now interfering with the image most people are trying to project. And it will help the elderly directly, and make them better and less frightened, lachrymose, and self-hating companions. All this can be brought about only by a change in the value system.

Will it occur? That is the focus of the entire book: the prediction is that it will occur, and in the coming decade, and that it will be brought about by the effective infusion of femininity as a force and by women as more effective participants in the society as a whole and in all its values. For the treatment of the aged in our society is essentially brutal, practiced by the next generation who themselves are under brutal pressure. Woman power will alleviate that.

Everything points to the likelihood that the family will be considerably stronger and happier in the 1980s than it is now, and much stabler. Extreme ideas of not being married at all, or of polygamy or polyandry of one sort or another, or of having childred reared away from their parents—old ideas, incidentally, all dreamed up by, among others, the Communists in pre-Revolution days and long since abandoned even in Communist countries—are all likely to be discarded. For it appears that the drive to monogamy is, on balance, stronger than the drive to polygamy, in the sense that a man and a woman, unless they are totally mismatched, as they so often are, can enjoy a special relationship when they have children together.

With growing harmony between the generations, better selection of mates resulting from improved consciousness, and because of all the other factors elaborated earlier, family life is likely to thrive in the 1980s. And the greatest boon to family life will probably come from woman power's current efforts to make unmarried females full-fledged members of society, thereby further reducing artificial pressures on them to marry and thereby adding to the number of marriages that are doomed from the beginning.

The Prospects. At this moment, when so many conservatives fear the family will disintegrate and so many revolutionaries hope it will, and when the family is so violently beset by strife between the generations, strife between the sexes, competition, inflation, war, and much more, the prospects on the whole seem good rather than bad. Everything points to a profound transformation in the average human being's approach to himself and herself, and to life and society around them, so likely to be produced in the coming decade by woman power and bringing with it a much better climate for family life.

But in family life, as in all other areas of human existence, no progress is thinkable, no adaptation to the changes wrought by technology possible, unless feminization takes over or at least begins to permeate in considerable measure all of family life as well. Man, as the exclusive master of war and peace, the master over capital and labor, over government and the sciences, over education, over the giant bureaucracies and the professions, has failed. He has maintained his mastery, but he has not made good on his purposes and promises. In too many ways he has turned peace into war, wealth into poverty, inventions into a curse, human love and labor into violence and injustice. He also has failed as the master over the family, as the *paterfamilias.*

As a result the *patriarchal* family seems doomed, but not the family. Nor is that family likely to become a matriarchal one; this would constitute merely a backlash and, like every backlash, would be unworkable and pernicious. Instead, in the coming decade, the patriarchal is likely to be replaced by the partnership family. Conceptually this may be nothing new. In Europe and in the Soviet Union a form of family called "comradeship marriage," based on roughly equal roles, existed in the 1920s. It never amounted to much because conditions were not suitable for it, and it was swept away in that last huge explosion of supermale assertiveness that ended in war and genocide.

That war and the subsequent wars in this century produced by male aggression appear to have been the last great paroxysm of an already defeated, already obsolete supermasculinity and patriarchality. The way now seems clear for men to begin living like men instead of as parodies and caricatures of supermen (and victims of supermanism) and to relax and let themselves be partners with women.

Once that partnership begins to flourish, the "closely knit family" may flourish with it. The "nuclear family"—depatriarchalized—may become the biggest "in" thing yet.

7

WOMAN POWER AND THE FUTURE OF FOOD

FOOD is a source of great anguish to most Americans, either because they eat too much or because they do not have enough to eat. What will be the approach to food in the coming decade? What effects will growing woman power have on our eating habits?

"Everybody," said the psychiatrist Edmund Bergler, "claims he likes good food, whatever that is." Whatever that is—for "good food" is a different thing for different people: it varies from country to country, from age to age, from class to class, from era to era, from person to person. Food is life itself—without it we would starve—and for that reason it is a powerful motivator of work. It dominates, in the form of agriculture, most of the country; it is a means of making and showing friendships; it serves a thousand other physical and social functions; it is a menace, by producing overweight and disease in one in three Americans; it is fashion, and can be slave-driver for the ambitious and sophisticated who wish to excel by producing or appreciating "gourmet" food.

Ever since World War II, America has looked with a jaundiced eye at comparatively simple eating habits and gone "gourmet" with a vengeance. Peoria matrons simmer their carrots in 1968 Chablis; homemakers everywhere serve Quiche Lorraine at the drop of a menu composed by Jacqueline Kennedy in the White House; hardhats, on their night out at the neighborhood restaurant, let a thin little Beaujolais roll around their tongues before authorizing the anxiously hovering waiter to pour that heavenly nectar for the rest of the folks. Like everything else that "takes" in the United States, gourmetism has exploded into a national industry, with millions of words about it printed in magazines and books every month, millions of dollars' worth of Japanese grasshoppers in sake being imported and retailed throughout the country, recipes of the most vexing composition carried in the daily press, Cordon Bleu competitions set up in the Dakotas, and menus printed in exotic tongues. Gourmet cooking utensils, pans, and casseroles imported from France and Belgium cost hundreds of dollars and are bought by sophisticated hostesses. And everywhere we see cooking schools where socialites scrub pots and pans for rude foreign chefs and pay them a king's ransom for the privilege.

Before one's recoiling inner eye one sees households across the nation in which determined gourmettes slave through the day preparing something-or-other Stroganoff, Niçoise, Zurichoise, à la Grecque, or à la Cambodienne, while the husband, back from work, would like nothing better than to sink his teeth into a steak and French fries. But he is out of luck, the brute: he will be confronted with several courses of exotic dainties. Needless to say, almost all the gourmet dishes served in American homes or restaurants are rather ghastly, partly because the ingredients are not of top quality, partly because the recipes are gross falsifications, and partly because our gourmette does not master the cooking art. For to prepare truly excellent food takes more, or less, than to study Craig Claiborne.

Why this incredible infatuation with gourmet eating in the first place? Ads describe long holidays at inns across the country or the ocean with one gourmet meal at the heels of another, and modern man more often than not is proud to be described with awe at cocktail parties as a "celebrated gourmet." And the phenomenon is proliferating: America is literally in the grip of a giant gourmet wave on which billions are being lavished annually. Actually there is not too much good food in this country on any social or financial level.

What is most striking, first of all, is that foodstuffs, from beef to peaches, from the lowest and cheapest grades to the most grandiose luxury products, have little real taste. Everything is flat, hardly tastes at all, as a result of the modern growing methods and in some instances for other and unknown local reasons: in California, for example, fruit never did have much taste. In any event, with beef and lamb shot full of growth-producing (and possibly cancer-producing) hormones, with insipid vegetables and fruit, with bread that usually does not deserve that appellation at all, and so on, American tastebuds quiver a lot, but in vain; and gourmet cooking, aside from being an outlet for "sophistication," aims at rescuing the eater from the nontaste of most ingredients. The trouble is that gourmet cooking does not transform inadequate ingredients into electrifying fare.

The flat and denatured food in America, against which gourmetism is really a form of rebellion, leads to gourmandise—that is, gluttony. The person who gets no satisfaction from quality consumes instead a large quantity, grows fat, and starts on the horrible roller-coaster of dieting, reducing, gaining, losing, fasting, gorging. No nation seems to have more trouble with its weight and waistline than America; in no other country is dieting and exercising and books on same such a multi-billion-dollar industry and, often, swindle. Except for the very poor, who still live as people have lived for thousands of years—that is, working hard and bending every effort to get three or at least one or two meals a day for themselves and their kids—most people are almost overwhelmed by the problem of food. Meanwhile, all the starches, fats, and other evils around invite illness and early death. Things culinary cannot and will not go on this way.

What, then, will be the future of food? The future of eating? The future of cooking? Of obesity? Reducing? Dieting? Gourmetism and gourmandise? What are the prospects? Like all other predictions, these too depend on a variety of "ifs." If life continues to be or becomes even more nervewracking, tense, frustrating, dangerous, food will become more and more of a problem. For food is the easiest and simplest way for anybody to find relief from tension and obtain some sensual gratification: it requires no partner, no time or money to speak of. Anyone who is angered or frustrated or elated but has no other outlet for his emotion can afford to eat a big amount of what to him or her is "good food." Everyone who is upset can use food as a tranquilizer. Food serves to celebrate our victories, console us for our losses and humiliations, pass the time at home or on trips. Food puts us, if we eat out, in a position of command: we are being served; others strain to please our every whim and, contrary to Mother, feed us exactly what we order, not what they feel we must eat. Besides there may be unconscious satisfactions on the deepest level: one psychiatrist has suggested that the sophisticated gourmet really wants to "show up" his or her poor mother for having had only one single and not very exciting item on the menu—milk.

People take their food terribly seriously—Samuel Johnson observed that men will pay such serious and undivided attention to few things as to their dinners. Look at people in restaurants studying the menu and you will not see people scanning something quickly and absentmindedly as they might a report in the office or a newspaper on the train. No, they deeply immerse themselves in those menus, hesitate, decide, hesitate again, as though picking a site on which to build a monument—at least. And even though a martini-drinking crowd may already be crocked when consulting the menu, the very importance of the impending decisions visibly sobers them. And the fat grow fatter.

Of course, Americans are not alone in being sore beset by food. Not only are the Germans suffering the same tribulations, but the Swiss, the Dutch, and other Westerners are not spared either. And in various other places, including the Soviet Union, waistlines are expanding, much to the distress of their owners, who want to hold them down for three reasons: vanity—in order to look good; fear—in order to escape heart trouble and other ailments; and general existential anxiety—in accordance with the perceived need to be or remain "in shape," "young," "attractive," and so on. Overweight in many of their people creates anxiety even in the armed forces, where it is felt, presumably for good reason, that overweight soldiers may lack the resolve and nimbleness to fight the foe effectively. The days when extra weight symbolized success or wealth are long behind us. Rubens would have a hard time finding models for his voluptuous nudes today, and he would probably be shown the door by every woman's (or man's) magazine if he were to try to sell them his finest paintings.

Will food overwhelm Americans in the 1980s? (To submit to a constant diet, with gritted teeth, is also to be overwhelmed by food, even if the scales remain steady.) Or will Americans overwhelm food and attain a reasonable working relationship with it? Will we ever see the day when two or three consecutive issues of a magazine will appear without long articles on a new effortless diet or new gourmet eating? This depends ultimately on whether people, on the whole, will be "happier" so that food need not serve the role of sop as much as it does now; whether they will find greater sensual satisfactions in areas other than their gustatory sense; whether they will be less anxious and tense, less in need of tranquilizing; and, importantly, whether they will be less bored, not just with their lives and tasks, but *with each other.* For food is particularly important to relieve the latter evil: if one has to share one's meal with a bore, whether at home or away, this experience can be made at least tolerable by a good big meal, with much to drink.

The principal reason for throwing oneself upon food, however, is sexual frustration. Says Dr. John W., a psychiatrist, "While you can find sexual frustration and inadequacy in every type of man or woman, I have never seen a seriously overweight person, or a person constantly groaning under the need to diet, or a person overly eager for gourmet eating who did not have trouble with his or her sex life. No glutton, male or female, ever has or provides adequate sex, nor do gluttons ever find enough, or the right, partners for themselves. Their sexual inadequacy may have many causes and many manifestations, and not every sexually plagued person overeats. But every overeater is a sexually plagued person. Gourmets and gourmands advertise their sexual problem." A look at the literature will provide wide confirmation of this view.

Whether Americans will find a happier and more reasonable relationship with food than they now have, and whether in fact they might even be creative enough to produce—as almost every other country has over the centuries—a truly indigenous and more satisfying cuisine of their own will depend in large measure on whether they will find a way to improve the quality of their professional, cultural, and sexual lives, at least to some extent. Should that be the case, everything concerned with food will also fall into place. And our prediction is that as the benign influence of woman power will help to improve the quality of life in all areas, it will help in the area of food as well.

What *will* people eat? Organic food? Health food? Here a truly gigantic battle appears to be shaping up. Before the health food rebellion, the human race, with America in the lead, seemed to be on the way to fulfilling those dreadful prophesies of the 1920s and '30s, to the effect that eventually everybody would live on pills, the ultimate artificial food. Then, side by side with the artificial food explosion, such as the vitamin explosion, came the hormone-raised steer and chicken, the chemically boosted fruit and vegetable—that is, what one might really also call artificial food.

These artificial foods are unsatisfactory for two reasons: their taste is insipid, and more and more evidence has accumulated that they cause a variety of illnesses, particularly cancer. So, apparently, do the thousands of additives, advertised to the public as a bonus, but in reality a means of making, directly and indirectly, some extra profit. Under the impact of adverse consequences of all sorts, and also for some neophilosophical reasons, the health food "craze" arose to drive back all the innovations and is currently in the process of becoming so extensive as to offer a severe challenge to the artificial, canned, and otherwise processed foods that now fill our markets. Which will win?

The "health foods" probably will, *if* for once, for perhaps the first time in modern history, people collectively embark upon what would appear to be regress rather than progress. Individuals and even groups of individuals, in fact often highly organized groups, have sometimes gone against progress: after central heating was invented some people began to sleep in the cold or outdoors; now that they have cars, many ride bicycles or walk to work; they wear handmade garments, and so on. Will people be able to cast off past technological progress in food processing? Will they return to a different nutrition? Eve J., a nutritionist, says, "In the first place, we do not know for sure how good or bad this or that kind of food really is. Science knows everything and nothing, in this area as in all others. But there is enough evidence to give researchers the general knowledge that there is something wrong with mass-produced and mass-packaged chemically treated food, to have aroused a general suspicion, a deep aversion. As a result, the health food fashion became strong, and is now going to assume major proportions. What will result? In the first place, we must expect extensive frauds in that area, as in all others; millions of tons of food will soon be marketed under new labels that, though not exactly wrong, will be misleading. Some ads will cry: 'No DDT on Our Product,' when some other pesticide may have been used, for example. The second development to be expected is that the big food producers will wage the battle of the wits and try to wash brains on a large scale. Like the cigarette producers, they will not give up easily. They may wage a campaign against organic food, or join it if they can't lick it. In fact, they already have.

"Curiously enough, the principal asset of organic food, namely, that it tastes better, rather than simply that it is 'good for you,' seems not yet properly appreciated even by most organic food eaters, according to our studies. Most people are in too much of a rush anyway or too tense or preoccupied even to taste their food properly. Those who eat organic food seem to eat it mainly for reasons of their health, with which they seem greatly preoccupied, not for reasons of pleasure. That too may change. People may relax to a point where they will demand to eat what tastes good, not just what is good for them, though of course the two coincide more often than not."

What about frozen or precooked food? The vice-president of one of the nation's largest frozen food manufacturers says, "We are assuming that the majority of people in the 1980s will eat mostly frozen food. In fact, we are cooperating with architects in designing a variety of dwellings that will have no kitchens at all. There will be a freezer for frozen foods and a slot in the dining-area wall in which they can be heated. Our variety of foods will be very large. People will be able to buy the most fantastic twenty-course Chinese dinners. Incidentally, some types of prepared foods are more suitable for freezing than others. Chinese foods, for example, or stews, such as Irish stew, or a large variety of dishes with delicate sauces, such as a truly great Sole Bonne Femme, are much easier to freeze and much better to eat than steaks or lamb chops. Thus, food *preferences* will change quite a bit, we think. There will be no labor and no garbage. This will save the time of the working woman. As to the looming battle between standard and organic foods, we are pretty neutral: we'll prepare and freeze whatever people will want to eat."

Will people really have no kitchens? For many people it is and probably will remain fun to cook, *if* there is time and energy and room left to do it, and as long as it does not have to be done every day, three times a day. It is when we look at food and its preparation that we can see best in how transitional, provisional, and obviously impermanent a style we really live at present. Where "everybody" had a cook a hundred years ago, now "nobody" has one, so that the vast majority of women (who still do most of the cooking) must accept this drudgery, together with all the other household drudgeries, in order to make ends meet and to benefit from that magnificently equipped modern kitchen. But if life should finally become easier and less hectic in the coming decade—and it probably will, not because of new technology, but because of society's new and better use of technology under the impact of woman power—cooking will remain a creative and at least an occasional pleasurable activity for most.

If life in other areas becomes better, eating will become a real pleasure. One might even say *again,* for there was a time in American life when the quality of the food at least—though we know little about the pleasure in eating it—was surprisingly advanced. If we look at the menus served at the turn of the century in the East or West, by the rich of mining or railroading, or by the men in the White House, we find truly exquisite selections of food and wine.*

* Though a man like Diamond Jim Brady was a glutton who eventually died of overeating, he had the true spirit of a man interested in food: at his own expense he sent the son of the owner of Delmonico's to Paris to serve a three-year apprenticeship at Prunier so that the boy would learn how to prepare a certain

The current desperate flight from mother's apple pie to gourmet cooking and eating indicates that Americans are at least beginning to seek a realistically attainable sensual pleasure in food and, the rest of their future life style permitting, will regain that pleasure as a matter of course in the 1980s. It will be then that the enormous natural resources and wealth of this country will also begin to produce the foodstuffs worthy of really good cooking (which can be quite simple). If the American people begin to appreciate food, even the prices for really good food, which at present are prohibitive, for a dinner in a restaurant and for the ingredients of a truly good dinner at home, may come down, for people will *insist* on it. People will demand it, and if they demand it, will get it. Probably they will even get better domestic wine; and even good bread will finally be baked in this country. Then people will be able to enjoy good, inexpensive, and simple meals.

Once the point is reached at which people have real fun eating, gluttony and obesity will probably decline, as *people will get from quality the satisfaction they must now obtain from quantity.* And if their now hectic search for other sensual pleasures is also reduced because of easier satisfaction, eating will become less of a substitute and therefore more genuinely enjoyable. This is likely to benefit the family greatly and other human relationships as well. It will make "togetherness" less of a menace and burden than it is today, and in general help the individual enjoy himself or herself more. In the 1980s, if everything goes well, and social life becomes mellower, saner, more feminized, better food will be both cause and result of a better life.

Truly good eating and the search for and consumption of good, simple wine—once the gourmet wave has abated a bit—is likely

---

dish—Sole Bonne Femme Prunier—to perfection. When the boy, now a grown man, returned, Brady and a host of friends, the proud father included, went down to the pier to rush the new master chef directly to Delmonico's kitchen to prepare the dish for twenty-four guests who, upon sampling it, declared it superb.

to become a new bond, a new common interest and activity for men and women. Men already have taken in large numbers to shopping and cooking. And even though, in the eyes of the hardhats, such activity is still deemed "effeminate," more men will take it up. It will be at the good table, jointly prepared (and presumably jointly cleaned up afterward), that the young men and women of the 1980s will celebrate their joint political or business or artistic or other accomplishments.

8

WOMAN POWER AND THE FUTURE OF SEX (I)

ONLY a few years ago America's sex life seemed to be headed for disaster. It appeared that within a few years women would jump off rooftops in droves, still clutching *Cosmopolitan* opened to the very page on which it was explained, once again, how that mind-blowing, soul-curdling, hair-raising, side-splitting, apocalyptic BIG O could be attained after all, by following thirty-seven simple rules, from stimulating one's own and everyone else's genitalia to undergoing sensitivity training with cyborgs in Colorado. Confronted everywhere with women insisting on permastay erections, sexual overkill, true romance, utter frankness, precoital candlelight dinners, and more, more, more, men were increasingly driven to prostitutes, homosexual relations, or grim masturbation, or *also* to jumping off rooftops, the same *Cosmopolitan* issue in hand, cursing Helen Gurley Brown. Fortunately, the worst of the crisis seems to have passed.

The young seem to be making out better, and the older generations, from people in their latter twenties to grayhairs in their eighties, observe the very young at play with a mixture of fascination and envy. But even all those not in the stage of utter youth, according to most sex manuals, can and must have vigorous and altogether fulfilling sex lives, whether they like it or not; and they are in trouble. Proud to have shed what they consider Victorian prejudices, to have brought sexuality "out in the open," to have mustered the courage to use the appropriate four-letter word for spade-calling, they feel they should now reap the fruits of their progress. But the more the media-besieged women have been crying for that BIG O, their million cries one collossal collective indictment of the American male, the more the increasingly impotent men shrivel up, become terrified, and make less than ideal partners for a roll in the hay, which, if it does not pass 5 on the sexual Richter Scale, is regarded by the ubiquitous sex experts and their diligent pupils as a fizzle, a bust, and a failure for both "partners."

Why? Why do both sexes seem frantic and schizophrenic? The women dress in hotpants and microskirts, disporting themselves sexually in probably the most provocative manner since the Stone Age. Their very attire screams: "Look at my behind, look at my thighs, look at the whole enticing bit, be enticed, get a hard on already!" But woe to the construction worker who whistles when the goods are portaged past his bulging eyes; woe to the man who is smitten by the display and wants the girl without first communing with her soul over several expensive dinners: they are just treating that girl as a sex object! Whether or not men do regard women solely or mainly as sex objects—and many, many do—women now display *themselves* as sex objects. And because the hotpantsed free-hanging girl can safely be assumed to be on the Pill (a circumstance that, as some of the interviews revealed, makes some women regard themselves as sex objects and makes men prone to feel that way even more), you have a bomb, if not on your hands, at least in your field of vision.

There is nothing "wrong" with this new attire. It is more comfortable and convenient, but it is presumably also a new outgrowth of the many forms of teasing—that sport that endlessly titillated and exasperated past generations. For the current highly skillful and imaginative female display, though it undoubtedly adds something agreeably stimulating to the outdoor and indoor scenes, still seems out of tune with contemporary sexual mores. Despite the display and the pornography and the "serious" or "frank" discussions on sex and its maddeningly involved mechanics—found everywhere from the cryptoconcupiscent *Reader's Digest* to the most explicit mag—men are really supposed only to look, perhaps to court, but usually not to grab, whistle, rape, or otherwise respond to what they see. And many men do not even see their own predicament and distress; in fact, they wink and inform each other that they are having fun. They engage in "girl-watching," followed, usually, by nothing. If they have fun nevertheless, there is, unfortunately, a reason for it.

They suffer from the perversion of voyeurism, and the girls, consciously or not, are stimulating this perversion. A perversion, by Freud's useful definition, is an activity that substitutes for, rather than accompanies, basic sexual activity. And from early burlesque to the explosion of first topless and now also bottomless bars, there have been innumerable places where the customers could and literally did buy frustration. "It is hard to know what is going on," says Gary L., a social psychologist. "Take the judge and his jury who went to a bottomless bar the other day in San Francisco to try a case involving indecent exposure and spent a couple of hours having nude girls dance for them in order to reach a verdict. Is the old goat fooling himself or others?" The nude bars are not the only sources of satisfaction for the voyeur, who today has at his command plays, movies, books, and magazines. And voyeurism, psychiatrists agree, is a form of sexual passivity on the part of the voyeur, causing frustration in those with whom he is involved. The fantastic display of anything from real bodies (as in contemporary fashion) to all the contemporary "art" is one indication of how widespread frustration also must be.

"All the contemporary display of bodies, pictures, descriptions of sex art is regarded by most people as part of their sexual liberation," Gary continues. "But there is a long way from saying 'fuck everybody' in female company to having a flourishing sex life. It is good, in fact a long overdue necessity, that people have made valiant efforts to cast off the crazy restrictions on talk about sex that prevailed so long. But they have now discovered to their dismay that some greater verbal and visual freedom and even more sexual activity may not be decisively helpful at all. Like horses that worked a lifetime in underground coalmines and could not see when brought to the surface, those conditioned through the generations often find, if they are men, that they cannot perform in what they think is the proper fashion, or if they are women, that they cannot enjoy the activity as much as they think they should. Once sex surfaced, impotence and frigidity also surfaced. If suppression was the bane of sex yesterday, inadequacy is the bane of sex today. And the misery is compounded by the 'Every-Woman-Can' fellows."

The sexual troubles of America (and the rest of the Western world, though to a lesser degree, particularly in Latin countries like Italy or France), had surfaced in the 1920s and '30s when psychoanalysis became the rage. Treatment was often sought for other reasons: increasing numbers of people found it increasingly difficult to conform, adjust, play one or another of the many crazy and insufferable roles society forced upon them. Yet when the psychoanalyst began to dig, there was always sexual trouble of one kind or another. "One need not be a Freudian," says Gary, "to accept the fact that every form of unhappiness is somehow connected with sexual troubles."

This has not changed. Francine B., a somewhat older student at Berkeley who today attends a lot of women's meetings, says, "It is amazing how unrestrainedly strangers pour out the most intimate details of their lives to each other. But it is equally amazing that these problems are almost always rooted in sex. These women, mostly women's lib sympathizers, have a terrible time with their sex lives." Let none of the male chauvinist pigs triumphantly say at this point, as they are wont to, "I always said so—all these women need is a good lay." First, this is not true: they may need the lay, but they have many other vital concerns troubling them. Second, even if they do need it, others who are not friendly to woman's lib presumably have as great a need. Third, he, the loudmouth male chauvinist pig, is probably the least equipped to provide it.

To all the sexual troubles and other difficulties that plagued their clients in the earlier decades of this century the psychiatrists brought the very long view. They believed that in order to bring about a change, their patients' deepest levels of personality had to be probed, uncovered, and restructured, in an extremely lengthy and costly procedure, after which the patients would be fit to enjoy the good life. And so great was the despair with their own selves of many that they braved the time, effort, and expense. But after years of effort it became apparent that most people were not helped by their analysis, at least "not really." As a result, many lost confidence and patience, particularly if in the sex department there was no real improvement; and apparently there rarely was. Then, with the extremism that is the premier hallmark of the human race, people jumped in the opposite direction, to opposite therapies. From the most circuitous approach to curing sexual inadequacy, via the labyrinthine depths of the unconscious, people turned to the most direct road, such as massage and manipulation and encounter groups; and instead of lengthy psychiatric treatments, stretching over years, they embraced the two-week road to instant potency at the Masters and Johnson clinic in St. Louis.

Premature Ejaculation. The claims made by Masters and Johnson for their insights and in particular for their method are nothing less than potentially monumental. The claims, that is. Masters and Johnson claim that they can, in their standard treatment of couples rather than individuals, requiring only two weeks, cure premature ejaculation, the number-one killer of sexual joy, Public

Enemy Number One of sexual satisfaction for both the female and the male. Actually, as is true of other clandestine vices or afflictions or habits, there is no information on how widespread this sexual crippler really is, but estimates range to well over 50 per cent of the American male population being afflicted by it all the time and a much higher percentage being afflicted by it some of the time.

The future of sex, regardless of what the women's movement might produce in that realm, would obviously be altogether different from current sexual conditions if the Masters and Johnson claim had real substance. Not only would the future of sex be happily affected, but the future of society itself—for it may be assumed that, just as a happy sex life tends to lead to a good personal life (or vice versa), a happy national sex life would tend to lead to a greatly improved social life, with a stark reduction of petty tyranny, violent hostility, omnipresent rapaciousness, crime, and even the apparently uncontrollable desire to make war.

But *is* the Masters and Johnson claim justified? Traditional psychiatry has wrestled from its beginnings with the disaster of premature ejaculation, and, as far as one can tell, not very successfully in most cases, but not entirely unsuccessfully either. The traditional view of psychoanalysis is that premature ejaculation is caused by a deep-seated hostility toward and/or fear of Mother, and thus all women, producing an unconscious desire to frustrate the female or some other psychic impediment. The analyst, by helping the male patient to bare this intricate internal mechanism, hopes to free him from his obsolete and immature relation to his mother or her image and of his compulsive though unconscious habit of equating with her every woman with whom he enters into a relationship.

Masters and Johnson try to take a wild shortcut: they pay little attention to the psychological genesis of the affliction at all, and to judge from their own writings and the two volumes produced by two couples who were treated,[1] they seem not to discuss it with their patients in any depth. Instead they simply ask their charges, first, to massage each other with some body ointment for a few days; to practice, second, some prolonged intercourse without motion or friction; and finally, to test their newly found powers to the limit. These very few who have published their confessions from the clinic attest to a newly acquired, albeit apparently somewhat shaky, potency. But such testimony is dubious, partly because with these ex-patients, who have spent much money and effort, the wish may be the father (or mother?) of the thought; partly because Masters and Johnson warn them that they cannot expect miracles, which may greatly distort their judgment downward; partly because they simply may not know much about sex and therefore be poor judges of their own performance; and partly, finally, because—curious though that may sound—Masters and Johnson may not know much about sex.

Everything indicates that, strange as it may seem, Masters and Johnson, the most "scientific" and long-term explorers of sex in this century, the ultimate authorities on "the human sexual response," the daring innovators who conducted research for a decade with prostitutes and others and used in their efforts the newest and most ingenious technological devices, indeed do not know much about sex at all, because they never observed normal sex. For people capable of having normal sex would not be very likely to expose themselves to sexual investigators. At this point some will explode: "There is no normal sex—you can't define it—just as there is no normal person!" But that isn't true. Some people—no one knows how many, but presumably there are quite a few—do practice what one can satisfactorily, even though not scientifically, define as "normal sex": the male is potent, the female is not frigid, both are roughly in harmony and balance in their desires and satisfactions, and their activities are centered on copulation.* And there is one other feature intrinsic to a "normal" sex

* Those who insist on scientific definitions for everything, the sophists and pseudoscientists who reject all common sense and in fact even the intrinsic wis-

life: a low curiosity about what others do and a low inclination to expose oneself—low enough, at least, never even to get close to the Masters and Johnson clinic.

It can thus be said with conviction that Masters and Johnson have never seen, observed, interrogated, photographed, electrically vibrated, oscillographed, or otherwise measured a normal male or female. Masters and Johnson expose their ignorance on the subject of sex by their *findings,* which, like most contemporary social science findings, abound with computerized figures and jargon, but are nevertheless personal conclusions based in this instance on observations made from a definitely unrepresentative sample—so unrepresentative, in fact, as probably not to contain a single normal person.

Masters and Johnson state that the most powerful sexual reaction in a female ever attained at their clinic was produced by an electric vibrator. This is probably true, simply because people with serious sexual problems usually react more strongly to masturbation than to intercourse. Politically, this finding has been a sensation, however, having been taken by the more extreme wing of women's lib to show that the female does not "need" a man and can do even better by herself or with one of the sisters. But the finding, though it may well be true for those few examined by Masters and Johnson, if generalized, is patently absurd. Only among people with psychological and sexual inadequacies can a mechanically induced orgasm—in male or female—be the strongest produced in the course of all the experiments; otherwise everyone would prefer masturbation to intercourse. This seems to be the classic case of a "closed system."

It can therefore be predicted that the Masters and Johnson technique, which at present is finding many disciples through the

dom of our language as it has developed, are the obscurantists, obstructionists, and philistines of our day, representing a great danger for a gullible population that swears by "science" and "education" and is constantly led down the garden path by contemporary intellectual quacks and quackettes in all realms of life.

country, will not revolutionize sex therapy and will *not* help America's sexual troubles. This does not mean that the prognosis in the realm of sex itself is dark; on the contrary. But the mechanical procedures as devised by Masters and Johnson cannot help any more, will in fact help less, than the previous (yet continuing) efforts made by psychoanalysis. The entire Masters and Johnson vogue is probably only a backlash against the lengthy and complicated psychoanalytical efforts, and will undoubtedly become the victim of a back-backlash in an area of human life that can (and will) improve only if the entire social setting improves, as it indeed promises to in the 1980s.

Frigidity. What about that mysterious affliction, frigidity? About few subjects has more been said and written than frigidity, and the positions taken are vastly contradictory. It has been argued that there is no such thing, that every woman can respond to the right partner in the right circumstances. And conversely, to the extent that it is accepted as a genuine affliction, frigidity has also been attributed to anything from conscious or unconscious inhibitions implanted by parents and/or society to the inadequacy of the male. Despite the controversy on the subject, some aspects are clear. There *is* such a thing as a constant or frequent inability on the part of the female to respond fully; and while it is often the male's fault, it is not necessarily the fault of that male, who may have had other females respond fully to him as the result of the same actions or techniques or exertions, and who therefore can tell the difference. The only mystery is what generates frigidity and what can alleviate it. And that really may not be that much of a mystery either. Apparently at least four interconnected factors are involved: the parents, the woman's psychic makeup, the men she has sex with, and the social-cultural-moral setting.

Needed: The Good Relationship. In one way the psychiatrists trying to combat male and female sexual inadequacy were probably on the right track. Besieged by patients whose batting average was poor (often despite considerable and promiscuous activity), they told their patients, by and large, that their views of sex and its enjoyments were too mechanical, too functional, that sex was not a sport, after all, but that a good sexual performance and its enjoyment required a good *relationship.* "Love," they probably thought, was too unscientific and archaic a term, so they settled for "relationship." And some men and women in quest of better sex have ever since sought a good relationship, perhaps quite grudgingly, with the attitude, well, anything for good sex. They even began to make heroic efforts to *communicate,* which is said to be the A and O of a good relationship.

But once again, many have been disappointed: they have found neither the good relationship nor the grand sex it was expected to provide. What they did not see and what most psychiatrists perhaps either did not see or did not want to see, was that our present society is *singularly unsuited for good interpersonal relationships of any kind;* that while good sex does indeed require a good relationship, a good relationship would require, for most, a better social setting than exists. A man who slaves in an office, even if it is his own enterprise, who is harassed and pressured by the endless agony of his job, frightened by the financial insecurity of his existence, irritated by the noise and dirt of the city, disgusted by his own servility to his boss or his clients, caught in narrow physical surroundings, and often in poor health or at least poor general condition because he lacks truly invigorating joy or labor, is a poor bet for a satisfactory relationship. And most women, whose ideals of the perfect mate and perfect sex have expanded because of their bondage to modern propaganda while the male qua male has actually declined, do not make very promising partners for a relationship with that man.

What at least the various older generations never seem to have faced was that all the realities of life—in fact, what by mid-century our way of life had become—was not exactly conducive to good relationships between the sexes or even between people of the same sex. For that way of life is not only taxing and irritating; it also puts a social and professional premium on keeping everything of true importance bottled up inside oneself—that is, it puts a premium on noncommunication. And it is also a depressing way of life because of the magnitude of efforts needed, the endless preparation for a truly good position, the inconstancy of attainment; and as everyone knows, depression and a good personal or even sexual relationship are not exactly natural allies. It is partly for this reason that so many of the young have copped out: they not only disapprove of or are bored with the careers held out to them; they also fear for their manhood or womanhood if they do enter the rat race. And indeed, a man who labors for twenty years to become president in order to begin, the day he is elected, to be pushed out again either by younger men or his own heart attack, is not an ideal partner for any woman.

Our way of life has brought it about that almost all men are now distinctly unattractive, unexciting; and sexual pleasures with unattractive, unexciting males are difficult to achieve for the women who live with them. These men are always overtired, nervous, suspicious, anxious. They eat and drink too much. They talk too little or, if they cannot have their say in the office, too much; they inspire pity and worse by identifying so ardently with their favorite sports heroes, whom they resemble so very little; they don't look well, smell good, dress well. They are now trying to lend some color to themselves by wearing flared pants and colorful shirts, but their sartorial daring only tends to underline their intrinsic meagerness. Contrary to what has come to be called, aptly and rather wistfully, 'the Beautiful People,' these men are the legions of the Unbeautiful People. This undoubtedly is one of the reasons for the present women's rebellion: the women are not just tired of serving man and being his inferior; they are tired of serving *contemporary* man and being *his* inferior. It is one thing to be carried across the threshold of a castle by a romantic knight, and quite another to share a narrow apartment with a pill-swallowing nervous wreck who ejaculates prematurely. Why cook for *him*?

So in a roundabout way much female frustration (unless its individual causes are deeply ingrained) results from male inadequacy, not so much purely technical, physical inadequacy, but a general human deficiency that makes the male unexciting to begin with, and therefore incapable of providing real satisfaction for which genuine excitement must be the first step. But women, in the current transitional state of affairs, have already learned a first lesson. Increasingly they no longer blindly push for the BIG O by a variety of techniques or try to acquire the ability to experience it by psychotherapy, as in the 1950s, but apparently have come to see that society itself needs changing if sex and men and all other aspects of it are to change for the better. The women's magazines don't know that yet, but the women do. Woman power, by transforming society, will provide the foundations for better relationships, which in turn will make better sex possible. And where psychiatry largely failed, and Masters and Johnson must largely fail, woman power will probably succeed, by providing a new social climate in which men and women can be less tense with themselves and each other, and thus function more normally. Frigidity will then decline.

What will sex be like in the 1980s, after our society has been feminized, saneized, rendered less violent, futile, compulsive, and barbarous? What will people actually do sexually? Will they be promiscuous? Monogamous? Very active? Free and open about it? Will there be orgies, interracial sex on a national scale? Will gay liberation be the thing?

Lesbianism. "Nonsense," says Christina M., a charming dark-eyed eighteen-year-old brunette. "The first thing to go in the 1980s will be the gays. Or at least their organizations, their crazy claims and demands, their high visibility. Who will need it? These people are sick, no matter what may have prompted their inclination, and they better learn it. Most people now in their twenties grew up in a very restricted way, I mean sexually and opinionwise; their folks were shocked by everything. So one way of shocking hell out of them is being queer and making a big production of it. That's one reason for being queer—for some. But the real reason people are queer is because their parents were monsters of one kind or another, and deformed them. When people become more human, their children will be less queer. I think in the future most people will really enjoy sex, I mean real honest-to-goodness sex, where you get into the sack with someone you dig, and *you go*! Who needs queers, masos, Mansons? Can't people just have a good time? Simple, man, simple, that's what we want. Who needs the Marquis de Sade? Who needs Myra Breckenridge? What kind of people get a kick out of that? Only the older generation that's tired of seeing Rudolph the Reindeer. Normal, man, normal. Normal is fun, believe you me. Normal is the future."

Others we have talked to do not agree. Ruth K., a beautiful and blue-eyed honey-blonde has this to say: "Well, I am gay, you know, have been ever since I started. I'm twenty-four. I started it with this teacher and I liked it. I have had boyfriends, sort of, but couldn't get with it, not with them. They sort of disgusted me. And they're all crazy. It can be very pleasant to be gay. But perhaps some of the sisters make too much of being gay, politically. I laugh at that. A little cunnilingus between sisters is not going to restore the ecology, do you think? But I'm all right the way I am. I really don't like men. I think they are strangers. They are insensitive. They are ridiculous too, the way they strut and boast."

If lesbians are proud of their habit, it connotes to them the ultimate independence from that dreadful creature, man, whom they dislike intensely (and, at least in our day, often for good reason). But some of the lesbians interviewed are not totally convincing, because their lesbianism seems partly ideological rather than "straight" and therefore presumably is less durable. If in the coming decade society becomes feminized, more sensitive, more gentle in the way that seems possible; if it becomes thereby more truly civilized, more responsive to people's true condition and needs, homosexuality is likely to decline drastically. In one way that would be ironic: the gays of both sexes, having finally attained a liberation and social recognition of sorts after centuries of oppression and persecution and contempt, would then more or less vanish from the scene just when they have managed to make that scene. Yet everything suggests that homosexuality is likely to be less widespread in the 1980s, among men and women, than it ever has been, mainly because the liberated female will be a better mother to her growing children, but also for social reasons.

Interracial Sex. "I think interracial sex will come to an end pretty much, soon, at least as something special or exciting," says Joseph W., an eighteen-year-old black. "My brother who is twenty-seven now, he used to lay every white chick on campus and they could never get enough of him. And he did like it! I mean, not just the screwing, but to get those white chicks to perform under his black cannon, and to see those honky boys know it and get mad and boiling inside. I guess it was fun for him and still is. And it is fun for me too. And as long as the man hurts us and spits at us and hates us—all that civil rights stuff don't amount to anything, you know—it will be fun for us to screw his women. And his women like it, too, the young ones, it shocks their parents. But even so, I have a soul sister for my steady. If we ever make peace with the man, that'll be all over, mostly."

The urge to engage in interracial sex has many causes, one of which may be simply that two people of the opposite race meet and decide they love each other. More frequently it seems to be—on the part of white women—the disappointment with white males; or—on the part of white males—the disappointment with white women; the protest, the novelty, and in some cases the perversion that leads people to it, as some interviewees indicated. People of different colors rarely seem really to fall in love with each other, regardless of the claims of so many observers. And most people, from what they say, seem really not to like an extended interracial physical relationship too much. There are always exceptions, but mainly there is the excitation of the brief interracial encounter. To the extent that the element of personal and social protest will go out of it, just as the element of protest is likely to go out of homosexuality, interracial activity is likely to decline rather than increase in the coming decade. What there will be of it will be accepted by society as a matter of course.

The Perversions. What, in general, will be the future of perversions? Dr. Beverly M., a psychologist with special interest in adolescents, says, "At present the perversions are enjoying a heyday that will not last. Of course, to start out with, many people say, 'What are perversions? Everything we do is normal.' Well, maybe. But some things are less normal than others. Homosexuality, sadism, wife swapping, group sex, sex in front of others—the list is long—are after all practiced by people characterized by two tell-tale problems: they suffer from some inadequacies in "normal," that is, private, man-and-woman one-to-one situations; and they do not get real or lasting satisfaction out of their practices. They are not happy. More precisely, even though few people seem to be happy these days, they are unhappier than most.

"Whether it's the chicken or the egg, people engaging in perversions are more plagued by the itch than others, which is the reverse side of never getting any real satisfaction. Their habits are a millstone around their necks. The perverts—and I know it sounds prissy to use such a word—think they are very sophisticated and mock straight sex, the 'missionary position,' and so on. But they really suffer from needing an extra stimulus. I personally do not believe that the perversions have much of a future. I think they are cresting. The young and the very young do not seem particularly interested in them. Nor do they show any inclination to revert to the earlier patterns of teasing and petting, which was a fierce perversion in its own right. Could it be that the new generations will be 'normal normal'?

"I have talked with lots of youngsters, sixteen-, seventeen-, eighteen-year-old kids. What do they do? They go to bed together, they have sex, they have no complaints about performance. I have not yet met a girl in that age range moaning and groaning about absence of orgasm, the way their older sisters with the romantic jobs on Madison Avenue or the wives of suburbia groan and moan about it. These young people seem to enjoy sex and to function right. They do not even use the plethora of dirty words with which our language now abounds. This verbal restraint I, for one, think is a good sign; I always felt that the use of all these words—if you can call them that—is not a sign of liberation, but of horrible frustration, particularly if used in mixed company, in which case their use is a sort of angry verbal assault. Anyway, these youngsters, from what I have seen, seem to get along with each other and with the fact that the human being is a sexual being. Not all, of course, but quite a few. Perhaps the key to it all is that they deemphasize sex differences in clothing and behavior, that—I know this sounds strange—they do not *hate* each other, and that they do not hate sex."

This does indeed sound strange, but it is not, for if one looks dispassionately, he or she will find that despite all the romanticizing and swooning, the sexes tend to hate each other, with men hating women much more than vice versa; and that on one level people hate sex, and men, despite—or perhaps because of—their never-ceasing, endless, and insatiable itch for it, seem to hate sex more than women do. More precisely perhaps, hatred of women and in particular of sex is not simple and one-dimensional, but rather part of a complex of feelings, of an ambivalence, which makes its "hate" component no less virulent. It is a true merit of Germaine Greer's to have faced and discussed that widely ignored, in fact carefully avoided psychic perversion in the chapter entitled Hate in her book, *The Female Eunuch.*[2] That chapter—significantly subdivided into Loathing and Disgust, Abuse, Misery, Resentment, and Rebellion—begins with the one stark sentence: "Women have very little idea of how much men hate them."

Germaine Greer is right. Men of this and past generations (yet, as said earlier, the very young may be different—we shall see) have had a strong streak of hatred for women, no matter what else they, ambivalently, feel for women at the same time; and men do generally hide their hatred from the women. Anyone who has ever been with a group of men (and even among men the hatred of women is usually fully vented only when there is a sizable group), be it in the army, at a sales meeting, a convention, or other gathering, knows the intensity with which men malign, befoul, despise, yet helplessly crave women—and sex. They talk about it constantly, joke (or what passes for joking) about nothing else, seem to think about nothing else, but almost always with contempt, hostility, anger.

A young soldier, now at camp, tells of an old sergeant, who after a few drinks liked to regale his soldier audience with his youthful exploits. The crowning piece, every evening, was the sergeant's World War II tour of duty in Shanghai, where the population was flailed by war and desperately poor. "Believe it or not," the sergeant would scream, "a piece of ass for a nickel! A nickel! Everywhere you went!" And his audiences would cheer him.

The point of the story is that it rests, not on sex, which is secondary, but on the humiliation of the unwilling females, who not only had to sell themselves, but to a man like that sergeant and for the merest pittance. Why would such a story generate tears of laughter and delight in so many men? Why would it give them such a kick? Only because, as Germaine Greer says, men tend to hate women, and many men really hate them with a vengeance.

Why? There are unconscious and conscious reasons. The view of most psychoanalysts, and as good a view as any, is that perhaps the manchild's extreme dependence on his mother, and the extreme difficulties in building his manhood against the strong drag in the opposite direction exercised by most mothers, answers the question on the deepest level. But there are more visible and accessible reasons.

One reason for men's hatred of women—and one that produces great resentment—may be that men resent the fact that for the most part they are so hopelessly and helplessly enslaved to the chase after the one thing only a woman possesses. And as Germaine Greer points out, the "lay," if finally granted, or an endless series of them, tends to make the womanhating man even more hateful and contemptuous. It may be that for most men sexual activity, far from being in any way satisfying, is endlessly and intolerably stimulating; it intensifies the addiction and makes the chains heavier. Then, quite naturally, the man hates women, no matter what ephemeral pleasure or relief he may get from them, just as the true alcoholic really hates the stuff he cannot do without but that poisons his every waking minute, whether he indulges himself or not.

There also appears to be a sociopsychological reason for man's anger against women that could be expected to vanish in the coming generations. As pointed out in Chapter 3, with few exceptions many men have lost their masculine role in the technological society, their natural habitat, their very manhood. They cannot use their bodies or their physical attributes, which, like all attributes unused, come back to plague their possessors. Many contemporary men lead an essentially passive, servile, and hypocritical—that is, cowardly and emasculated—existence. They are dependent upon the whims of others. They can only feel and assert their stunted manhood through sex, at least superficially. Symbolically this may go a long way toward explaining why men are so obsessed with sex and invest it with all the male aggression for which they can find no other outlets, and which, because woman is not a very suitable target for that aggression, turns to hatred.

It may be equally important that man in the technological society already knows, in his soul, though generally not on a conscious level, that almost no matter what his position in society, a woman could now easily take his place. Where once he had to fear only male competitors reaching for whatever his position in life, he now sees female competitors as well by whom—except for producing sperm and performing the act of sex in his way—he can be replaced. And he is primitive enough to let fear and apprehension of the inevitable changes in society that will soon occur turn into hatred and anger, though he may not dare to express this directly. But he does express that fear and hatred all the more strongly indirectly, in his brassy talk with other men about sex (which talk they regard as a display of virility) and in his actual contacts with women. Yet as his hatred of women is often as unknown even to him as Germaine Greer says it is to women, it expresses itself not merely in brute physical aggression (though often it does that too, as in beatings), but more frequently in one of the many forms of impotence, predominantly in premature ejaculation, the phenomenon that is one of the links in the pernicious chain of poor sex, poor relationships, poor society, poor sex.

Can this hostility between the sexes, cause and result of untold personal and social misery, come to an end in so short a time as, say, a decade after having been around so long? (It is not known how long—it does not seem to have been so irksome, or so public, a fact of life in the preindustrial ages, although, as the women's movement rightly points out, hatred of women was stimulated and cultivated by the churches for two thousand years.) It would appear that way, merely from the better, more natural, casual, unhostile fashion in which the very young now get along with each other. While the older generations scoff at "unisex," the social and in particular the sexual relations among the young appear to be much more effective, normal, satisfying, and vigorous than the widespread and vicious teasing-being-teased cycle was to their teeth-gnashing forebears. The very fact of "unisex" seems to suggest that very young men at least no longer seem to feel the exasperating need to preserve and assert their manhood in every aspect of their appearance or behavior, which would indicate that they feel more secure about that manhood than the closecropped and husky types who secretly loathe and fear women.

Young men who are not afraid of resembling women externally would appear to indicate that they do not feel the need to assert themselves, to defend themselves, to establish beyond the slightest doubt their otherness and superiority; that they feel their sexual identity can be maintained and developed without the customary social props. And if, as they seem to, they also feel secure enough in their masculinity to permit women to take their rightful place in society, to let the feminine element pervade and civilize the society in which we live, they would therefore automatically also not be prone to the ingrained hatred toward women. This in turn would make it easier for women to take their rightful place and have true and amicable relationships with men, and both could then attain mutually satisfying sexual relationships. Hatred of women, to the extent that it is not an atavistic or psychotic trait independent of the social climate, should then largely disappear from the scene. The doors would be opened to the social and sexual progress that cannot occur as long as that hatred is so strong and widespread and mostly so unconscious that it cannot even be properly perceived or confronted.

Here too woman power will be the source of a better life for both sexes. For woman power, first of all, will demythologize women, will make women *real,* to themselves as well as to men, so that men's now so contradictory fantasies about woman as the angel, the mother, the madonna on the one hand, and the slut, the bitch, the "cunt" on the other—will simultaneously give way to a less romantic or satanized perception of female human beings. Men's sexual inadequacy was undoubtedly contributed to by this unreality of women, the wild ambivalence that perceives the Virgin Mary as too magnificent to be sullied with sex, and the predatory slut as not worthy of affection and dangerous to be with besides. When women step out of their enforced distant and often unnatural roles, when the pernicious propaganda about women abates and women truly appear on, and change, the social scene, men (and women too) will probably shun both extremes of their ambivalence and as a result become sexually more adequate, without psychoanalysis or Masters and Johnson.

Will Sexual Activities Be "Free"? Sexual freedom currently appears to mean to most not just promiscuity widely tolerated or encouraged, but doing "everything" that can be done, and doing it more or less openly—that is, either doing it publicly or at least talking about it publicly and displaying what one does. These anxious efforts at deprivatizing sex, whether in bars, where it is practiced by hired performers on a piano, or in general, with the claim that "it's all natural," is in itself a strange perversion. It is attributable to the sexual tenseness in our day, the strong desire to cast overboard all that inhibits sex, on the assumption that such casting away of external inhibitions must increase the quality and quantity of available pleasure. But as much of the tenseness goes out of sex, as it probably will in the coming decade, sex is likely to become reprivatized and therefore more pleasurable for everybody.

For sex is not like riding a horse or singing: the pleasure *is* enhanced by privacy. To witness the act, whether with one's eyes or by hearing every detail about it, may be exciting, but it does devalue the act. The singer enjoys his song more rather than less if others listen. But except to various types of exhibitionists—that is, people plagued by a deviation that, like all deviations, interferes with the giving and experiencing of sexual satisfaction—the sex act is not enhanced by display or public discussion of specific individual activity, and the current fashion of exhibitionism may be regarded as a mere rattling of the chains that have so long inhibited all sex. It is not likely to endure.

The relations between men and women have been so deeply poisoned for so long, and hostility between the sexes is so great (aside from all other factors already discussed), because of the twin plagues, the twin terrors: VD and unwanted pregnancy. For many centuries both were lethal. The man or woman contracting VD could not be truly cured, was poisoned for life, as often as not produced, if it was syphilis, monsters for children or, if it was gonorrhea, blind offspring, and suffered other terrible scourges. People went mad, suffered hell physically and mentally, and were despised and shunned by their fellow creatures as impure, a horror to themselves and others. As for out-of-wedlock pregnancies (and even unwanted in-wedlock pregnancies), the consequences were equally devastating. Only rarely did the unwed mother not suffer a socially incurable fate and anticipate a degraded, intolerable life compared with which suicide was often preferable. No wonder that these twin monsters drove terror into people's souls, and fear and anger as well. Driven by the overwhelming power of sex, men and women would "weaken," only to be sobered, terrified, and despairing the next moment, and perhaps forever. So great were the dangers inherent in sex, and so virtually unavoidable, that people had no choice but to forego sex as much as possible; to fight ever-present temptation with their feeble and forever melting will power. To the man, the woman was indeed the worst possible, the most dangerous temptress; and to her he was the worst possible tempter. Parents, whatever their religious or moral views, had no choice but to warn their children in the sternest terms against the other sex, planting fear in their hearts. It is only natural that in those conditions men and women, consciously or unconsciously, came deeply to fear and hate sex, and, via psychological transposition, *each other.*

"Modern pharmaceutical control of VD and pregnancy," says Jungian analyst Robert S., "are the most fantastic steps forward the human race has made in thousands of years. By taking the actual dangers and the commitant terrors out of sex, these new devices have opened entirely new perspectives to the human race, not just for the enjoyment of sex—that is the least of it. People will, as a result, be able to see and live with members of the opposite sex differently, no longer as the enemy, the irresistible yet potentially poisonous source of untold delight *and* horror. This is now over. As a result, man's and woman's attitudes to each other and to their own lives will change radically, for the better.

"One can say that freedom is now within reach," he continues. "Not just political freedom, but human, individual freedom. For all the political freedom is not worth too much, in fact, ultimately is not even possible, without human freedom all around, and in the days of unconquered VD and pregnancy there simply was no human freedom for most. There now is a chance that relations between the sexes will undergo a fundamental change. No longer will every girl be the snake in the grass, deadly with danger, for any man who seeks sexual enjoyment, and no longer will any handsome or attractive and lusty male be the potential Devil Incarnate for every maiden, leaving behind woe and death after a brief moment of bliss. Why, the sexes will be able to begin *loving* each other without reservations, mark my word!

"Of course," says Robert, "the full benefit of the new devices controlling VD and pregnancy cannot have their full impact overnight: the human race has suffered too much too long. A person freed from a concentration camp after years of experiencing and witnessing the most terrible things cannot fully enjoy his freedom the first few days of his release, in fact he cannot believe his good fortune. At night his dreams continue to be nightmares. It takes a while. Of course, there are so-called epidemics of VD now, but they are not all that important: VD *is* no longer a killer, it *is* essentially under control and will soon be altogether."

There is today a VD epidemic, particularly of gonorrhea. Troublesome though this is, however, and even though some of the strains are impervious to antibiotics, the sting has nevertheless been largely taken out of these diseases. They are still serious, and do a good deal of harm. But the high incidence and prevalence—though regrettable—are also evidence that these diseases are feared much less than they were, and rightly so, as the new cures usually do work. It is not good for people to have VD, needless to say, and the problem of its ultimate control is still unsolved. But the terror has been largely taken out of it; psychologically, this is the most important factor. Few parents now describe these diseases to their children in the same lurid, fear-producing, hate-engendering ways as formerly.

Robert S. continues: "With the disappearance of the evil consequences of sex much of what people lived by will go out the window. Look at the stern moral, social, religious, educational injunctions of the past which even most reformers did not like to tamper with, as the hazards of sex were so great and real for male and female. Small wonder that so many people were ground into psychological and intellectual cripples by the two giant millstones of sex: its irresistible attractions and its unspeakable consequences!

"For both men and women any person of the opposite sex—and, ironically, in particular any attractive or lovable person of the opposite sex—was the potential source of terrible damage, something to be dreaded. And dread always generates hostility. For parents, girls of all kinds were indeed the greatest threats to their sons, as boys were for their girls; and their warnings, and what all the growing youngsters could observe all around them or read in books or see in plays, could not but generate immense suspicion, anxiety, anger. And all three modes of behavior that followed—abstinence, hobbled sex such as petting, or full consummation followed by terror and remorse—further increased the hostility between the sexes and poisoned the lives of young and old alike. Believe me, with the means of controlling pregnancy and VD the human race has made a find like a poor downtrodden embittered man finding a twenty-carat diamond he can keep. These things will transform all aspects of life once people have deconditioned themselves from all the past repressions that were really not so much generated by religion as by the terrors of sex. But it will take time, though perhaps only a decade."

We agree with the enthusiasm of the good doctor and with his thought that the ultimate social and political consequences of VD and pregnancy control are so vast that a human race conditioned for thousands of years to the inevitable repressive attitudes toward sex, and thus society, cannot free itself from all these in one instant. The young seem to have taken the first step: they no longer stand in awe of the sexual freedom medical science has provided. Hence they have every chance of remaking the world in just those very few years it will take them to grow up. And woman power will help fulfill the sexual revolution and benefit by it. In social and political life, with men hating and fearing women less from boyhood on because of people's liberation from the twin plagues, men will place less resistance in the way of women taking their place. And in relations between the sexes the ability to have and enjoy sex, and the ability to love and respect the other sex without gruesome reservations, will finally obtain. Sexual activity will then be truly "free." Presumably only the older generations—mainly because of anterior conditioning—will not be able fully to partake in any of it, neither in the enhanced sexual nor the greater social freedom.

9

WOMAN POWER AND THE FUTURE OF SEX (II)

PORNOGRAPHY. If the human race did not have the capacity to adapt overnight to some very strange developments, the current porno wave and its manifestations would seem utterly incredible to most people. How could it happen and what is its true meaning? That it indicates widespread sexual frustration is only a facile and unsatisfactory explanation, and that it represents a new page in human sexual freedom is obviously nonsense, just as it is obviously nonsense that the porno wave must be guaranteed its existence by the First Amendment. Perhaps the best point of departure for examining the phenomenon of contemporary pornography is an examination of the strange reaction so many claim to have in response to pornographic displays.

Nine in ten people claim that "it's boring," that it "does not turn them on," that it is "always the same." But they are all liars. True, it may not turn them on sexually, at least not physically. But the viewing of pornography is nevertheless exciting for most people. Why? One reason is probably that pornography is a release and a promise: a release from the crushing taboos that, like all previous societies, our society imposes, and a promise of more release to come. The entire social corset seems to be loosened a notch or two when pornography is viewed. Besides, we like to see other people's bodies, and men will no more tire of seeing women's sexual accoutrements than they will tire of sex itself. Finally, it is a curious quality, innate or inbred, that people like to see or watch strangers. Because the nude girl displayed in a magazine or a film is a stranger, the excitement is increased, precisely for the same reason that all our taboos are intended mainly to inhibit us in the company of strangers. Pornography's unspoken promise seems to suggest that if some of the restrictions will fall, *all* of them may fall. Therefore, pornography *is* exciting, no matter what most people say, and that is why it is such good business.* Therefore, too, "conservative" people—who are just as sexually eager as anyone else and just as interested in "dirty pictures"—fear pornography, rightly, as something that might corrode a wide variety of apparently unrelated institutions. Which is exactly why "progressives" or "revolutionaries" insist with such ludicrous intensity that the right to produce, sell, and obtain pornography must be preserved: they too must somehow expect it to help bring down the social structure.

One important reason for the disclaimers of interest in pornography (which would actually die a quick death if the disinterest were widespread) is that, for most people, to advertise an interest in pornography is to advertise one's sexual frustration, sexual failure, indeed sexual inadequacy. People like to play the jaded or at least fully satisfied citizens; they want it known that they need no substitutes, because they have more than enough of the real thing. They fool themselves, though not others, on both scores; for their claimed disinterest in pornography is rarely convincing, and besides, an interest in pornography does not necessarily advertise frustration or inadequacy at all. Fully satisfied people (to the extent that any person can ever be fully satisfied sexually) are as in-

* The partial failure of the last pornography fair in Copenhagen was probably caused by many factors too extraneous to analyze here. In any event, as is patently obvious, it did not spell the end of the porno wave.

terested in or excited by pornography as anyone else, just because of its metasexual promise of an infantile wonderland with *no* restrictions, and because of the anarchical aspects already mentioned.

Why does the subject of pornography always appear in discussions of sex, and why is it so hard to abandon? Despite the current intensity of pornographic activities and, perhaps even more significantly, despite the perplexity of the courts and other authorities as to what to do about it, it is a symptom, not of sexual emancipation, but of the disturbed sex life of our era. Even though, given the opportunity, the "normal" and "satisfied" person may also view pornography, it is a sign of frustration and rebellion when it plays so strident a part in society. It is most interesting that those who must establish rules in the (male) establishment are in such a quandary about pornography, and that so many invoke the First Amendment so fervently when defending someone's right to produce, display, view, or sell it. To people a generation ago, had they had the power of prophecy, this aspect of pornography—that is, the weighty and tortured exculpations given by the pillars of society—would have been even more unexpected than the porno wave itself. And far from being evidence of a truly broad mind or of a great respect for the Bill of Rights, it is more likely to be evidence of an essentially restricted and prurient national mentality attempting to justify itself.

The insistence by authorities that all pornography must be permitted is not dissimilar from current efforts to do away with the death penalty. Rather than the sign of humaneness they are advertised as being, such efforts are mainly designed, consciously or not, to obscure the fact that the same authorities have conducted and are still conducting a war, and still need to mollify their consciences. The fight against the death penalty says: "Look how humane we are." The tolerance of pornography says: "Look how enlightened we are, and how seriously we take our First Amendment!"

Probably the most powerful stimulus behind the porno wave is a factor that, visible or not, pervades all of contemporary society: hostility between the sexes, particularly the hostility of men toward women. By fully exposing the female body, man strikes blows against female modesty and shame. He figuratively rips the clothes off collective woman and forces her to assume suggestive postures, to see her all the better and degrade her all the more, and in return for his vileness, she must beckon to him to boot, as the unclad ladies of the pornos invariably do. *That* is probably the biggest source of man's excitement and insatiable quest for pornography. Many men experience, in response to pornography, the curious feeling of being left relatively cold sexually, yet fascinated and excited, probably because of the satisfaction of their *hostility,* the enjoyment of the vicarious rape of the stranger forced into a demeaned sexual position and—as testified by her enticing smile or lust-laden mien—made to like it.*

If this interpretation is accurate, we can predict that in the coming decade the prevalence of pornography will greatly decline. First, a more natural and satisfying relationship between the sexes, in particular a reduced hostility of men toward women, will reduce interest in pornography. In a society reshaped by woman power a good many of the reasons for the current spread of pornography are likely to disappear, not least because the women will—as evidenced in women's lib publications—meet the wave head-on once they have more influence in society. Second, a cleaner and more direct and self-assured national conscience will enable people to say, simply, "Most of the stuff has nothing to do with the First Amendment." We will simply forbid it. Caught between reduced interest and stiffer laws, the porno wave is then likely to abate considerably.

* There are many other types of pornography, of "sexploitation," that cater to and are equally exploitive of those whose tastes are for sadomasochism, male or female homosexuality, and so on. These, however, are beyond the scope of the present discussion.

What about Prostitution? Vivian M., former prostitute and drug addict turned Synanon member and law student, says, "If anything is insane in our society, it is the prostitution laws, the whole incredible slapstick circus of evil vice squads and crotchety judges and horrible jails and matrons and pimps and Johns who are flimflammed and rolled and infected and beaten senseless and left in gutters with broken skulls. As though society has nothing better to do than track down women who, as it is called so dramatically, sell their bodies. The lot of a prostitute in our enlightened society is truly horrible, an absolute inferno. But that she must sell her body is the least of it.

"The principal enemy of the prostitute is the cop on the vice squad. He is a strangler, a blackmailer, an exploiter. He demands sexual services free of charge, he beats the girls, he takes money that is not taken by the pimp. He is hard to deceive or escape; he knows the ropes. He is, mostly, a tough and depraved person. There are some exceptions—at least they don't blackmail or force prostitutes into submission. But they are brutal too, believe you me. They think they save Christian womanhood or something. They *hate* prostitutes. Being on the vice squad, they are real psychos, like the rest of them. As for jail, I don't want to go into that—you probably know yourself what is going on there from the papers.

"The next mortal enemy of the prostitute is the pimp, but not always. What is a pimp, anyway? He is different from what the newspaper reader thinks. The pimp, even if he has several girls, is really more or less a husband, without the ceremony, or the alimony when things break up. Some pimps are perfectly decent, but most are vicious, greedy men on whom the prostitute is dependent and who take all her earnings and terrorize her. In that respect the popular imagination is correct. But why the pimp? Learned psychologists—men, of course—write long and well-paid articles saying the pimp is a father figure, that the girl needs to lean on him, derive emotional security. Nonsense. If the law and the whole machinery with which it is enforced were not what it is, a girl hardly would need a pimp. The power of the pimp is furnished him compliments of the police and the courts and the jails. They are such that the girl needs the protection of a criminal fellow."

There are three basic positions on prostitution these days. The first is the traditional one: prostitution is a crime; the girls must be hunted down and punished and jailed when they are caught; and the Johns go free. The second is that prostitution should be legalized. The third, now generally accepted as the women's lib position, is that prostitution should not be legalized but that the John should be punished, not the girl.

If all factors are taken into account, the probability is that none of the three positions will prevail. The traditional approach is not likely to remain unchanged in a society in which women and the feminine way of doing things will be more influential, as they can be expected to be in the coming decade. The second is not likely to materialize, at least not in this century, for Christian ethics as well as other motivating factors are too deeply ingrained to make such a course of action likely. The third is equally improbable, because while men will have to surrender a great deal of their power to women in the coming decade, they will not surrender all of it; and whatever they keep they will use to prevent such new legislation, simply because they expect that they will want to continue to visit prostitutes. What, then, will happen?

Most likely, in a society that is more harmonious and more sensitive to human needs and dignity, the mad, vicious, and depraved hunt of prostitutes and their ludicrous trials in court and wretched treatment in jails will abate. In a sinister way the treatment of prostitutes has come to be tied in with drugs, not only because many prostitutes become users (or many users become prostitutes), but also because the ballooning of the drug affliction has swelled the ranks of vice squads and their venality. Even though the evils of drug use and the evils of vice squads may diminish, the prostitutes will still have to suffer greatly, not just from customers and pimps, but from "law enforcement."

Still, prostitutes may look forward to somewhat better days in the 1980s. They will not disappear; they will never disappear. Men like Marx believed that socialism would do away with prostitution, which he saw as a purely economic phenomenon; he was wrong, as evidence from Communist countries shows. Others, be they evangelists or women's libbers, see other ways of doing away with prostitution, and they are probably wrong too. From an economic point of view prostitution, as has often been stated, is a special but not untypical transaction at one end of the societal spectrum. The prognosis on prostitution is that in the coming decade people, who will be more sensible and cooperative with each other once the partnership society between men and women has evolved and taken hold, will be kinder to their prostitutes.

Prostitutes will never have an easy life. But some former civilizations have at least treated their prostitutes well and with respect, sometimes even according them a place in their temples. In no event is prostitution likely ever to become a desirable profession or condition. But a society that madly persecutes and exploits prostitutes, while madly promoting and sanctioning pornography, cannot live forever with such contradictions. In the saner partnership society there is likely to be some equalization, with prostitutes becoming less persecuted and pornographers more.

Monogamy? Polygamy? Men and women, throughout recorded history, have always gotten into trouble, but also obtained much pleasure and diversion, because they are monogamous as well as polygamous—and inclined to be both simultaneously. After various trials and errors over the past ten thousand years, monogamous marriage established itself as a nearly universal institution. Though that alone does not prove its value or guarantee its durability, marriage seems likely to remain mono, at least for the period we are here contemplating (see more about that in Chapter 5).

We probably will see changes, however, in what is called infidelity. Though almost universally practiced, infidelity is a risky business, not so much because the law gets into the act—that too—but because any form of it, no matter how unable to produce real satisfaction, so often contributes to the destruction of the marriage and thus the family. The married man is acceptable as a sex partner to most unmarried women only if he is "serious," which implies his promising, honestly or not, that he will get a divorce, which, if he promises it long enough, he might get even if he did not intend to initially. Though many unfaithful men manage to string their mistresses along for years, the price they have to pay for sexual activity away from home is in many cases their marriage, or most of it. For in our present society, more females are predatory rather than hedonistic in their inclinations, predatory for the legal possession of their man and for reasons inherent in society more than in the female.

Married women, on the other hand, though they dislike the double standard that, at least in this country, they have quite successfully abolished, can take greater liberties more easily. A married woman who feels inclined to have sex with a man other than her husband does not almost have to promise marriage to the stud to get him into bed, nor take him out for dinners or to the opera along the circuitous seduction trail that a man must generally follow to reach his aim (which even then is elusive and uncertain). Contrary to common legend, there are many more opportunities for a married woman than for a married man, and if she indulges her whims, she can even dissemble better than the man: she is at the market (unsupervised), he is at the office (supervised). But does she do it? A twenty-six-year-old woman, married for six years and so far childless, said, "Well, at this moment I would not contemplate it. That is, I would contemplate it, but I would not do it, probably. If I did it at all, I would do it only if the sexual attraction were overwhelming—that is, if nothing else were involved, if the whole thing would not hurt my relationship with my husband. So far I haven't done it, but yes, I probably would, under the circumstances I mentioned."

Presumably, in the coming decade, thanks to the more realistic and relaxed society resulting from a stronger feminine influence on all its aspects, infidelity will become even less of a disaster if found out than it already is, less of a first step to the divorce court. The family as a unit would thereby be strengthened, because people would not have to be "seriously involved" with outsiders to rate their attention, nor unforgiving when infidelities occur. In general, as people come to view each other less as sex objects, so that sex can genuinely become less dominant as the principal lien in marriage, they will find new and more satisfactory ways of being what they really are: polygamous *and* monogamous.

The reader may say that this is not much of a prediction, especially since infidelity seems already to exist on a much larger scale than in the past. To some extent that is true; but the retention of the term itself, or its equally sinister-sounding companion term, adultery, indicates that basic attitudes have not really changed. What we are likely to see in the different social and sexual climate of the 1980s, brought about in part by woman power, is that emotionally and terminologically the act of having sexual relations outside of marriage will be divested of the connotation of breaking faith, of betraying, cheating the one person most people are generally most attached to. It is a reasonable prediction that the terms "infidelity" and "adultery" will soon be designated by Webster as "archaic."

Group Sex. From wife-swapping, which seems to have become quite common and is presumably a consequence of life in the suburbs, where couples rarely meet anyone except other similar couples, an unknown but apparently considerable number of Americans have graduated to "swinging." Group sex, practiced by one couple with another, or in larger groups, calls for much variety and a complicated network of nationwide connections and reliance on advertising. A slender volume, *The Group Sex Scene,* by

John F. Trimble, Ph.D.,[1] presents what purports to be the experiences of a California couple who began with a little conservative wife-swapping and eventually went on to bigger things. It is amusing to follow their amatory itinerary.

The two played it conservatively and tell us they avoided the "nuts" and "psychos" and "crazies" who are forever trying to "horn in," such as "singles" who are "bad news," or "bestialists," or people "who bring their teenage daughters." Somewhat surprisingly the couple, when just swapping wives and husbands (the initial stages of group sex), found that they tended to be *jealous*—not over their wives or husbands either: if the couple they "went with" flirted with another couple at a party, they would be troubled. The two principals of the book soon overcame this impediment by expanding. They went on trips on the basis of advertisements, so frequently, in fact, "that all our time together was devoted to sex and planning of sex. We hardly looked at television any more." On one of their safaris into the outskirts of Los Angeles, Lorraine and Don, the heroes of the tale, met Doris and Brad in midmorning by the latter couple's swimming pool, and it was "all systems go" from the start. Don reports that Doris began by "reaching into a heavily iced picnic cooler and bringing out three bottles of the best imported Dutch beer." Don smiled at Lorraine (his wife): "They might be country, but they have class."

Within minutes, literally, of their arrival, Doris (the hostess) had dragged Don (the male guest) into the basement to show him hundreds of dirty pictures, and a lot more. Meantime, by the pool, Lorraine says, she "felt a bit ill at ease when Don left me alone with Brad. I don't mean that I was afraid of him or that he repulsed me. . . . It was simply that I wondered what in the world we might have in common to talk about." She need not have fretted, for Don was "no unsophisticated clod" and knew pretty well how to start the conversation. "You know, honey," was his swift opening gambit, delivered in a "cute drawl": "Those legs you got make me want to get moving!"

These words were quite literally the Open Sesame! for Lorraine: "I brought my dress up by placing my hands on my thighs. The young stud unzippered his fly and produced (what else? Ed.) his very hard penis. I (continued Lorraine) was more amused than shocked, and I was also titillated . . . I am not used to drinking beer," she confides in the reader "and that strong imported variety was making me adventuresome." Brad, the subtle conversationalist, then asked "whether I had ever been screwed out in broad daylight like that, and I could not help but break out laughing (Why, Lorraine?)." Anyway, "ain't nobody gonna see," Brad assured Lorraine—not only "very sincerely" but also "waving his penis proudly." "You can hear anybody drive up front," Brad told Lorraine, and continued, "Besides, I got a system where you can keep all your clothes on. Come on over here and set (!?) on my lap, and I'll show you." As Don said—real class.

Lorraine then muses: "Was this really *me?* I wondered for a moment." But not for long: "I gulped down the rest of my glass of beer, removed my briefs, hiked up my dress, and went over and lowered myself to his lap while he penetrated me with—(with what? you guessed wrong!)—with surprising ease." And in the meantime Doris and Don were not wasting their time in the basement.

Gratifying though the experience and others like it were, Lorraine and Don then aimed for larger groups. They made new contacts, again via an advertisement, this time for genuine group activity in a large mansion. The first person they met at the mansion where the session took place, aside from the—obviously—stark naked host in the doorway, was a fellow Don had met previously (he underwrites the industrial policies for Don's company. Don's reaction: "I'll be damned"). And Don adds, "We were in high society now, and we knew it. This was the league of swingers we had always wanted to be with." Much as the reader might like to learn details of the party that ensued, we prefer to deny them to him. Let him merely be informed that it was an apocalyptic gang-bang, serenely surveyed by a portly psychiatrist, sitting naked and alone in an overstuffed chair, masturbating and giving directions to the revelers.

The reader is left uncertain whether Lorraine and Don are having a good time. They do not, it appears, have a bad time, nor a good one either. It is not clear why they engage in these activities and what all the activities give to them. More than anything else they appear disingenuous, like people pursuing some hobby, "doing their thing." As to their activities, these may—as in the case of pornography or the use of sex words in indiscriminate profusion—appear to some as sexual liberation, a newfound freedom. But they actually suggest that they are the end of a line, the end of a transitional response to former suppression, *a false start.* The activities as described appear essentially ridiculous, as does the language in which they are reported, a sort of colossal sexual joke, played *on* the participants more than *by* them, yet not a tragedy. One senses that these two just will never "make it," certainly not whatever it is they are trying to make, much like the man playing golf with a tennis racket will never make it.

Group sex does not fit into the more sensitive and more genuinely liberated society foreseen for the 1980s. Despite its current great vogue, it will disappear before the decade is over, at least as a national phenomenon even though there will probably always be individual orgies of one kind or another.

10

WOMAN POWER AND THE FUTURE OF SEX (III)

WHAT about sex as a sport, a performance, a challenge, a competition? Almost everywhere the emphasis on the sporting analogy for sex, such as performance, number, and type of conquests, has always been extraordinary. In the 1950s in particular, when the media began their frantic stressing of the Big O, and the refinements of sex were discovered in the wake of World War II (much like Camembert cheese or Fiat Spyders), it almost seemed as though sex, which had always been to many a test of prowess and something to brag about, might indeed become the poor man's karate, with black belts being given out by junior chambers of commerce. In his wild yet penetrating parody of American life, *Why Are We in Vietnam?*, Norman Mailer envisaged it this way: "Yeah, the time is coming, thinks Rusty, when fornication will be professional athletics, and everybody will watch the national eliminations on TV. Will boys like Tex and D.J. be in the finals with a couple of Playboy bunnies or blackass honeys? Well, shit-and-sure, fifty thousand major league fuckers will be clawing and cutting to get into the big time to present their open flower petal pussy, or hand-hewn diamond tool and testicles in happy magnification by Color Vision RCA. Only thing holding this scheme back is the problems of integration. What if the Spades run away with the jewels?"[1]

Well, Rusty, that time is *not* coming. The trend will be in the opposite direction. Not only will the athletic performance and competition factor be taken out of sex to a reassuring degree, but under woman power's influence the exhibitionism, the crude, actually animal-like, display is likely to yield to a reprivatization of sex in word and action.

Together with the performance rage and the many trying acrobatics advocated by the books and the women's magazines, the female's frantic hunt for the male will also largely disappear in the 1980s. That amazing best-seller *The Sensuous Woman* may have been the last gasp of the frenzied. The book recommends that after you (a woman) have gone through ten sensuality exercises (Exercise Number Six: "The tongue again, and this is the wildest one yet. . . ."), you go out and find your men: "Where are these men? All around you. Take another look at your children's piano teacher. Or the piano tuner [!!!]. How about your golf pro or that muscular gentleman who gives you tennis lessons? Newspaper reporters. . . . Portrait photographers. . . . Get out the phone book, make a list and go portrait shopping. . . . Get that handsome landscape architect to do your hedges and more. . . . Grab yourself a professor." However, "Insurance men only want to sell insurance. Fuller brushmen are too square." Dance instructors often "like other men." Plasterers and painters don't seem to have any strong urges. . . . "Forget supermarket managers and shoe salesmen." Why? "By the end of the day they hate women." There are other fish to fry. "Doctors are nervous about hanky panky during office hours," but that is no problem. "You [must] entice them out of their offices if you want a *complete* physical. . . ." "And then there are all sorts of repairmen, delivery men and delivery *boys* ["J's" emphasis]." And so on. Finally this crowning piece of advice: "The *best* ["J's" emphasis again] way for a married woman to meet prospective lovers is through her husband." [2]

Future generations, reading this book in the knowledge that it sold millions of copies, will be puzzled as to whether the author was writing a beautifully funny parody of the frenzied sex-seeker, or had approached her subject and audience straight. They will find it hard to believe that it was the latter, that her advice was taken as seriously by many readers as advice to shipwrecked sailors by Billy Graham, no matter how bizarre that advice seems. Presumably a million or more women, after having learned from the book to apply, for instance, the "Butterfly Flick" on discomfited partners, really fanned out in search of prey, "J's" book in hand. But historians will find it hard to accept that sexual frustration, sexual despair, could have ballooned to such proportions that such books not only could have been written, but they could even have become best-sellers; that society was in such dismal sexual straits and that the methods advocated and practiced to combat the problem could be celebrated as signs of sexual liberation. While future generations may pity the Victorians as we do, they will undoubtedly pity the frenetics of the 1940s and '50s and '60s even more.

Sex Manuals and Sexual Enlightenment. The multimillion circulation figures of such primitive and elementary tracts as Dr. David Reuben's *Everything You Always Wanted To Know About Sex But Were Afraid To Ask* or his *Any Woman Can!* which created, at least terminologically, "The Sexually Marooned Woman" and told her where, or rather how, to get off, are a clear indication, not of sexual enlightenment and progress in our day, but of stark ignorance and naïveté in sexual matters.

Who can tell how much people know about sex? It does seem, in any event, that people are surprisingly ignorant in sexual matters, if some of those interviewed for this book can serve as an indication.

Ingrid B., an ardent adherent of women's lib, said on the subject of sex publications, "It will do a lot for sex in general as more information comes out. Just little tips in there, like how much fun it is to be on top—it significantly changes people's relationships because they go home and try something out." Considering that Ingrid is twenty-three, a feminist, and a contributor to sophisticated women's magazines, one is astonished that so simple and universally practiced a sexual position as "to be on top" is not known to her except through published materials, and that she has to "go home and try it out."

It is hard to imagine that such simple mutations of sexual intercourse were not practiced even in most Victorian England or in the Catholic countries, where explicit sexual literature was not available until very recently. Perhaps people do know very little and the vast reading matter on the subject is of help to them. What does it consist of? Where the psychoanalysts have insisted that all that is needed for good sex is a good relationship, where others may see the panacea in vigorous exercise of the pelvic muscles, even under the hairdryer, where there is really nothing much else to do, contemporary sexologists see the solution primarily in techniques designed to enhance a sexual relationship that is not sufficiently satisfying or has gone stale.

Our interviews indicate that people do not seem to realize for how many years such advice on sex techniques has been openly published. Whatever else it is, it certainly is not evidence of great sexual progress or some newfound freedoms. The granddaddy and true "first" in the realm of sex education was a book by a Dutch physician, Theodor H. Van de Velde, *Ideal Marriage, Its Physiology and Technique.* It appeared in Europe in 1926, where it was read by millions, and was brought out shortly thereafter in New York by Random House and has gone through some forty printings, the most recent being a revised edition published in 1965. It contains descriptions of all the positions with all the necessary diagrams, including those of male and female organs and charts of orgasms achieved under various conditions. Can the new literature provide much in the way of enlightenment if the old—Van de Velde's "ultimate" book has now been available for half a century—has not helped in the past? No matter. The burgeoning sexual "how-to" literature swamping the country may on balance be a positive sign in the sexual development of the nation: at least, as Ingrid says, the people "go home and try it out" and it may improve their performance and reduce their chronic frustration and all the social and political ills it engenders. Many may even learn to change their relationships into a mutually pleasure-giving and pleasure-taking partnership.

But that is not likely. Even though ignorance in sex matters is certainly not bliss (nor greatly conducive to it), the knowledge of what "others do" with supposedly good therapeutic effect or more information about *techniques* is most unlikely to improve the sex lives of sex students. Only as relations between men and women improve and the social environment becomes more conducive to sex will America's collective sex life improve. Sex manuals and especially the so desperately fought for and so highly touted sex education in schools will then largely disappear. It will become unnecessary.

Rape. Never before, it seems, has rape been so widely practiced as in our day. Rape is not merely (or even mainly) the result of unfulfilled and unfulfillable overwhelming sexual needs. On the contrary. A recent article in *The New York Times* established the fact that almost all apprehended rapists were shown to have other sexual opportunities at their disposal.[3] Why do they rape?

In part the reason is simple sexual pathology: the combination of sex and stranger and sex and violence arouses some men, who indulge their inclination to a limited extent with wives, mistresses, and acquaintances, while others actually rape strangers, and others again relegate such drives to their own imaginations. But there are further reasons, such as bitter hostility between races, classes, and the sexes. Eldridge Cleaver, in *Soul on Ice*, says,

"Many whites flatter themselves with the idea that the Negro male's lust and desire for the white dream girl is purely an aesthetic attraction, but nothing could be farther from the truth. His motivation is often of such a bloody, hateful, bitter and malignant nature that whites would really be hard pressed to find it flattering." [4]

Such feelings do not, of course, account for most of the many rapes committed daily in this country. The secondary reasons—legal and social—for the phenomenon are at least as important as, if not more so than, the primary ones that make men rape a woman. On the legal side, a conviction for rape requires corroborating evidence from someone other than the violated female. Because that is generally impossible to produce, rapists feel relatively free as far as the law is concerned, and also tend to go free after a trial and be on their violent way again.

On the social side, most women are too embarrassed to report a rape. More important, if a woman is assaulted—whether in daytime or at night, in an empty lot or at home—people who hear her cries or even witness the crime seldom come to her aid. Many civic crocodile tears have been shed over this by armchair heroes. But people might as well recognize that John Q. Citizen, even if he is perfectly honorable and courageous, or at least as honorable and courageous as his basically sedentary, nonviolent, mostly verbal life has conditioned him to be, is not going to risk death or mutilation and horror for his family by rescuing unknown maidens from the grip of knife-and-pistol-wielding maniacs. It happens occasionally, which is good. But women cannot expect to be protected against rape by gallantry on the part of the average Rabbit Redux.

The high incidence of rape, then, is merely one more indication that ours is a violent society in which a large number of people are in the habit of taking anything they want—sex, money, life—simply by using force. There are more murders committed daily in a *city* like New York than annually in a *country* like

Switzerland, and, embarrassing though this may be, apparently many more murders or rapes than in countries like the Soviet Union and China where—however visitors may disagree on other aspects of life—no one seems afraid to walk around alone at night.

As long as our society is not at least to some extent freed from its violence, rape will continue, just as the killing of policemen, holdup victims, rivals, judicial witnesses, and others will continue. Only a change in the social climate such as we anticipate for the coming decade, brought about by an infusion of what women have to offer on a big scale to all social institutions, can defuse that society of its violence and thereby significantly reduce the incidence of rape as well. Society will then also find more effective ways to curb the rapist, mainly by easier convictions and longer sentences. The latter will be necessary, because the typical rapist, no matter what his conscious motivations, is a deviant, a pervert, a psychopath, and a true criminal who can be curbed only by force. He may also be curable, but that will be in any case a long and uncertain process.

Perhaps the most unfortunate aspect of the rape wave is that for every woman who is actually raped, many thousands of women must fear rape, fear men, see sex in terms of danger and hurt at the very time when the former specters of VD and pregnancy have been partially curbed. So women flock to the karate schools and develop obsessions of their own: they will have to fight wherever they go; they will be "hassled" at every corner; they must wear boots "to kick them in the groin." Reliance on self-defense seems a sensible response by women in the current transitional state, the prepartnership society. It will largely disappear in the partnership society that will follow.

There is another reason for the increasing prevalence of rape: many women go out or live alone, and more of them all the time. The opportunities are multiplied for the habitual rapist. Will that trend continue into the 1980s? There can be little doubt that even more women, young and old, will live alone or with each other, and go places, day and night, without men or travel without them. Therefore, unless other facets of the society change simultaneously, the rate of rape might rise astronomically.

The partnership society will be able to find ways of preventing this, if only by changing attitudes. The aforementioned *New York Times* article on rape notes, significantly, that those secondarily involved in rape, such as policemen, detectives, and so on, get an unmistakable sexual kick out of the whole thing ("Did you have fun at least?"). Such attitudes show that the (male) establishment is likely to be lax in the prevention and persecution of rape on all levels. Such attitudes will change, and the most important development in curbing rape will probably be in the laws. Many people now insist that the thrust of modern law is much too far into victimless crimes and that law generally places undue emphasis on property rather than people. For both these reasons the state does not deal with the rapists as effectively as it could and should. When woman power can exert more influence over legislation and law enforcement, rape will decline.

Casual Sex. Most men like "casual" sex, but most women dislike it. Still, there is a great deal of it, with "Don Juans" and "nymphos" in every corner. They seem to enjoy their activities and then again they do not. "On the whole," says New York psychiatrist Michael P., "my patients are overactive rather than underactive sexually, and the Don Juans and nymphos often seek help. On the one hand they always want lasting attachments. On the other they seek to develop reliable psychological barriers against their constantly and suddenly arising overwhelming desires that make them have the flings they almost always regret." But casual sex, instant sex, sex without long and involved preliminaries, sex as the result of sudden irresistible attraction has, as an idea at least, a powerful appeal for most people. It is well known that most people's sexual fantasies revolve around such episodes.

The man who has been better able than any other to put such daydreams on paper is Henry Miller, and Kate Millett has selected a passage from one of Miller's "instant intercourse" fantasies for the most prominent place—page one—in her *Sexual Politics.* She quotes Miller describing an episode: "I would ask her to prepare the bath for me. She would pretend to demur but she would do it just the same. One day, while I was seated in the tub soaping myself, I noticed that she had forgotten the towels. 'Ida,' I called, 'bring me some towels!' She walked into the bathroom and handed me them. She had on a silk bathrobe and a pair of silk hose. As she stooped over the tub to put the towels on the rack her bathrobe slid open. I slid to my knees and buried my head in her muff. It happened so quickly that she didn't have time to rebel or even to pretend to rebel. In a moment I had her in the tub, stockings and all. I slipped the bathrobe off and threw it on the floor. I left the stockings on—it made her more lascivious looking, more the Cranach type. I lay back and pulled her on top of me. She was just like a bitch in heat, biting me all over, panting, gasping, wriggling like a worm on the hook. . . . Not a word was spoken. . . ."

Not a word was spoken. Not one word. To Kate Millett this is—rightly—the crux of the entire passage. She says, "Without question the most telling statement in the narrative is its last sentence. 'Not a word was spoken.' Like the folk hero who never condescended to take off his hat, Val has accomplished the entire campaign, including its *coup de grâce,* without stooping to one word of human communication." [5] In Kate Millett's view, presumably, the ability to say something is, after all, what distinguishes man from beast. (And when Val does say something, finally, she does not like what he says.) Her reaction to Miller's lascivious imagery does not really demonstrate that Miller (or his hero) is a rake; it does demonstrate that Kate Millett is, to some extent, a romantic. More so, surely, than Germaine Greer, who quite mercilessly castigates Denis de Rougemont and his famous work, *Romantic Love in the Western World*, in her own book, *The Female Eunuch.*

Miller, one might say, has his own way of daydreaming—his books are daydreams, after all—which is rather explicit and not to everyone's taste. But the core of his dream, the often recurring theme, that events might just take their course, that no word need be spoken, presumably has an attractive, exciting quality for many, if only to judge from Miller's enormous success. Contrary to popular myth, merely writing explicitly about sex does not a best-seller make: there has to be much more in a book to make it truly appealing to large numbers of people. There has to be identification, and people apparently identify with Miller's fantasy of, dream of, desire for instant sex—sex that becomes all the more powerful and exciting and satisfying by being sudden, straight, undiluted, like a shot of whiskey or a fortune won by a throw of the dice at the gaming table.

The fantasy of the wordless "conquest" also appeals to many men because they do not trust their own line of talk when they are out for "conquest." A rather primitive man, asked by an admirer for the secret of how he managed to be so obviously successful with women, gave the ultimate chauvinist pig reply: "I never talk to them. If you do, you only screw yourself up." When aroused or enticed, yet forced to look forward to a long delay and an uncertain seduction ritual, mainly verbal in nature, men often fear that "their line of gab" will be rather counterproductive, as indeed it often is. So they would like more instant sex. Presumably, that inclination will stay with them. The question is, Will women also like that?

In the current social circumstances, surely most do not, though, as the interviews reveal, women often permit themselves to think in such terms too, and find the fantasy by no means unpleasurable. But not only are the social taboos against it a strong deterrent; the social dangers are even stronger. This holds true for the male as well, though to a lesser degree. Anyone, man or woman, who should give in to a sudden urge to "pick up" a person of the opposite sex, has an even chance, if that other person is willing, to come to some form of violent physical grief in our crime-infested society. The general injunction not to pick up or go along with strangers is not just, perhaps not even primarily, a moral injunction; it is also a security measure. As such it may become obsolete in a more harmonious society of partnership between the sexes.

Then, when things are physically safer, more women may not only permit themselves to respond on occasion to an extremely brief—that is, almost entirely wordless courtship after an incidental meeting—but take the initiative in such encounters. All factors considered here, such as better cultural and physical relations between men and women, less danger of VD or pregnancy, a lower crime rate, and fewer moral injunctions, do point to a much higher future incidence of casual sex than exists now. In one form or another, perhaps in a somewhat less crude and salacious form, Henry Miller's dream of frequent episodes of casual (though perhaps not entirely wordless) encounters, pleasurable to a high degree for both female and male, may well come true in the coming decade. Perhaps that is why Miller's reputation has undergone such great change, from insignificant pornographer to significant sociosexual prophet. The women's movement decries him as the super-male chauvinist pig of our day. Kate Millett, whose prime target Miller is, says that "to confuse [Miller's] neurotic hostility, this frank abuse, with sanity, is pitiable. To confuse it with freedom were vicious, were it not so very sad." [6] This is probably true: Miller's great evocative artistry is full of wild hostility, and his use of four-letter words in such apocalyptical profusion is a compulsion, *not* a sign of freedom.

Yet Miller, like Hefner, cannot be "all bad" as, curiously enough, both share with the women's movement quite a few views on the (male) establishment, and on such matters as war, repression, and race.

In any event, if and when woman power brings about the changes envisaged here, sexual relations between males and females will obviously undergo fundamental changes, all for the better; and levity and lasciviousness, frustration and tragedy will ebb in equal measure.

Love. What about the future of love? The psychiatrists discovered early that sexual inadequacy and sexual frustration were largely a function of the absence of love. They also discovered that people were painfully ambivalent on the subject of love. They wanted to love but were afraid to love, to "get involved." The psychiatrists attributed this mainly to early negative experiences, concluding that people who in childhood had been hurt because their love was disappointed had come to associate love with pain and therefore to shy away from it. There is much to indicate that this is true. But it is not the whole story. And while the theory probably holds true for men and women, there is another, perhaps even larger factor standing in the way of love where men are concerned.

Men in our society are afraid of the very emotion of love as it would so seriously be in conflict with their entire life style. They may love objects—a house, a painting, a car, or an organization they have built—but to love people is too dangerous. One could say, well, why doesn't he at least love his wife and his children—that ought to be safe? But that isn't safe either—wife or children may turn against him or be taken from him. And the human psyche does not appear to be made that way: love cannot be so neatly compartmentalized. People do not have to love everybody as, for example, St. Augustine tried to, but they either love or they don't.

In our time love is too great an impediment in the race for success or indeed mere survival—it is too great a risk, an obstacle, a time-waster for most people to love other people. Modern man would not be able to compete the way he must if he felt love—he cannot afford it, it would literally ruin him, first emotionally and then with respect to his job, his career, his business. True love, *agape* as the ancients called that which was stronger even than Eros, is a luxury man cannot afford in our era. Nor can he permit himself other kinds of love: love of God or love of himself. Organized religion has driven the love of God out of him; and he is unable to love himself because he feels he differs too greatly from that he-man image of himself he carries around in his head—the great, rich, powerful, successful, irresistible, imperturbable superman. He would rather cry and berate himself than love himself when he looks at himself.

And everywhere his love is blocked. Besides, he has at his command means to overcome the vestiges of love should they assert themselves in his breast: he can get drunk, get busy at the office, take a trip, go to the gym. The state of nonlove has long become chronic in modern man, so he does not have to worry too much about its erupting and plaguing him. As he is not usually a cold fish, much of his inborn love turns, once stifled, into hatred. And modern man, no matter how soft-spoken, is probably history's record-holder in the variety and depth of his hatreds.

All this keeps him from giving and experiencing love, and makes him in turn unlovable. A man who cannot love may, if he is "attractive," drive love-seeking or power-seeking or husband-seeking females crazy, but he cannot make them love him. Aside from their own sexual and erotic idolatry, which prevents them from loving in general, they cannot love him because, unloving, he is just not lovable. He may be impressive or arresting or exciting, but he does not inspire love. The he-man is—though he fails to know it—not only unlovable because of his emotional deficiency, but he is doubly so today, when most of his he-manship finds expression daily in his unloving attitudes toward others. And he is triply unlovable when he aims at being the he-man but is really a (ninety-pound or two-hundred-pound) weakling, just dreaming to be Atlas in business, in government, on the tennis court, in the bedroom. How can any woman love him?

No matter how deprived he may be, he feels instinctively that love is too dangerous. If he were to begin loving his fellows in general, without which he cannot truly love any individuals either, where would he be? He would find that all his views *and* his own life style would need changing, and in such a fashion as to bring upon him the disdain of his brethren and the loss of his position in society. He could not do for another moment what he now does, or do it as he now does it, if he had love in his heart.

The rise of woman power is also a rebellion against a loveless, hate-filled system replete with unloving and unlovable men. The young already are different in large numbers. Elsewhere we have said that many of them refuse to enter the rat race because they feel it would deprive them of their manhood or womanhood. They also think it would deprive them of the need to love and be loved which cannot be squared with the requirements of "modern" society. So they are opting out. But few adult women do. They want to change the world. The world that liberated women are striving to establish is a world in which people would be freed, not only of some of their social and political fetters, but freed to love.

That is a very tall order indeed. But it is not inconceivable that as a result of woman power's exerting its influence, people might become more able to give and take love. In that case sex would largely disappear as a problem, a frustration, an inadequacy.

11

WOMAN POWER AND THE FUTURE OF NUDITY

WHAT effect will growing woman power have on fashions and the display of the body, in particular, of course, the female body? The "of course" points to the circumstance that the unclad, or partly unclad, female body has a different and stronger effect upon the male than the sight of the unclad male body has upon the female. Has anyone ever heard of a female voyeur—or shall we say voyeuse?—peering through keyhole or shutters to see a man undress? They may exist, but surely they are rare. Voyeurism in its aggravated form, when it actually becomes a substitute for sex mainly for reasons of inadequacy or age,* is a sexual deviation. But the desire to look at the unclad female form is both part of and stimulus for most normal sexual activity. That display generally creates sexual tension between men and women except under conditions of long-term habituation. Such habituation sets in only in the case of the same partners, not just from viewing the female form as such. With any new female form seen the tension arises anew. Seeing the female body is, for the man, not akin to

* In "Joie de Vivre" (*Harper's*, January 1972), Simone de Beauvoir informs us that organized voyeurism is often the exclusive sexual pastime of wealthy octogenarians.

inspecting something (like a carburetor), for the purposes of gaining knowledge, but a sensual stimulus, a sensual pleasure, and therefore, like all sensual (in this case visual) responses, capable of being aroused and satisfied repeatedly.

The female, depending on her era and culture, apparently likes to display her body but also to hide it. Her hiding all of her body in the Victorian and other eras must have been primarily on her initiative, not that of males, and so must be her current readiness to display a good deal of it in public. Why? The reasons are a mixture. First, there is today the greater freedom of movement, the greater informality in appearance and manner in general—that is, *convenience;* second, there is the greater emphasis on the blessings of sun and fresh air and unencumbered exercise—that is, *health.* Beyond that there is the less easily assessed sexual component.

In the "normal" female the freer display of the body presumably is a conscious and guiltless means of appealing to men. In the more compulsive female it may be an outgrowth and cresting of teasing. When teasing plays a role, the display blends in with and intensifies the institutionalized teasing of the public practiced by the advertising media: the live figure in hot pants, on the contemporary scene and in its effect on the brain of the beholder, blends in with the giant cardboard figure on the billboard and signals to the beholder one more pleasure in addition to that glorious trip to Trinidad he is missing. Thus the display of the actual person in the street or office can be mockery, whether intended or not, of the beholder, adding to his frustrations. Finally, public display can be aimed at those, and they seem to be numerous, who actually prefer stimulation to consummation.

In the current and perhaps last phase of the battle between the sexes, the freer display may therefore serve a variety of good and bad purposes and have a variety of effects. It can be a lure to attract men desired as companions, or a weapon against others, particularly older men, fathers and father figures, who can be distracted and reduced in their authority when they respond; or it can be part of a game in which men of all ages, once they respond, if only by ogling, can be dismissed as "wanting only one thing," and used as confirmation that they are all chauvinist pigs. Finally, extensive undress can be an unconscious or conscious weapon against Mother, who had so much power over the girl while she grew up but is now, compared to the daughter, at a distinct disadvantage in microskirt or hot pants.

What is most interesting is what the fashions and customs will be in the coming decade, when woman power will have greater impact than ever before on all aspects of life, customs and fashions included. How will women be attired on the beach, in the drawing room, in the convertible? * There are at present two widely opposite trends coexisting (or in conflict?). Young females use ever new forms of generous and stimulating display; but they also wear sex-hiding jeans and boots and jackets. To the extent that one can generalize, the essentially anti-lib woman—that is, the conservative sort—seems to display herself much more than the pro-lib woman. This is somehow at variance with the situation a decade ago, when the conservative women dressed conservatively, with a minimum of display, while the progressive woman dressed more freely. Would this indicate that as woman power becomes increasingly successful and self-confident, fashions will tend to deemphasize rather than emphasize the attributes of the female body?

It is striking that at the large political gatherings at which members and sympathizers of woman power play a dominant role, such as meetings assembled to hear Shirley Chisholm, the dress of women is antiprovocative; these girls and women seem to underline their serious interest in the business at hand by their unsexy attire, so much in contrast with past customs of going

* Incidentally (Detroit, take note!), in the coming decade there will probably be a return to the convertible, in the wake of a general liberation from today's grimly functional life style.

somewhere to be seen and admired and perhaps even striking up an acquaintance with the help of the outfit one was wearing. The attire of a young woman attending a political meeting is as chaste and functional as that of astronauts going to the moon.

People do and presumably will, at least in the coming decade, signal to others (but also to themselves) by their clothing what attitudes they wish to take in certain situations. The storm trooper wears heavy boots, not an old pair of sneakers—not just because they serve the purpose of violence, but because they signal to others, and to him, that he means business and that his business is rough. The executioner, if there still is such a functionary in the 1980s—and there may well be, or be again—will always be dressed for the occasion; he is not likely to wear a California shirt and John Weitz socks when throwing the switch. People express a great deal through their clothing. Therefore, if we want to guess how they will dress or undress in the coming age of woman power, we should start by trying to guess what they will want to express and project of themselves.

If this text's general prediction holds and woman power does enter dominantly into the affairs of society in the coming decade, and society consequently does see a turn toward greater social sanity and a true partnership between the sexes, then the prediction must be that woman's fashion will be businesslike in business, playlike for play, and so on—that is, in harmony with the situation. They may go nude on the beach or at a poolside cocktail party, but women are likely to be most unprovocatively attired in their offices or other places of work. In other words, the postulates in *Sex and the Single Girl*, which admonished its disciples to go to the office attired as provocatively as possible, in desperate cases even without underwear, will be upset. At play, on the other hand, nudity is likely to increase.

To what extent and in what fashion? It is generally predicted that within the next few years the female bosom will be as freely displayed in public as the male chest. But a variety of reasons make this improbable, even though the bosom is likely to be increasingly displayed. A considerable limitation is likely to remain on the display of the female breast because such display, it seems, does have an intrinsic rather than merely a more habitual impact on the male. An ankle displayed in the age when skirts had to trail on the floor was presumed to be stimulating, particularly when it was shown with flirtatious intent; but now that every woman is showing her ankles, ankle-baring has lost its titillation appeal entirely (except perhaps for fetishist "ankle men"). Similarly, the display in a bikini of virtually the entire body, except for what the people in the swimwear trade call "the critical areas," is not particularly stimulating when seen on the beach, though it probably would have rendered men delirious in the 1890s. Habituation and "naturalization" do set in. But it is not likely to set in automatically with regard to the bosom. It just is not probable that barechested man will meet barechested girl at the swimming pool during a stockbrokers' convention and, impervious to the display, plunge into a conversation about the Dow Jones averages, as he would with another man or a fully dressed woman. Rather, the display is likely, even a decade from now, to generate considerable static on his brain.

If we trust Desmond Morris, the author of *The Naked Ape*, the role of the bosom and even its genesis is far more mysterious and sex-related than most people realize. In his theory the bosom was a curious afterthought of nature, added to the Naked Ape only when the latter changed over from walking on all fours, as he had for millions of years, to the erect stance, and thereby radically altered interpersonal postures before and during intercourse. Where everything had previously been dorsal, first the display and then the coitus, now everything became frontal—attraction, courtship, and coitus. The breasts, says Morris, only then grew, in order to substitute for the other side of the anatomy: "The protuberant, hemispheral breasts of the female must surely be copies of the fleshy buttocks. . . ." They served the purpose of shifting the male sexual response from the latter to the former. And as additional support for his thesis Morris observes that only nipples (not breasts) are needed to feed the young and that only the Naked Ape, because of his (and in this case her) hairlessness, can effectively display the bosom.

"The enlarged female breasts," says Morris, "are usually thought of primarily as material rather than sexual developments, but there seems to be little evidence for this. Other species of primates provide an abundant milk supply for their offspring yet they fail to develop clearly defined hemispheral breast swellings. The female of our species is unique amongst primates in this respect. The evolution of protruding breasts of a characteristic shape appears to be yet another example of sexual signalling. This would be made possible only . . . by the evolution of the naked skin. Swollen breast patches in a shaggy coated female would be far less conspicuous as signalling devices. . . . In addition to their own conspicuous shape, they also serve to concentrate visual attention on to the nipples and to make the nipple erection that accompanies sexual arousal more conspicuous." [1]

Both the covering and uncovering of the female breast seems to serve in helping to regulate human sexual activity to some extent, and is therefore—and is likely to remain—strongly connected with sexual activity, so that displaying it as casually as an arm or a leg does not seem to be in the cards. Even if the next generation should free itself to some extent or altogether of the sexual hang-ups plaguing its elders, a completely uninhibited display seems unlikely. Within limits, however, females will "think less" of uncovering the breast—at least in public—and so will the males. To the extent that women will uncover their breasts, they may find it emotionally sustaining. As one attractive redhead observed, "To be told by the swimming pool that you have nice boobs helps you through the day." Even so, the display will remain limited, though perhaps not so ritualistically as in the past.

What about nudity at home? Though it is also on the increase, it too is likely to remain limited. Mother will not serve the Wienerschnitzel—if in the 1980s she will still *serve* food at all—with her bosom uncovered. Nor will the teen-age daughter display hers when eating that Wienerschnitzel. For the display of the bosom in the family would be however mild, an invitation not to mere sexual thought but to incestuous thought, and incest is not likely to make the scene generally or officially in the period here under consideration, if ever. This does not mean that families will not ever engage in full nudity on the beach. But the home, with the omnipresent couch or bedroom and the easily available privacy, is another scene.

What about nudity below the waist? Will women go bottomless too on the beaches and by the pools and elsewhere in summer and winter or even indoors in mixed company? A young woman to whom the question was put, said, "It's already happening." Perhaps the interesting word in her reply is "already." It suggests that she extrapolates along a straight line, assuming that anything we see now is just the beginning of something more along the same lines. It need not be that way: certain developments may just be false starts, just as, perhaps, frenzied group sex might be a false start in the direction of sexual liberation.

Public bottomlessness, except as a business, in bars or brothels, is not likely to become widespread. One reason may be that the display of the entire female body, so shocking to the philistine, may lose its present symbolism as a gesture of social protest in a society in which fewer things will be deserving of protest; another may be that genuinely liberated people will give up the essentially silly insistence that they are or can be just free and "natural," children of nature, innocent as babes, beings without guile or sin who can return to Paradise. Perhaps, too, while people may no longer feel the *need* to be covered, they may no longer feel the need to be uncovered either. Nudity as a behavioral symbol, like short hair for women in the 1920s, may become obsolete.

When Hugh Hefner was asked in 1971 why he was beginning

to show pubic hair in his centerfolds, he said, "God put it there, *Playboy* didn't." A very neat answer that evaded the issue. There is a difference between a living female's displaying her natural endowment, and a female's being displayed in a photograph. The girl in the photograph is displayed for men's enjoyment; the liberated woman undresses primarily for her own enjoyment. The display of her body by Hefner's printed nude may or may not be designed to appeal to that mysterious and elusive quality, prurient interest; liberated woman's taking off of her clothes definitely does not aim at that interest. Hefner's reply actually illuminates the curious collision course of the *Playboy* "philosophy" and the liberated woman's philosophy. Both favor greater sexual freedom, fewer restricting conventions, more enjoyment so that they may appear to be close; yet as everyone knows, they are regarded as entirely antithetical.

And yet. . . . Hugh Hefner's role in society and his true aims, other than making money, are hard to discern and harder to judge, even though most liberated women regard him as a panderer to male chauvinism and the ultimate advocate of the woman-as-sex-object approach. But did Hefner not help make the nude body respectable? Is that not of some merit? One might say that he did it sort of through the back door, in a dishonest way, by loading up a girlie magazine with respectable reading matter—dressing up the girls, so to speak, in Sartre and Greene, so that the readers needed not have the magazine delivered in a plain brown wrapper and could read it openly in the living room or during a skyjacking to Cuba.

The *Playboy* pictures seem to run toward the deindividualized female, the "great chick." But did Hefner not at least try to pay some respect to the girls displayed in his centerfolds by showing them also in dress, at work, at play, and with a background story about them (which no girlie magazine would trouble itself to do)? A recent issue of *Time* on women dismissed Hefner on the grounds that "the *Zeitgeist* has passed him by." One wonders.

There is more to Hefner than "chicks." His views on a number of issues are quite humane. If we can believe in the increasing humanization of society through women powers, Hefner may be, not behind the *Zeitgeist*, but actually ahead of it. Of the many antagonists woman power has in this country, Hefner may not be the worst.

In any event, woman power, which will transform our sexual mores substantially (see Chapters 8–10), will also make nudity or quasi nudity much *less of an issue.* With less social protest needed in the future, with better and more satisfying sexual relations between people, with less widespread sexual inadequacy, and with the resulting reprivatization of sex under new conditions, will nudity actually decline? Its practice or nonpractice will probably not be *uniform.* People of the same social persuasion or age and in the same circumstances will behave differently. Not everyone will be nude at the beach, just as not everyone will be clad by the pool; people will just feel freer, on the whole, to display themselves (or not) if and when they feel like it, and produce less of a stir (and surely no legal action) if they do. But more often than not they may not feel like displaying themselves.

What will be the effect on fashion of this new approach to nudity? Katherine H., a dress designer, starts off by saying about Rudi Gernreich: "You can get caught in an image. That's what happened to Gernreich. He's a creative person, but I find that today his designs are really uncreative. He started to philosophize, and now he can't design any more." Gernreich himself did indeed "philosophize" when he created the topless swimsuit. But he would not agree with Katherine that he is now caught in an image and uncreative. He has recently talked about the possibility of people using uniforms, presumably not because individuals would be all that uni-form, but because their individualities would be so *strong* that they would not need to advertise differences through dress. They would be more concerned about their inward feelings than the outward images they were projecting to others. This is a very interesting point of view when applied, for example, to our new friends the Red Chinese, all of whom, male and female, seem to be going around in tunics, even on the stage. We tend to regard that as evidence of sameness, collectivism, regimentation; Gernreich indicates that the opposite may be the case.

When asked what she predicts for the future, Katherine says, "I don't think you can predict. The only thing is that people will want to wear comfortable clothes." But, "Do you think that women will ever go back to really *uncomfortable* clothes? Bustles and corsets?" Katherine: "I dare say it could happen." One thing one can perhaps predict with a certain measure of confidence is that the current women's lib uniform—jeans and boots, with or without some kind of sweater or jacket—will largely disappear. That type of outfit—unless it serves the purely functional purpose of protecting the wearer against harsh weather—symbolizes and exudes a certain hostility to men and society for which there will be less reason in the future.

Once woman power will successfully penetrate the (male) establishment and help transform it, the current boots-and-jeans fashion will decline proportionately. Like soldiers who take off their uniforms after victory, women will probably take theirs off once their militancy has borne fruit. Whether they will, in public, take off everything else with it will depend on the woman and the circumstances. It will probably matter much less than it does now.

12

WOMAN POWER AND THE FUTURE OF THE LAW

ONE level of government on which women will probably exercise a great and beneficial influence will be the judicial. Once they take their places on all levels of the judiciary, women are likely to bring about true changes for the better in the entire system. It is encouraging and significant that young women are now flocking to the law schools. Once they penetrate the law, not just as judges, but also as lawyers and prosecutors, the law will become more human and more genuinely progressive.

In the first place, always proceeding in this analysis from the core chapter on the current—culturally or otherwise produced—different traits of men and women, woman's greater compassion is likely to produce a different climate in the courts: greater equitability coupled with greater realism.

Many worry when they hear what to them is a four-letter word: compassion. They feel that their lives depend on their keeping woman from the bench, lest she coddle all the criminals with which they are surrounded. But compassion as a guide is not the same as softness. Women on the bench can in fact be extremely tough.

The real problem with contemporary justice is neither, as the hardhat insists, that it coddles criminals, nor, as the sentimentalist believes, that it is totally cruel and repressive. That is just one of those fundamentally faulty dichotomies that plague us. Rather, because of certain male attitudes that operate in the courts, many criminals are treated lightly who should be dealt with severely, while many who deserve leniency are treated cruelly and injustly. Richard Speck, the murderer of several nurses, was at last report living comfortably in a private cell in a penitentiary and had taken up painting—a most agreeable and soothing pastime for which many a talented artist on the outside has neither the time nor the money. Trivial offenders, on the other hand, are given harsh sentences that must be served in evil jails, and are in danger of being beaten or killed. Perhaps at no point in the establishment machinery is the male mystique as powerfully at work as in the realm of the law, particularly criminal law. But women in the American judiciary will be the catalyst in today's crotchety, largely outmoded, and insensitive judicial system. Men, as they are wont to, clamor for more money to remedy the situation, but money cannot bring to the system the qualities it needs most. It is the old frontier days to which our courts and laws often seem to be geared, but there are now many more types of offenses whose judging demands a reasonably clear view of contemporary society and the causes of the crime.

At a charity dinner in splendid surroundings a prominent judge told his elegant audience, over fine brandy after a fine meal, what he thought was an amusing story. It concerned a black defendant whose first brush with the law, in Texas, had resulted from the theft of a bicycle, for which said defendant, then nineteen years old, had been sentenced to seven years in jail, every day of which he had served. That horrendous, murderous sentence was not, however, the point of the anecdote—which actually related some new misfortune suffered by this young man—it was merely background. Nevertheless, it seemed to register on the women present who gave the gently smiling raconteur noticeably less of a hand than his more ebullient male listeners. Would a woman judge have treated a young bicycle thief in this fashion? Would she have considered the entire story—no matter what the ultimate joke—a felicitous choice of subject matter with which to regale an audience? Possibly but not probably.

Naomi C., a senior in law school (UCLA), says, "Women, we can predict, will be tougher on the real criminals and not let them forever escape and repeat, as our present system does, merely because of some technicalities or perhaps some unconscious intrusion into the case by the masculine mystique. It is well known, for example, that some of the worst crimes of violence and brutality rate very high in our penitentiaries as prestige items in the eyes of the other inmates. Murderers, bank robbers, holdup men, and all sorts of killers and people who have done others, as the legal phrase goes, great bodily harm are treated with deference and respect. Rapists are also not looked down upon as a general rule, unless they are child molesters, which the other felons disdain, presumably not so much because of the harm done to the child as because of the unmanly nature of the transgression."

Could it be that, consciously or not, the males on the bench react similarly and act accordingly? In connection with the frequent injustice of current procedures, with both the harsh and the light sentences often going to the wrong people, an increasing presence of women justices may therefore be very much to the benefit of society.

Women are also likely to be better judges of other women than the male judges are. Female crime rates have increased greatly in the last two years, a fact often attributed to women's liberation. Statistics being what they are, it is hard to know just what the situation is and what the most likely causes may be. But more women than ever stand before the bars of justice for all sorts of crimes, especially crimes connected with drugs and prostitution, but also for crimes of violence or murder. These women are then judged by or at least sentenced (which in many cases is the more important of the two legal steps in a criminal case) by male judges who may have little idea of what makes those women tick. Would women not do better in sentencing other women?

Women are likely to be more aggressive than men in calling for a reform of the archaic, ponderous, expensive, and time-consuming jury system. The jury, as the book says, must have a "reasonable moral certainty" that the defendant is guilty. Every jury ever seated asks what those mysterious words might mean, and is then given a baffling explanation by the judge. Women, as newcomers, may be less respectful of such antiquated formulas, and in this as in other areas of the law, as reformers or legislators, they will help adjust the current system to current situations.

"Women," continued Naomi, "are also likely, once ensconced in the legal affairs of this country, to exercise a powerful and beneficial effect on the excessive attention in our day to 'no-victim' crimes. The no-victim crimes, such as prostitution, public drunkenness, drug abuse, and even some sexual practices between adults consenting only too gladly in the privacy of their bedrooms clutter up the courts, occupy tens of thousands of venal vice squads, and are detrimental to the effective administration of justice."

It may be that this vast and futile pursuit of no-victim criminals plays a greater role in the maintenance of the masculine mystique than is generally recognized. Sinners are proverbially often the most sensitive to sin: they love to uncover it, persecute it, punish it—in others. The very righteousness of the establishment male—and perhaps also his basic conviction that the peasants should not have too much fun lest they become lazy or rebellious—produces an undue emphasis on all these no-victim crimes which female judges are not likely to share. They are likely to be more interested in real crimes, and will perhaps go still a step further (as judges and lawmakers) and make a much needed greater distinction between crimes of physical violence and crimes against property. It makes little sense that the thief of a bundle of stock certificates should be punished as harshly as, or ever more so than, the killer of a little girl, yet that is often true—and women may not want to perpetuate this.

Finally, and very importantly, one can assume that woman power will reform the jails. Here again, men barricade themselves behind the good-for-all argument that reform is proceeding just as fast as it possibly can but that it cannot go very far or fast because it requires so much money. Billions of dollars are said to be required; but there is no reason to assume that even if they should become available (which they never will), they would do the trick. While the physical plants of most penitentiaries may be terrible and in need of large expenditures for improvement, the true horror in them stems, as does all true horror anywhere, from people who behave viciously to other people and who in turn are commanded by callous overseers. That has nothing to do with money, not even with the always bemoaned fact that the low salaries available for the "correction officers" attract the wrong men. Prison guards could easily be controlled if a different spirit reigned. So could those worst criminals, who generally get the best treatment and as trusties acquire the most power over inmates, like the kapos in totalitarian concentration camps, because it suits the prison administration. Money cannot alleviate such evils; only a change of attitude to the imprisoned can, a change of attitude of which men, left to themselves, have never been capable anywhere at any time.

The entire system of jails, with all its cruel and flagrant *injustices,* is typically man's work. Some old-fashioned female warden or guard in a women's jail may have paid her own entrance fee into the (male) establishment by mimicking male wardens or guards, but these women are not as typically female as male guards and wardens are typically male. The more typical feminine qualities, once they appear in the form of woman power, will be applied to all aspects of the judicial system, reform that system beyond current dreams, and help bring about a cleaner, juster, and therefore also safer society.

Contemporary attitudes toward crime are outmoded, if they ever did fit reality at all. Even a sociologist (this one specializing in crime), the Englishman Stanley Cohen, admits that "in America and Britain the sociologists in the field of crime have been left behind by two major developments." "The one," says Cohen, "is the (necessary) interactionist approach to deviance and the other is the emergence of civil disorder, revolt and protest movements in America, centered around the anti-war cause, students and negroes." [1] By "interactionist" Cohen means that crime and delinquency cannot be properly understood unless they are treated as "joint enterprises," involving not only the rule-breaker but the rule-makers and -enforcers as well. In other words, not only the deviant's direct environment, such as his family or neighborhood, must be taken into consideration (as it already is), but much more. But we do not like to look critically or analytically at the "makers and enforcers" of rules, so our scientific analysts of crime—let alone the unscientific ones—omit a vital dimension and operate in a vacuum.

The other and perhaps even more important factor that has "left sociologists in the field of crime behind" is the arrival on the scene of ideologically sparked deviation and violence. As Cohen points out, particularly in the United States the distinction between criminal and ideological violence has become "altogether ambiguous." When, he asks, does stealing become looting, hooliganism rioting, vandalism sabotage? Do the everyday encounters between American black youths and the police really lose their political character if a massive riot isn't in progress? The "new" crimes that have arisen as a result of new social and political situations are different from crimes with other motivations. That does not mean they should not be punished. But because prevention rather than punishment is the avowed aim of the (male) establishment, new approaches to understanding and dealing with new, and old, crime are needed. Of this the (male) establishment is incapable because of its essentially he-manist, sclerotic, and vindictive basic views. Will woman power help? One would think so.

Besides, whatever the crime or its motivation, the punishment neither fits it nor does it perform the tasks it is advertised to. Everybody is his own armchair penologist and explains to others who know it already that jails are breeding grounds for crime, veritable finishing schools for criminals. The cure for that, as to anything else in the view of the cognoscenti, is money: more pay for the "correction officers," who all too often seem to be sadistic, cunning ruffians. Also, vast new prisons are talked about, a new parole system, more courts, and so on.

Why are prisons breeding grounds for crime? The pat answer is: because the first offender is thrown in with the habitual criminal, who teaches him the ropes and is a repeater—eight out of ten crimes are committed by former inmates. But this close association is not likely to be the principal reason that first offenders, once in prison, become habitual criminals, unless they are already the type who become habitual criminals. The real reason is probably the way in which prisons appear to be administered, with a power structure of cruel and racketeering criminals *and* guards forming two parallel pyramids with which every inmate must learn how to deal. He does not begin to learn about professional crime as soon as he enters prison; he begins by turning his back on a society that treats him with injustice, brutality, and contempt. He may be guilty of his crime, but he still deserves *justice*, no matter how harsh, and must have it if only to be taught better and not to be turned permanently against the society in which he has lived and to which he will return. It is not the association with professional criminals that makes the novice a professional, any more than a person on the outside becomes a professional criminal merely by associating with criminals. It is the treatment he receives that gives him an insight into how vile and hypocritical can be those who have now absolute power over him, perhaps for years. Probably for the first time in his life he meets persons of real power and authority—wardens, chaplains, doctors—and what he sees is what turns him away more than before from society, and makes him seek friendship and help and criminal training from those who have already turned against society.

"In prison," says a Synanon member who served time on several occasions for a variety of offenses, "you find yourself face to face with a world so horrible, words cannot describe it. It is not just the punishment inflicted, mind you. The self-righteous go around and ask for drastic punishment of criminals. What exactly do they mean? Less food? Corporal punishment? Solitary? I guess they savor all these possibilities. But these are practiced anyway, and they are not as dreadful as other things that go on in prison. In the first place, you are in constant danger of being killed by another prisoner. The guards know who the killers are, but use them for their own purposes rather than isolate them. You also are constantly in the middle—the authorities demand one thing from you while the prisoner code or individual criminals preying on you demand another. I really never hated or despised anybody until I went to prison. Then I began to hate a lot of people, some of them fellow prisoners, some of them the prison personnel."

"They can really begin to convince you that you're a criminal beast," an undercover agent reported after spending some time in Nassau County Jail.[2] It is interesting to note that the agent-observer did not say that prison can turn the prisoner into a criminal beast, but that it "can really begin to convince you" that you are one, make you believe you are one, from which belief, presumably, there is little possibility of escape. And the agent-observer was not even a felon.

Why are people incarcerated for long periods of time (and years *is* a very long period of time)? Three reasons are given. One is punishment, which in turn is to serve two functions: it is to do justice by inflicting pain on those who have inflicted it on others, and it is to be a deterrent for all, criminals and noncriminals. The second reason is protection of society: while the criminal is locked away he cannot do harm to his fellow creatures. The third is rehabilitation: the criminal as prisoner is to be turned into a law-abiding, God-fearing, hard-working, and highly skilled gentleman by the law-abiding, God-fearing, hard-working, and highly skilled gentlemen who run the institution.*

Some of the results proclaimed *are* attained in many cases. Prisoners *can* get reformed in prison, if only because of the horror of the experience, and certainly many others are deterred. Society *is* protected against criminals while they are locked up. And a certain amount of justice, without which human society would not be able to exist, *is* being done, a certain retribution, a cleansing of guilt. Punishment, if it is fair, serves a purpose: it is unbearable to think that people should not only commit crimes of violence against others, but get away with it.†

And what has all this to do with the coming age of woman power? The purpose of this chapter was merely to point out that in crime, as in most other areas, he-manism—as exemplified by vengeful or callous attitudes, slick public relations, deception of the public, cries for more force and more money and more costly studies by machine scientists designed to confirm ingrained prejudices—stands in the way of change for the better. With regard to law and penology, force and money actually may be required in greater measure than in other problem areas of social life, but it is the orientation that counts, the views of and feelings toward other people, empathy and understanding, an open mind. The fight against crime—whether directly, by curbing criminals or apprehending and reforming them, or indirectly, by helping alleviate at

* One wishes the silly arguments as to whether punishment, including capital punishment, deters or not would finally stop. Punishment—any kind—obviously deters some but fails to deter others.

† How about women in prison? As the situation seems to be roughly the same, it has not been treated separately.

least some of the factors that make society increasingly crime-prone—requires compassion, firmness, equitability, patience, and a divorce of the task from crude politicking and sterile "science-eering." And woman power can be expected to bring its qualities to bear in this area.

13

WOMAN POWER AND THE FUTURE OF POLITICS

WHAT will woman power do to American politics? Will there merely be large numbers of women in Congress, perhaps as many as half the total membership? And if so, will that affect the shape of society as little as woman's suffrage did even though it made half the electorate female?

No one can claim that male rule was much altered by the female vote. Not only did the men retain power and the positions they already had; they also perpetuated the same policies with that power in the realms of war, social issues, economic issues, politics. Perhaps no victory in human history was more Pyrrhic than the suffragettes'. It produced no change, mainly perhaps because women were as susceptible to the new infectious mental disease of the age—propaganda—as men were, at least until very recently. Will history repeat itself now, with more women getting in on the action, but with the action remaining the same?

Ideas of women taking over the reins—or speculations as to what that might accomplish—are very old. Twenty-one hundred years ago Aristophanes wrote a play called *Ecclesiazusae*, which, freely translated, means "The Female Parliament." In the play the women of Athens have decided, under the leadership of a clever woman named Praxagora, to reform the constitution. But the women are trying to do it in a way different from women today: by disguising themselves as men.

The women dress like men, beards included, and occupy the seats in Parliament, in order to be able to command a majority of votes in the next public Assembly. Praxagora believes that, first of all, women are better speakers than men: "when they have anything to say, they can mostly find words to say it." The women then hold a midnight meeting in order to rehearse their speeches and to get accustomed to their new clothes.

Praxagora herself makes a speech that is generally admired. She complains of the mismanagement in public affairs and asserts that the state's only hope of salvation is to put the government into the hands of the women, arguing that those who have so long managed the home successfully are best fitted to undertake the same duties on a larger scale. The women are described by Praxagora as highly *conservative,* and "therefore safe guardians of the public interest":

They roast and boil after the good old fashion,
They keep the holidays that were kept of old,
They make their cheesecakes by the old receipts,
They keep a private bottle, like their mothers,
They plague their husbands—as they always did.

Even in the management of a campaign they are depicted as more prudent and competent than the men:

Being mothers, they'll be chary of the blood
Of their own sons, our soldiers; being mothers,
They will take care their children do not starve
When they're on service; and, for ways and means,
Trust us, there's nothing cleverer than a woman.
And as for diplomacy, they'll be hard indeed
To cheat—they know too many tricks themselves.

Praxagora's speech is unanimously applauded; she is elected president by public acclamation.

In the next scene two of the husbands appear, greatly perplexed, one wrapped in his wife's dressing gown and the other in his underwear and barefoot. They want to go to the Assembly, but cannot find their clothes. While they are wondering what their wives might have done with the clothes and what has become of the women themselves, a third neighbor comes in. He has been to the Assembly and reports that the place is quite full already, and of strange faces too. And a handsome fair-faced youth (Praxagora in disguise), amid the loud cheers of unknown voters, had proposed and carried a resolution that the government of the state should be placed in the hands of women, an experiment that had found favor with everybody, chiefly because it was "the only change which had not as yet been tried at Athens." The men are somewhat confused by the news, but congratulate themselves that their wives will now, at all events, have to see to the support of the children and that "the gods sometimes bring good out of evil."

Praxagora then declares, "there shall be no more poverty; there shall be community of goods, and so there shall be no lawsuits, and no gambling, and no informers. Moreover, there shall be community of wives,—and all the ugly women shall have the first choice of husbands." She goes off to her public duties, to see that these resolutions are carried out forthwith. The fantasy dissolves into a banquet.[1]

As we know, the women did not take over in Athens, or anywhere else. What if they were to now? Or if they were at least to enter the male political establishment on equal terms and in equal numbers?

What would happen?

For some atavistic reasons men crave leaders, and they appear to crave them much more than women do. Men surpass women in needing, searching, and clamoring for leaders: they invest their leaders with prodigious virtues and powers, and eagerly turn over to them their meager resources and small freedoms. They think that in a "democracy" it is they who ultimately control their leaders and thus the course of events. They debate fervently about to whom they will, at the next opportunity, donate their tax money, destinies, good reputations in the world. And they always think they select a leader who will do what they want, what they elected him to do, what is needed. They think they are like lords hiring coachmen, but really are more like coachmen hiring out to lords. And everywhere politicians offer themselves as servants in order to become masters.

But is it not true that the leader can last only if the "people" not only elect him but also keep supporting him? If the leader did not do what the people want, would they continue to support him? Those who lend the leader support do so on "information" and "positions" and packaged views sold to them by that leader, so there is a cycle at work here, but not a good one. The leaders sense certain emotional needs in the electorate and tailor a propaganda program to fit those needs, and the people then "demand" from their leaders what they have been asked by their leaders to demand of them.

One young woman interviewed, a member of the Kerner Commission on violence, said, ". . . the United States says that it is operating in a democratic way, yet in reality it works in an authoritarian way—people at the top making decisions and then going to the people for reaffirmation of those decisions. They're not saying, 'What should we do?' and then acting on the policy the people want. The most tragic thing about it is that the people of the United States seem to accept this, because we're so used to the fact that someone over us is going to make the decisions."

Who wins? Who stays in office? Simply the best semanticist.*

* Khrushchev's rise to power has been traced to his use of semantics, superior to that of all his rivals.[2]

Doesn't his performance count? Not really, for in our increasingly intricate situation the war, inflation, employment, the dollar devaluation, alliances, the control of pollution, and everything else is merely a matter of interpretation. Besieged with billions of words, on issues so involved and unclear that no expert's word is worth much and every good semanticist (demagogue) can make a good case for or against anything, the citizen's mind is swamped. That the experts and the semanticists in and out of office often contradict each other in public—a fact advertised by the same experts and semanticists as evidence that democracy is working—in no way helps people to know whether their leaders' performance is good. Somewhere, but remote, there is a reality: people are being killed in Vietnam, the cities are full of smog, there is crime in the streets, prices rise, people are unemployed, minorities are discriminated against. But the responsible citizen wants to know the *causes* and true dimensions so that he can decide on proper courses of action or evaluate the performance of those he has instated to act. Yet it is precisely that knowledge that he cannot obtain.

As a result, with politics becoming increasingly opaque, the led surprisingly, have become, decreasingly demanding: they no longer even look for *promises,* which the astute candidate, in this age of easily communicable and retrievable information, would hesitate to make anyway. The voters now mainly select their leader on the basis of what he says on any given subject, on the "position" he takes, or what they think he said or was the position he took—that is, on the basis of the "noises" made by the leader on any given subject at any given time. One therefore wonders whether the candidates will ultimately simply enunciate only certain words, such as "ecology, ecology, ecology," or "Communism, Communism, Communism," or "segregation, desegregation, segregation, desegregation," and leave the voters to salivate like Pavlovian dogs.

In the face of all the vagueness leaders receive more rather than less support because psychologically man, rather than woman, feels lost without a leader, abandoned, weak, perplexed. And nothing is easier to find than some man, often without even a decent profession, who out of the will to power and fame will "lead." Leaders and led alike act from weakness: men need their leaders because they are weak without them, and leaders need "their" men because they are nothing without them.

Still, political leadership, which led to such excesses as the rules of Hitler or Stalin, and which now seems to be growing stronger in America, is also under many pressures. The young, particularly the young women, view it with growing skepticism. Helen B., student of political science, says, "Why do people need leaders anyway? One of the things that bugs me when I listen to the older generation is that they always wring their hands and call for better leaders. The older folks seem bright enough to notice that we do not have exactly the best choice of fine candidates. They also say we have great problems. The greater the problems, the greater the leaders they have in mind who should solve them, and the more anxious they are that leadership must become stronger and wiser. Only there are no good leaders, at least not in our day, because leadership is obsolete. Not intellectual leadership, I mean, but political control over people.

"Incidentally, that is one reason why our generation, or those who just won't play ball with the system, are much more numerous and much stronger than they appear to be. We have no leaders because we don't believe in leaders. Leadership and the reverence for leaders is one of the big things in the system we don't like. If we had leaders of our own, we would be much more visible of course. But we don't need leaders, we have no use for them. That's because we have no use for all those things people need leaders for: war, imperialism, economic exploitation, propaganda. Freedom and leadership are incompatible. People who think they serve their leaders freely because they have gone to the polls are just fooling themselves. And leaders who convince themselves that they serve the people also fool themselves.

"In fact," added Charles M., a political science major, "this whole business of making it a sacred duty to go to the polls to select those leaders and representatives is very objectionable. 'Get out the vote,' they all shout, 'we don't care for whom you vote, just vote.' And they measure the success of an election by the turnout. Just as in the Soviet Union. The Soviet leaders always come in with over 90 per cent of the vote to show they are wanted by everybody. We do the same, except that two fellows instead of one compete with each other for the advantages of being the leader. Naturally, any man who votes for Humphrey for President will also cheer Nixon as his leader when his own horse fails to come in. And the winner benefits by the big turnout: it gives him what he calls his mandate. Well, no one is going to get any mandate from me unless I really like him, and as for representing me in Washington, like senators or congressmen say they do, I don't need to be represented in that place, or any place, and least of all by a professional politician."

Perhaps for the first time in history, the entire idea of national political leadership is in trouble. (Except for the Anarchist movement, which has long since died, or similar efforts of little consequence.) In essence, *the women's movement is a rebellion against the leadership principle,* and the women's movement is much bigger and stronger than earlier antileadership movements have been. It also is much harder to combat, for incumbent leaders, because the thrust of woman power is aimed not against individual leaders or parties, but at leadership per se. One of women's main objections to men is that on all levels and in every conceivable way, men aim for leadership rather than partnership, even among themselves, which means suppression of others. Increasingly weakened as individuals in a mass society, men apparently can feel strength only as leaders of families or of small groups or, better still, of large domineering groups that, to be large and domineering, need a strong leader. That leader has to have, as all pundits and political scientists have discovered and keep repeating, *charisma,* an overused but meaningful term.

Charisma describes that quality in a leader (and in his followers' response to him) that in earlier days was less satisfactorily called "magnetism" or something like it. It describes the leader's ability to appeal to the led in other than intellectual, factual ways, to sway them, hold them, arouse them with his charm, his "image," his "personality"—that is, with all sorts of qualities irrelevant to the political issues. Charisma means that a leader can command the loyalty of the led no matter how he fails them, even though, semantically speaking, he can never fail them, for part of his charisma, as long as it lasts, is precisely that the led will love, admire, and appreciate him and willingly go along with his insistent claim that he has done and is doing great things for them.

If anything reveals the abdication of the intellect or of simple rationality in our era it is the appearance of charisma, a dangerous phenomenon, greatly furthered by TV, with the charismatic leader looking deep into the eyes of each of his people, personally it appears, and emoting with them. The essence of charisma is *unquestioning acceptance* and *blanket forgiveness.* It is the *surrender to a personality rather than the selection of person,* the submission to a "magic" that is hollow and treacherous. [It is interesting that Hitler, perhaps the greatest charismatic leader and male chauvinist pig of all time (though the Germans, like disaffected suitors, now deny they ever loved him), used to say that "the masses are feminine in their response." He believed that the qualities of irrationality, illogic, excitement, supineness, adulation that masses display are feminine qualities. But it becomes more and more apparent nowadays that they are more specifically *male* qualities.]

Perhaps the most encouraging recent development is that the women's movement does not seriously support charismatic leaders, male or female. The last orgy of women's support for a charismatic leader seems to have largely spent itself on John Kennedy, even though men like Nixon or Agnew or Wallace or Ted Kennedy undoubtedly still hold charismatic sway over numbers of "unliberated" women. The women's movement, though it may never have said so specifically, is profoundly anticharisma, suspecting (in fact rejecting) this particular phenomenon on the contemporary political scene. And the women are not likely to compromise with it. The women, of all people, for whom not so many years ago the "glamorous" candidate—the fellow for whom one voted regardless of the issues, whom one *always* believed because he was so irresistible—seemed tailormade, have turned away from that political threat and will have no truck with it (while men seem to go increasingly the other way).

We predict that one of the first wholesome effects of woman power on the American body politic will be the disappearance of charismatic leaders. Women who "want" a man like Ted Kennedy will take him to bed and not to the White House, and not even as a substitute in the White House if they cannot take him, or someone like him, to bed. This will, in the coming decade, have a sobering, detuning effect on the overrevving political machine. It will also lead to reduced campaign expenditures as the frenetic, professional, smooth campaign designed to overpower a hundred million emotionally keyed-up voters will become less effective, and eventually even counterproductive, in the post-McLuhanesque age that woman power in politics may well usher in. Politics, of course, will and must continue: even the young lesbian-feminist interviewed observed with a shrug that two hundred million people in one place need some kind of government. But the charismatic leader, that half step away from the dictator (in countries that do not already have total dictatorship), will decline under the impact of women in American politics.

This may have far-reaching consequences. For with the charismatic leader disappearing from the highest office, he will disappear as well from the lower ones, to the extent that he is not replaced by women in any event. All the little politicians in local office, as well as congressmen and senators in Washington, to the extent that they face the voters are also charismatic leaders or try to be, conjuring up before the voters some qualities that they hope will help them into office and keep them there.

Curiously, women are generally regarded as more gullible, less rational than men. If that were the case, they would be the perfect pigeons for the charismatic demagogue. Apparently, however, this, like so much else that is believed today, is propaganda. Or if women once were oriented that way, many no longer are. It is the men who, for reasons of fear or frustration or simple stupidity, and also because they live through them vicariously, quite obviously are more emotional about their political leaders than the women, more easily fooled, more irrationally loyal to them, cheering leaders who often do them great harm and lie to them outrageously. It is the very gullibility of contemporary man that has made it possible, indeed inevitable, that almost every contemporary political personage is a *professional liar* first and anything else second.

Professional liars, it must be added, are also believers, to varying degrees. They do not wholly believe what they say; they may lie to the people about an issue, generally by manipulating, before the eyes of the baffled populace, the very "facts and figures" the individual insists on having in order "to make up my own mind." But they are believers nevertheless: they believe in the righteousness of the (male) establishment.

Whether because they have the detachment of the uninvolved bystander or for more fundamental reasons, women are now withdrawing their support from that (male) establishment and will do so increasingly, thereby changing the entire political system and everything else with it. This does not mean that all active women politicians appeal to reason. In fact, Shirley Chisholm, sometimes uses the charismatic approach too, saying, "I am a good woman, an honest woman. Trust me, come to me." And though she may indeed be a good woman, her approach is not likely to be successful or representative of the politics of the future. Once they acquire more power and are given a feeling of political security by it, women will demand rationality, low-key discussion, honest effort from their representatives, female or male, rather than TV spectaculars or mere popular cliché's or simple evocative sounds emerging from carefully made-up and smiling or grimly determined lips.

Women in Positions of Power. This will make the playing with the people more difficult for male politicians. It is easy for them now, for man is emotionally so unbalanced at present by the runaway technology and other pressures closing in on him as to be fair game.

When women candidates begin to play the game differently, trying at least to be serious and honest with the voters instead of mainly pursuing the conquest of office and power, the entire electorate will respond. What will then come to pass is that the more rational and less violence-prone males, who often have nowhere to go with their vote in today's political situation, will in very large numbers begin to vote for *women candidates.* At that point woman power will make a quantum jump—presumably still in this decade.

What will the women do with their (large) share of the power on the local and national level? Once in office will they, like the men, use all their time, aside from representing special and often invisible interests, to campaign for reelection to the same or higher office? Will they, in the words of the most chronic campaigner of them all, also become "chronic campaigners"? That just is not likely, for women are not likely to be as infatuated with power as their male colleagues on the political scene. As everyone knows, women can be just as power-hungry as men, as status-hungry, as hungry to be honored, fussed over, to be "insiders"; and perhaps most of the women who have "made it" so far fall into that category. But it is unlikely that most women coming to the fore in the coming decade will be of that type. The power-hungry, male or female, are likely to fare less well in the coming decade, mainly because woman power as a whole will probably take the wind out of their sails.

Will women then deal effectively with the issues? It is hard to say, of course, whether these issues are still manageable. It can be said, however, that they will not be manageable if those elected to deal with them do not have even the intention (or the capacity, because of all the political constraints on them) of dealing with them; and many of the current politicians have no intention or ability to deal with the issues. The issues, to them, are merely lances with which they spar or horses on which they ride or vehicles for their rhetoric when they confront the public. It is not that these politicians are all fiends, and many may even embark on their careers with good intentions. But the present system makes intelligent and effective effort in any problem area very difficult.

Women in politics will have a sobering, soothing influence and will help create an atmosphere in which people and their politicians will be able to communicate factually and seriously without too many slogans, emotions, suspicions, or doubts cast on their patriotism or loyalty. Women representing woman power will be more practical, more sensible, more tolerant for all the reasons mentioned in Chapter 4. And they are likely, as discussed there, to bring one additional important quality to bear upon the political scene: a greater respect for money, a better sense for the value of the dollar.

It is hard to realize how revolutionary an effect a different posture toward money—always, as said before, the fruit of someone's labors—can have upon the broad spectrum of the political scene. For the (male) establishment has now brainwashed itself into believing—perhaps because of the American or the capitalist tradition—that except for force, money is the answer to everything. Whether it is drug addiction, the decay of the cities, desegregation, pollution, education, crime, drugs, the male politician's, in fact any male observer's, reflex is that this can all be solved with money, and only with money, but of course only with *billions* of dollars. But this is a fallacy, a form of playing truant with problems, a megalomaniacal fantasy, a (conscious or unconscious) desire to prevent society from seeing clearly the nature of all these problems. For if society did see them in their proper light, it would perceive that not lack of money but the general posture of the (male) establishment toward society as a whole and all individuals in it, the lack of compassion, the premium on toughness and aggression, the disdain for "bleeding hearts" and their ideas, the drive for more bureaucratic and other power—and *not* lack of money—are at the root of all the problems.

Several aspects of this general cry for unimaginable sums of money are quite curious. They represent simultaneously an overvaluation and undervaluation of money. It is an overvaluation of money to think it can cure all the ills now plaguing us. It is an undervaluation of money to call cavalierly for the spending of a billion dollars for anything. A form of pathological compensation may also be involved: the less able a fellow is to make his mortgage payment on time, the readier he seems to see his government spend a billion dollars. Aside from being just another three hundred dollars out of *his* paycheck, which he can ill afford, that billion is, as a sum, an almost metaphysical figure, a sort of imploration: if this does not do it, nothing will. The voting for or spending of vast sums of money also exonerates the politician, who equates money with "action" and tells the voters at reelection time: "Look, I've spent a billion dollars on drug abuse. I've set up a huge machinery. No man can do more." And the voter—himself a money-worshipper—believes it.

If all these billions the politicians call for were available—which they can never be, unless the average taxation is raised to perhaps three-quarters of all incomes, with the state then taking all a citizen's earnings except for a Saturday-night allowance—they would buy very little, for drastic inflation would diminish their buying power. More important, their being spent would lead to new superbureaucracies, new immense agencies on drug abuse, pollution, crime, and so on that would absorb all these funds like a gargantuan sponge, creating new parasitic power nuclei, staffed by ever more bureaucrats and fed by ever more studies by machine scientists.

But with such money spent on whatever the evil is, the evil itself is helped to institutionalize itself. In fact, those "combating it" become institutionalized with it. Imagine for a moment that drug addiction and poverty and pollution should go away or be reduced to easily manageable proportions: a great many people and institutions would be out of work! Perhaps the only thing harder to reform than a drug addict is a student of drug addiction who has become addicted to writing papers about it.

It is unlikely that woman power will tolerate this, will permit such activities, will waste money as barbarously as the (male) establishment often wastes it. Nor will women be as impaled by the necessity of seeing these problems as technical. Bringing compassion to them, and not toughness, reliance on money, "hardnosed" approaches, controls, wasteful studies, or (and this is of equal importance) mistaken theories, women will be better equipped to understand what is happening and to cope with it.

Social Problems? In an article, "The Problems with Social Problems," which appeared in *Politics and Society* in the fall of 1971, an Englishman, James B. Rule, castigates the scientific bureaucratic community for deliberately confounding *social problems* and *political conflicts.* "Race, pollution, poverty, the cities—all of these so-called 'social problems' amount to contests between various groups over the control of desirable resources, including wealth, privilege, and, above all, the application of political power. These issues turn on clashes of interest, and thus represent *political conflicts.* And yet, in the language of the prevailing coalition between government and social science, they are treated instead as *social problems,* as forms of 'social sickness. . . .' This unwarranted application of clinical language to politics is misleading and dangerous. For it suggests that political conflicts can somehow be resolved a-politically, through the dispassionate intervention of experts instead of through political action. And this suggestion, in turn, paves the way for the imposition of partisan measures in the guise of non-political 'solutions' to 'social problems.' "

Rule continues, "Similarly, government bodies sponsor countless studies and 'action projects' aimed at the 'solution' of the 'poverty problem,' 'the racial problem' and the like, doubtless with the hope that the public will interpret these gestures as signifying unanimous opposition within the government to these evils. But it does not take much reflection to see that racism or poverty would rapidly cease to exist if it were not to the satisfaction of certain elements in society that they should continue—and that these are groups on which the government depends for its existence."

And, he adds, ". . . the participation of social scientists and other experts in problem-solving efforts entails a political advantage for those who hold power. For, if questions of opposition of interest are officially ignored, the only debates left are discussions over technique, over the best means. . . . And since social scientists are seen . . . as preeminent experts on the workings of society, who would be better qualified to hammer out the optimal solutions to vexing social problems? The visible presence of such experts, hard at work in their problem-solving efforts, is bound to enhance the credibility of the notion that everything possible is being done to set the situation right." [3]

Our prediction is that once woman power becomes operative in the American political system, social problems will again be seen for what they are—social conflicts. Because women do not yet have as much to lose from social change as even the lowliest member of the (male) establishment, they will see through the game of bureaucrat hiring expert to tell him how to spend money so that it appears credible to the public that the problem is being tackled, attacked, put on the list of priorities. Women will easily see that today's scientific experts are merely attempting to depoliticize genuine political problems (which, of course, cannot be done), are serving as a public-relations bastion facing the gullible public and the gullible or cynical media writers, so that the (male) establishment can perpetuate itself *and* its billions-of-dollars-consuming, yet rapidly proliferating "problems."

Women may have the intelligence, which will be sparked by compassion and the absence of fierce partisanship and bizarre loyalties, to see these problems for what they are; and they have the sense not to consider them all as problems to be solved by more studies, more bureaucracy, more force, and more money.

This, in turn, will finally enable many men to see the calamities of our day in a different and more manageable way. The new revolutionary approach by woman power to our hidden contemporary political conflicts (which really generate all the contemporary problems) will be of great social and political value for the nation, and it will occur in the very near future.

Depoliticization? At the same time as woman power asserts itself in government and conventional politics, it is likely also to deemphasize government and politics altogether, paradoxical though this may seem. One of the troubles with modern society, as Jacques Ellul has stated in *The Political Illusion*, is that people and all issues are "politicized" as never before. What Ellul means is that modern man—and modern woman too, but apparently to a lesser degree—seeks political solutions to everything, whether the problem is freedom or justice or peace or prosperity or happiness. Anything not political does not arouse widespread interest and is thus not accorded independent existence in our hyperpolitical world. As a result of this politicization of all of life, and because of the entropy of all thought and energy in the direction of politics, people turn increasingly to the state for a solution of all their problems, though the state could not solve them if it tried. And this increasing inclination to turn to father (or mother) state leads, everywhere, to three evils: a boundless inflation of the state's size and power; increasing dependence on the state by the individual; and decreasing control over the state by the "people," who think they control it but who really only surrender their power—and money—to it.

The appeal of a man like Ralph Nader in this country—significantly a greater appeal for women than men—is not just that he takes on vast machines and thus projects the cherished David-versus-Goliath image, but that he is "honest"; he protects the people; *he works outside of political channels,* even though he works within the system. An interesting article by Stephen Schlesinger, "The Young Good Guys," sketches the dimensions that extragovernmental efforts toward societal improvement have already reached, and discusses how strongly some intelligent, well-educated, and dedicated young women are involved in them. "Aileen and Geoffrey Cowan, representing an environmental and several other groups devoted to the public interest, have come to feel that developing movements *on the outside of the electoral process is more effective than depending on political campaigns* [emphasis added]. Aileen says: 'There is a tremendous freedom about doing a well-researched, honest study which need only be responsive to the facts at hand, not to the political needs of some candidate. Nader's approach is severely accurate; it doesn't compromise beliefs or make mistakes. That sort of thing makes it very difficult to think about reentering the political process [in which Aileen had previously been active].'"

Tracing similar views and actions by other young men and women, the author concludes: "These, then, are some of the 'new independents' who are avoiding straight politics and have evolved intellectual guerrilla operations to reshape American life." These efforts on the part of young people, especially young women, to free themselves from the government and its professional political pyramids—not to battle it as an institution but to bypass it wherever it interposes itself—seem highly significant. To work through such extragovernmental, extrapolitical channels, which are not "subversive," however, and remain within "the system," requires that one dedicate oneself to the matter at hand, without seeking, on the side or maybe even as the principal goal, personal advantage through political power. It is paralleled by the increasing reliance by some people concerned with social reform on the so-called NGOs (nongovernmental organizations) that are springing up everywhere and are creating their own international network. To work outside government seems a natural vehicle for young woman power. And this can ultimately lead to the acquisition of power as well. Schlesinger observes that next to the President, Ralph Nader is the most powerful man in the country. And even though that is somewhat hyperbolic, Nader's power obviously is considerable. What those who, like Nader, make their social and political efforts outside of government have recognized is that the political machine, the government, is not only an insatiable money-sponge, absorbing any amount of it, often without a trace, but also a great sponge of *individual effort and idealism,* absorbing those too, often without a trace.

Once Woman Power will be partly channeled through avenues other than conventional politics, the behemoth of the state, increasingly blind, greedy, haughty, and saurian, will be brought down to size, and for all we know, dismissed from first place in human society and the human mind. For thousands of years people had many other and better things to think about, give their loyalty to, further and cherish than the state. Only in our day, in which the individual feels increasingly helpless, has the state assumed so unique a position. But woman power is likely to help return it to its place, not just in the fabric of society, but even more importantly, in the minds of—particularly—men. That will perhaps be the outstanding effect by women power on politics in the coming decade.

14

WOMAN POWER AND THE FUTURE OF WAR AND PEACE

MEN love war. Men love war even though, from the humanist point of view, war is the ultimate disaster for individuals and nations. Feebly or vociferously, they deny this; but the thief also denies to the very last that he is a thief. No matter how much men protest, how many international congresses they convoke or attend, how fervently or volubly they proclaim their love of peace, they love war in most of its forms and manifestations, they love its rewards and rigors, the violence, the cruelty, the waste, the excitement, the victories, the women.

What is the evidence? There is the universal hysterical contempt and hatred directed at pacifists by most men, but few women. Confronted with a pacifist, most men sputter with rage, heap ridicule on him, accuse him of cowardice and treason, treat him worse than a leper. Tony A., a Vietnam veteran turned antiwar, says, "Nothing is as obvious about our ways as the disgust with pacifism. Maybe pacifists are not always right, and maybe Hitler had to be fought, and all that. But people do not just disagree with the pacifist, they despise him."

Psychiatry has demonstrated that people who continually have certain experiences they claim they are trying to avoid, whether a disastrous fight with the boss or a barroom brawl, *want* those experiences, at least unconsciously. They suffer from a "repetition compulsion," they seek out these events, at least unconsciously, or at least they are not sufficiently anxious to avoid them, do not dislike them enough to change their own modes of behavior. The bully may not like a fight (or he may), but in any event he loves his aggressive behavior enough to risk subsequent fighting, which, even if he dislikes it, he dislikes less than giving up his aggressive behavior. And most of the time he loves the ensuing fight; in fact, his aggressive behavior is generally designed to provoke it. Either way, he always fights, and if he protests between bouts that he does not want to fight (but must, of course, defend himself), we can disregard his words, which also say that in addition to being a compulsive slugger, he is a compulsive liar. Man's constant warfare proves that he is a war-lover.

But what if the other fellow makes war on us? he asks indignantly. It is discouraging proof of man's stupidity that he really believes this to be the situation. Why does he believe it? Because, feeling guilty about his lust to break the Fifth Commandment, man sets up a strawman on whom to exercise his provocative behavior and then his vengeance. If he did not love war so much, he would not forever create situations in which war is inevitable.

War is also a welcome challenge to most men. At first they are scared to death, then they struggle fiercely with themselves, mainly in order to prove themselves in the eyes of their comrades, but also in their own eyes. Then, if they make it, they feel like "real" men, who can face death and cause it without batting an eyelash. In our generally unheroic times that gives their egos much more of a lift than even a promotion. For they fear nothing more—from early childhood on—than being called *"coward,"* a term to which they give an entirely anachronistic interpretation—that is, they call people cowards who consider it foolish and frightening to have their bodies torn apart and their minds extinguished. And for the men who stay home, for the men in industry and government, war is even more welcome as a challenge than it is for the soldiers.

Finally for our purposes (to furnish all the other available proofs that men love war would fill an entire book and bore the reader), any man who has ever been in a war or who, after a war, has met any of his ex-comrades knows beyond the shadow of a doubt that men love war, even most "cowards." The causes of this are to be found in a million male urges, including the "noble" ones. This is not the place to examine them, and the point here is merely that men love war, whether they acknowledge it or not, realize it or not, welcome this emotion in themselves or not. The company commander of a Marine unit in Vietnam, when asked why so many men reenlisted after their year, said, "Well, there are lots of good things for the men in that dump. Good pay, plenty of ass. Even outlets for their idealism. But don't forget, the men also sign up again because they *love* to fight and they *love* to kill." And so, incidentally, does this man, as the author knows from personal contact with him.*

Beyond such primitive drives that make men love war so much, there are practical reasons for at least condoning it. "Wars are occasioned by the love of money," said—not Marx—Plato; and only a brainwashed person can deny that wars are profitable for many people. Even though the war-lovers cry "Communist!" when this is mentioned, it is nevertheless known very well to all economists, all businessmen and labor leaders, and politicians as well. Naturally not everybody wins, and the costs of war harm many. Still, both World Wars were tremendous boosts for the economic and technological growth of America and the source of accumulations of money and power.

---

* If the reader still has doubts, the words of Maj. Gen. James F. Hollingsworth in Vietnam may help dispel them: "When you can kill hell out of them out there, goddammit, you feel good." [1] Hollingsworthism will, we predict, be dampened by woman power in the coming decade, and the defense of the United States will gain rather than lose by it.

War also derives an impetus from a powerful, power-hungry, ambitious bureaucracy that thrives on it, emotionally and professionally. And yet another impetus from powerful contemporary ideologies, mundane religions fanatically adhered to by many and cynically dispensed by others; ideologies that have such a strong hold on people perhaps because there is so little genuine religion left. That makes all wars crusades, and men rather than women are crusaders.

War is also furthered by the fact that those opposed to it generally are mostly mild in their opposition, disliking war about as much as they would a carrot stick in a martini. Or they oppose it for utilitarian reasons that are not effective: the war costs too much, it is not really necessary, it takes too long, it creates problems of one kind or another. Still others, who spurn the argument that the war costs too much, argue that it is immoral, thus bringing down on their heads the scorn of all those who, when they hear the word "morality," consider their he-manism challenged (as well as what they call their "realism").

Hardly anyone ever combats war simply because it is war, and therefore mankind's greatest evil. Richard Barnet, co-director of the independent Washington-based Institute for Policy Studies, said recently, "When we asked one of the most strategically placed doves in the State Department why the moral issue was never raised, he replied that such a discussion 'would be as if from another world.' "[2] Such a frontal attack would lead the attacker nowhere except to be laughed out of court, or beaten out of court, as a pacifist or a fool. The Naked Ape is pretty hard to budge when it comes to his favorite sport, outlet, pastime.

What makes war even more secure is that men lie about their feelings on war, to others and to themselves. Not only do they deny publicly that they are war-lovers, but they deny it to themselves. Ignorant of history or anthropology, which, foremost among contemporary sciences, could furnish them with a clue, they romanticize and glamorize humankind's positive, civilizing, and sensible proclivities and pass over in silence or embarrassment its perhaps more elementary, aggressive, and deceitful other half. Like the alcoholic who does not admit to himself his irresistible penchant for alcohol and who is therefore its easy victim, the Naked Ape is no match for his martial inclinations.

But man does not listen to scientists who do not please him. His attention is very selective, even though he professes and apparently feels a deep admiration for some "experts" and the machine social scientists, usually much to his detriment. Yet he would derive considerable benefit from listening to the very voices he disregards: for example, a behavioral geneticist at the University of Colorado, Dr. Peter A. Corning, who says, "In an age when the masculine virtues are becoming less adaptive for our survival, government by women may actually prove to be a superior adaptation in evolutionary terms. Judging by the available biological and sociological evidence, women would probably be far less likely to get bored with peace. Women would be less likely to go to war for irrational reasons, too. On the other hand," says Corning, "they would probably not shrink from war when it became necessary for survival. Neither Golda Meir nor Indira Gandhi are timid souls. . . ."[3]

Corning suggests, in effect, that the only possibly effective antidote to war is woman power. Even comparing women's dominant traits with men's, however, one wonders how strong an antidote woman power really is. Women have historically had their own share in supporting war. They have worshipped heroes from Alexander to Napoleon to the bemedaled boy on the block and supported war and their warrior men in many ways. There were probably reasons for women's being unable or unwilling to be more of an antiwar force in history than they actually have been. Perhaps now that women are beginning to liberate themselves, not just from social institutions they do not like, but also from the intellectual bondage to ideas, ideologies, tenets, superstitions posing as patriotic or scientific, and to jettison such mental impediments in order to attain a clearer view of *what is*, they may become the first effective opponents of Mars. For to combat war, love of peace is not enough: one must first see what is going on.

Richard Barnet observed about the genesis of war: "All great nations play the game . . . to keep the game going you must be prepared to be flexible about your enemies, ready to change them when the game so requires . . . there are not winners, only losers . . . success is claimed if disaster is averted. . . . When his term of office came to an end in the ignominious stalemate of Vietnam, Dean Rusk looked back on his eight years with satisfaction, he said, because nuclear weapons had not been used.

"For the national security manager, the *game* is what makes the job exciting. Assistant Secretary of Defense John T. McNaughton who had been working fourteen hours a day, weeks on end (in the early stages of the Vietnam war) once exclaimed to an assistant: 'I couldn't stand this job if I didn't love it!' What makes the game worth unending hours of dreary meetings and sleepless nights? One national security manager to whom I put the question answered immediately: 'The sense of playing for high stakes.' . . . When the Vietnamese agreed to meet in Paris, [an] official told the *New York Times* proudly: 'There we were right off the bat—eyeball to eyeball on a question of prestige as well as procedure. And they're the ones who blinked. Now we're one up!' "

A lot that got us!

Barnet continues: "All killing in the national interest is done in strict accordance with certain scientific principles. . . . It is these principles that persuade Presbyterian elders, Episcopalian wardens, liberal professors, and practitioners of game-theory rationalism alike that bureaucratic homicide is neither wanton nor purposeless. Killing and threatening to kill foreigners are rational, necessary, and effective instruments for building what President Nixon calls 'a generation of peace' and what Dean Acheson called twenty-five years ago 'positions of strength.'

"One of the first lessons a national security manager learns after a day in . . . the Pentagon, State Department, White House, or CIA is that 'toughness' is the most highly prized virtue. Some of the security managers of the Johnson–Kennedy era . . . talk about the 'hairy chest syndrome.' The man who is ready to recommend using violence against foreigners, even where he is overruled, does not damage his reputation for prudence, soundness, or imagination: but the man who recommends putting an issue to the U.N., seeking negotiations or 'doing nothing,' quickly becomes known as 'soft.' To be 'soft,' that is, unbelligerent, compassionate, willing to settle for less, or simply repelled by mass homicide, is to be 'irresponsible.' "[4]

Most men, each in his own way, will always make war, and if "central" war has by now become a little too difficult and dangerous because of the existence of nuclear weapons, they invent "limited wars," counterinsurgency wars, conventional wars, police actions, which make even less sense than the wars of yore because they can never decide anything or even really end, for all the major players keep their big weapons in reserve. Limited wars merely kill. And the men who play the game, the thousands fresh from the universities who annually enter the government, from the very first day can never again extricate themselves from the need to be aggressive, hard-hitting, destructive, deceptive. For if they were not, they would, at any level, be destroyed by their peers. If ever a trace of humanity does stir in them, a trace of doubt, a trace of compassion, a trace of common sense, it is always too late because a career must be preserved and furthered, and there is only one way to do it: by showing that one is just as "hardnosed," in fact more so, as the next fellow. Unfortunately, singularly few of these men ever experience such stirrings.

This, then, is the situation. But some of the younger people, especially young women, are beginning to see the light. Gilda A., a young assistant professor of political science, says, "I think we—the younger generation—have learned something the hard way.

When we first started to take an interest in political affairs, we were shaped in our views by our leaders and the media, and of course by our professors. Without exception they all opted for what they insisted was peace but turned out to be war. All their theories on international politics, advocating deterrence, coercion, compulsion, and tough bargaining, produced war, not peace. And will always produce war. And of course one reason why our opponents were such fierce opponents was because *they* knew that all our policies meant war. I do not mean to say they are better; far from it. They too seem to believe in nothing but force and propaganda, just as we. But we have been had, I mean the younger people, the students, the people. We *know* now that continued reliance on force and propaganda, at home and abroad, spells war. But we don't yet know what to do about it. The one thing we can do is not to teach mindlessly to our students what we pretty mindlessly absorbed as the facts of international life ourselves."

We must look at semantics. The enemy: we're told we are surrounded by the enemy. Who is that enemy? Why, even the gentle, avuncular Walter Cronkite has spoken every evening now for seven years of "the enemy" with a perfectly straight avuncular face! What is he talking about? Male chauvinists apparently just need an enemy, but the United States doesn't. We do have real antagonists, such as the Soviet Union and China, and they are our antagonists partly because they are much as we are—belligerent, aggressive, paranoid—and partly because of what we try to do to them. And as when men arm-wrestle, it's hard to get disentangled. But the wrestlers really do not want to get disentangled: each wants to win. No one knows the answer, except that it is not what our leaders and defense intellectuals say it is. The answer may be woman power.

There were times, not long ago, when naïve men and women thought that the League of Nations, or the United Nations, or World Government, or disarmament conferences, or socialism or

Moral Rearmament would be the answer to the scourge of war. But that is ineffective, for no matter how archaic the sound of the trumpet, coming in over the handsomely designed intercom or the cheapest radio, the old warhorse in men rears up, forever ready. The entire baneful psychological chain—men wanting to dominate and aggrandize themselves and/or their tribe, men taking great chances in doing so, men striking arrogant and aggressive poses, men challenging the smaller and the bigger, men ready to fight, kill, coerce, subdue, rob—prevents peace. This can never change except perhaps, finally, by the infusion of woman power into the system. Woman power would dilute the martial aggression endemic in the male-dominated society, and thereby even help men to become more mature, more civilized, less aggressive, less violent, less irrational, less infatuated with war and death.

But first it would have to dilute all the disguised and hidden war propaganda. To do this, women would have to conquer strong positions in the nation's foreign-affairs machinery. For there the chain of events begins: intelligence analysts report home that this or that enemy is now "vulnerable"; ambassadors apply pressure to outwit the other fellow, who can no more be outwitted than they; negotiators sally forth with professions of good will but in fact try to bring home some big advantage they never will bring home; then there is stalemate, hate propaganda, more stalemate, more faulty analysis of the "enemy," and finally war. In all this the Pentagon generals often play the least nefarious role. They generally hesitate to fight, either because they feel, as generals always do, that "we are not ready" or for other reasons—often good ones. The colonels and majors and captains—that is a different story. They want war in order to get the decorations and promotions they cannot otherwise obtain, but that is an unimportant technical detail: these men have "nothing to say."

It is just more propaganda, firmly believed by Americans because George Washington thought so, that the military are more belligerent and therefore must be kept in check by the civilians.

In an age in which computerized war is conducted via telecommunications from air-conditioned offices, civilians have emerged as distinctly the *more* belligerent of the two.

However it is not the military, not the civilians, not the "merchants of death," not the vainglorious bureaucrats who cause war. Rather, it is universal he-manism, active as well as passive: the active he-man loves to fight personally, and the passive he-man—more numerous by far—loves to fight vicariously, to teleview the active he-man charge; the passive he-man identifies with the active and cheers him on and supports him, drink in hand, from his overstuffed chair. Men, not just certain men, but *men* make war because they love war, always have loved war, even though the (male) establishment has overdone it with three wars in one generation, so that a sizable number of young males now seem to have turned away altogether from that pernicious passion. These young males will be the natural, though minor allies of woman power likely to enter into and remodel our social and governmental structure and our values in the coming decade. And because similar inroads are apparently being made by woman power elsewhere in the world, Mars may eventually be in trouble. Woman power may yet bring about peace in our time, not by brandishing an umbrella, like Neville Chamberlain, but by seeing war as it is and doing what is necessary to curb it.

15

WOMAN POWER AND THE FUTURE OF THOUGHT

One of contemporary man's most catastrophic qualities—and the affliction *is* found predominantly in males—is that he cannot, dare not, will not think. This may sound strange in view of the rampant intellectualism that is reaching and titillating millions of people, or in view of the rapidly proliferating "education," and the large numbers of scientists, experts, professors, think tanks and foundations that lavish large sums upon what they consider original or useful thought. The concern with "education"—or really what goes by that name—is quite obsessional, considering the low quality of teaching and learning that is visited upon the young. Ex-Texas schoolteacher Lyndon B. Johnson was a prime example of those who saw all blessings for everybody as springing from education, while Johnson himself, though one of the craftiest, was one of the least educated of men. But his most "educated" advisors were not very educated either.

True education, above all, should teach people how to think. Yet contemporary man is not taught to think. Instead he engages prodigiously in what might be called "antithink," in elaborate and cunning public-relations and propaganda efforts for political, personal, ideological, or economic reasons, or perhaps occasionally just for the mind-blowing sport of it. It does not really do to say that war is a failure of man's morality. Earthman's morality was never much to brag about. Besides, in that department, as in most others, man has always been ambivalent: he is moral, but he is also amoral or anti-moral, good and bad. But could it be that, all his pretensions and convictions to the contrary, he is, though cunning, unable to think well? If this is so, it would be the ultimate irony, for just in that one respect man never has any self-doubts.

Man will accept that he is no angel, that for various reasons he is at times weak, that he can be a victim of passion, that he may not be the best of fathers, husbands, football players, citizens. He accepts many of his human frailties and foibles, at least in "moments of truth." He is aware of and usually makes no bones about his ambivalent nature. But stupid? Unable to think? Not *that.* And not in a democracy teeming with "intelligent laymen" and even more intelligent experts! On the contrary, he is smart, his leaders are smart, his country is smart. And he is smart regardless of social or educational background. If he is uneducated, he has "common sense." If he is a trained man of the mind, an intellectual, a professional, then he has all the modern "tools" at his fingertips, he has his methodologies, his computers; he "factors out" his bias; he goes about his thinking scientifically. How, then, can anyone assume that he is unable to think or that a generation may be growing up which, without any more gray matter and perhaps less formal education, will be able to use it far better and be able to think more clearly and apply the results of their thoughts more effectively to their lives? Most fantastic of all: could it be that women are able to think better than men?

And yet, much suggests that the future generation, strongly influenced by woman power, will think much better. An inability to think, or a collectively distorted or restricted way of thinking is nothing unusual in history. We laugh at the endless arguments among the most learned of medieval scholars about how many angels could dance on the head of a pin. To them, this was a serious matter—which makes it seem all the more ridiculous to us. We also conclude, probably rightly, that men who turned their intellectual powers to that problem and used their theological methodologies to attack it were talking nonsense, not only on that subject, but on *all* subjects; that they could not think very realistically. We probably would not put great stock in what these same men had to say on other subjects.

Similarly, we laugh when we hear that the Chinese, if faced with a problem or argument, brandish the Little Red Book of Mao's Thought, believing and insisting that it contains all the answers. Or we laugh at the Nazi view that the Jews dominate the world, whether we hear it in the form of a curse from an illiterate storm trooper or a reasoned volume by a Nazi "philosopher." We laugh when we hear the Communists insist that America is planning aggression against the Soviet Union and that all their military efforts are necessary as protection against this danger.

But we don't laugh at the thoughts our own elites proffer, at what our own economists, political scientists, psychologists, strategists, criminologists, biochemists, politicians, generals, businessmen, labor leaders, church leaders, or commentators proclaim. We readily accept that men of an entire era, such as the Middle Ages, could not think reasonably, what with witches burned and angels dancing on pinheads, or that even in our "modern" age entire nations cannot think well, like Russia or China or the Germans under Hitler, when they are in the thrall of propaganda. But *we* can think, we think, all the more so as we have an "opposition," an "other side," that is such an important part in a democracy, and that keeps the debate going, challenges self-serving deceptions, and guarantees that thinking remains on an even keel. We have, we say, freedom of expression: everyone can say anything he wants; and surely there must be some among the two hundred million citizens who can think straight, even if thinking in some quarters has gone awry, and these will speak up and therefore sense will always be made.

But we forget a number of things. People—especially men, and especially men of great "intelligence" who are professional thinkers—find it almost impossible ever to admit, to themselves or others, that they have been or even can be wrong. If one could eavesdrop on the confessional, one would presumably hear people castigate themselves over every kind of failure, but confessions of merely having thought wrong are probably rare. People will not admit it, partly because they do not even see anything much wrong with being wrong: "Okay," they say, "if I was really wrong, I can change my mind; after all, I'm not infallible, even though I *am* pretty smart." Moreover wrong thinking appears more often to come from without, at least initially—that is, it is the result of propaganda; and false thinking engendered by propaganda seems to be even harder to avoid than self-generated mistakes. What often seems to happen here is that a false sense of modesty takes over: people think they could be wrong, but their leaders or their favorite columnists or their current darling or hero surely cannot be wrong. And the intelligentsia is the most frequent and easiest victim of propaganda, just because, among other reasons, its members think they are too smart to fall for it.

A young woman philologist, Susan O., made this observation on propaganda: "He who swears by words is lost. The modern propagandist—who is both victim and victimizer, originator and conveyor belt of the untruth—knows that people have no way of gaining firsthand knowledge of all the things at home and abroad they feel they must have an opinion on or should debate or should participate in. He knows they will jump at his words, more precisely, his noises. If he says we must assert ourselves in the world, it seems to be a different noise than if he speaks of satisfactory compromises. The citizen compares speakers, propagandists, and then picks those that make noises that harmonize with his own ego rumblings. If he thinks of himself as a gentle, cooperative, broadminded sort, he picks one noise; if he thinks of himself as a no-nonsense man, an American fundamentalist, he picks the other."

When the President or someone in the center of the power structure, or who wants to get there, describes a course of action and calls it "fair to everybody," the listeners respond favorably. That's fair, they say, and that's the best we can expect. That fellow is okay, he's fair. At least he tries to be, which is what counts. Moreover, he is honest—he doesn't claim too much for his scheme; he just says it's fair. The leader or aspiring leader of our day has learned to manipulate one simple semantic secret, so simple it is astonishing: there are four sides to every notion, two positive and two negative and he operates perfectly in this four-cornered box.

For example, the spending of money can be wasteful (negative) or worthwhile (positive); the nonspending of money can be thrift (positive) or stinginess (negative). The spender of money can be described as generous (positive) or wasteful (negative); the nonspender as frugal (positive) or stingy (negative). And he can always describe himself in terms opposite from those his critics use. Thus a virtue *or* a vice can be made of the spending *or* the nonspending of money. A daring fellow is either courageous (positive) or irresponsible (negative); a less daring fellow is either careful (positive) or a coward (negative). In the propagandist's paradise that is the modern (male) world, any posture can be defended or attacked by propagandist and counterpropagandist, and usually without the listener's having much chance to apply his own judgment intelligently or to verify the claim. It is therefore the better semanticist who wins, in government or elsewhere. All we judge is the speaker, his posture, his inflection, and, in the TV age, his mien.

A newsman says, "Of course, to be successful a politician needs the largest number of votes, so he must strike the right chord with the mostest. To prepare for this, he uses the 'opinion' polls, launches trial balloons, sees how his noises are going over; and, of course, the polls, once published, further consolidate what he has picked as his favorite set of chords." At the same time, all the politicians and all the media flood the hapless citizen with their secondary propaganda, which tells him he is a well-informed person, a person of keen and responsible judgment, a person who has the facts at his fingertips and knows how to make up his own mind on the basis thereof. Read the daily newspapers, *Time, Newsweek, Reader's Digest, U.S. News & World Report,* says the secondary propaganda, and you will be the best-informed citizen in the world. And because this dovetails with his own wishful thinking and his idealized self-image, the propagandists have a patsy: the citizen really thinks he is well-informed and capable of good judgment. And from there on in the speakers, writers, politicians, leaders, scientists have easy sledding.

Why is it that way? Those critical of the contemporary political and social system may overlook the fact that the public has been bludgeoned into such a state of intellectual conformity, regardless of surface quarrels over "issues," that any really deviant voice would hardly even be heard. This process takes place with the full cooperation, one might say unconscious connivance, of the public, the victims. The lambs lead themselves to the slaughter. They insist on their daily dose of propaganda. Therefore leaders—and all leaders, alas, are today political leaders—could not deviate if they wanted to. With their help the public has conditioned itself to a certain semantic line on all subjects. And woe to him who steps out of the magic box within the semantic confines of which there is no room for real thought.

Words have taken on the role of thoughts and things and actions. Much of what is said in official quarters on any of the important issues is not just untrue, it is logocide, and logocide cannot be perpetrated without grave consequences. The public-relations men denature our language, and without language there can be no thought, no civilized society. It is never properly considered why the Nazis and the Communists spent so much money, time, and effort on internal propaganda *after* coming to power. Why should they? In our imaginations they ruled by "terror"—so why waste money on words? The reason is simply that they didn't rule just by terror at all, and terror cannot function anyway without millions of true believers who enforce the terror, who are fed on words. Therefore they had to slay the language—it was their number-one enemy.

Susan, the philologist, continued: "What makes the average American a particularly easy victim for logocide, propaganda, heedless follow-the-leader, and so on is that he is so conditioned to 'taking sides.' He has sucked it in with his Pablum, I guess, that to take sides is a sign of freedom, of democracy, of an active intellectual life, of free and vigorous thinking. So the victim-victimizer semanticists dish up a phony choice, and the people fight over it like dogs over a bone. It is not just the choice of political candidates that is often a phony choice—many people already know that. It is the 'two sides' of the issues that are phony. And the ensuing discussions always have one thing in common: the citizen is asked to take sides in a simple dichotomy—for or against this or that specific, limited, ill-defined thing. But all these choices are nonchoices. They are as though the people were asked to take sides on whether two times two is five or three. If millions debate the question in these terms, heaping argument upon argument and evidence upon evidence, is there some man—or woman—courageous and independent enough to say, even to himself or herself, 'Maybe it's neither. Maybe it's four. Maybe they are giving me a phony choice.'? Very rarely. And men still smile when they see boys on the debating team throwing nonsense at each other until one 'wins.' But, unexpectedly, women dare to question this entire ritual in ever greater numbers and with ever greater conviction. They sense that the truth is filtered out in the conventional mental process."

The potential significance of this female intellectual rebellion is not yet understood by the male intellectual establishment.

Contemporary thinking, like contemporary action, is perhaps best described as lacking human understanding, compassion, generosity or decency, common sense, or the other predominantly feminine traits. What, cry our "thinkers," have such irrelevant sentimentalities to do with good hardnosed thinking? The answer depends, of course, on what people think about. If the problem is to build across a river a bridge that must carry a certain amount of vehicular traffic, people should leave sentiment at home and take out their sliderules. But in thinking about human affairs, a suppression of human feelings, instincts, wisdom is likely to produce undesirable results. For example, only a dehumanized kind of thinking could have prompted the world's most "advanced" nations, including the "leader of the free world," to be so soft on Hitler for a full decade just because it seemed a "smart" move in the "struggle against Communism." This kind of thinking led to the deaths of many millions of our fellow men. But in all the ministries *and* universities this form of thinking continues, carried forward by arrogant and power-hungry men, not just on the subject of war and peace, but on all subjects of concern to people.

The leaders in America today really all think in the same ways, and insignificant differences among them are magnified out of all proportion. Senator Fulbright is not nearly as different from Senator Stennis, nor James Hoffa from any corporate president, as it appears. This is why so many young people now totally reject the establishment: they feel that the thinking done by it is all pretty much the same and not suited to advance the fortunes of the human race. What the young critics probably are not aware of is that it is the *masculine* element, *the male principle of thought,* the principle of *logic* as defined by men that is responsible—in the American as in other Western establishments today. That is what mainly stands in the way of all reform, of adjustment of the human race to the new dangers and opportunities produced by technology.

Male thought's greatest danger derives from its formalism, its clinging to formulas, its ritualism, its inflexibility. A formula is sort of a miniprinciple, an archaic incantation. Men, aside from being formalistic, also are ritualistic. When they think "scientifically" about society, they think in formulas, schemas, shibboleths, "principles" that often are obsolete and arrogant and empty.

Is it likely that the more feminine ways of thinking will become part of the collective national mind as it faces the 1980s? There are two obstacles to this. First, the (male) establishment fights all intrusion on other than its own terms. But it merely succeeds in immuring itself in a steadily shrinking perimeter of untenable positions.

The other obstacle, or rather danger, is that women storming the male fortress may, in the process and for the purpose, masculinize their own thinking to such an extent that it will ultimately make no difference who operates the levers of power. But that is not really likely. Thinking, we predict, will be feminized in the next decade.

To say that thinking will be feminized, means that it will be humanized. Buddy W., a philosophy student, says, "To the extent that our generation thinks at all about the massacres perpetrated by our societies in our century, it is astonishing to see the lack of true emotion, lack of sorrow, lack of interest, even, with which people, women included, view what has been done, and how little significance 'thinkers,' even theologians, attribute to all this. Somehow, ever since Hitler, it seems, lack of feeling has dominated Western thought. If you tell people in responsible positions what is really happening to human beings here and abroad, they look blank. All they are interested in is the GNP or some strategic position or the next Presidential election. They are not sadists or fiends. They just seem to lack a dimension somewhere. Perhaps it is the feminine dimension. Anyway, they don't seem to think."

Contemporary thought—materialist, limited, schematic, statistical, bloodless, pseudomoral, and arrogant—is but a shadow of what the human mind could produce if it operated in conjunction with the human soul, human feeling, in which the modern intellectual bureaucrat in government, business, or labor has little interest. Women who seem to be endowed with a different mode of thinking, a more intuitive, sensible, direct form of thinking, have so far made little effort to infuse their own feelings into the type of thought dominant today. The reason may be that up to this point in the feminine revolution, many women were really conservatives—that is, they accepted the male mode in the world of thought as in all others, or they were takeover types who, in order to succeed individually but also collectively as, say, bureaucrats or lawyers, followed male modes of thinking for opportunistic reasons.

It is not a foregone conclusion that women can humanize our thinking and thereby civilize our society, for the male forms of thinking are strongly ingrained. Men seem largely incapable of acting or reacting humanely, because of their early conditioning and because of the eternal struggles into which they are plunged at an early age. Perhaps because they have been deprived of their primitive clubs and other weapons, and because many channels for personal violence have been closed to them, men are using their brains, their thoughts, like clubs, battering rams, rapiers, guns—and the effect is what can be expected.

Women, says the Jungian psychologist Robert S., "still have the lines open between the brain and the heart, the mind and the soul, thinking and feeling. Men do too, perhaps, but in a different way. They no longer *know* what emotions their thinking serves, so that far from being conscious of their own aims and motivations, they are by now far more unconscious of the true reasons why they act and think the way they do, and therefore are much more dangerous. If women could only gain confidence in the fact that their way of thinking is much better. . . . Well, they are still intellectually unencumbered enough so that they probably will see it soon, now that they have begun to doubt the entire mode of masculine thought."

Anyone reading the books women have produced recently will readily see that women—whether they have "the answers" or not—have begun to *think* in ways different from men, that they have begun to express their way of thinking freely and powerfully, to apply their own mode of thinking rigorously to all they see around them. They have left most of the simple choices behind. What is perhaps most impressive in the books by Friedan, Millett, Greer, Firestone, Elizabeth David, Elizabeth Janeway is the newness and power of their thought, the revolutionary nature of that thinking, the insights produced by that thinking. This becomes even more apparent when one compares such works to the books produced by male observers of the local scene, the antiquated nature and rigidness of the male approach, the infatuation with technology or politics or power, the paucity of new insights or ideas. The women deal more with life, the men more with machines, structures, abstractions, empty shells.

The new way of thinking by women, and the growing confidence women display in *their* thinking—often the result of a definite change in their own intellectual developments—also emerged very clearly in the interviews conducted for this book. Women have begun to think for themselves, and they are not only enjoying it (for thinking is the exercise of a great human gift, it is fun, and it has been dormant for a long time), they are also using it to remold society. Thinking will bear the stamp of women in the 1980s, in every domain.

So much for the theory of the future of thought. Concretely, the first major breakthrough and breakaway will occur when the people throw off the intellectual yoke of the "expert" at whose desk they now worship. The expert says he *knows,* and his followers *believe* he knows. They *want* to believe it. But he does not know, and his followers will have to accept this eventually. Only woman power, however, will have the freedom and courage of thought finally to acknowledge this.

Important distinctions are to be made here. The genuine expert has his place in our society. If you need brain surgery, you are better off to have it performed by an expert than by your bright little son with a toy doctor kit. If you want to have anything fixed, built, made, done—as long as it is within the realm of the physical, tangible world—you need an expert, and there are many. But the experts have spread out and arrogated to themselves expertship, and with it power and leadership, in areas in which they are not only ignorant to a large extent, but are motivated by questionable philosophies and often self-serving objectives more likely than not to be at odds with the interests of the people at large.

There are no real experts or authorities on any of the most currently urgent social, political, racial, economic questions. There are people who know a lot of detail with which they can make a good case for their personal opinions, but their opinions are still only gut opinions, often unrealistic and unhuman because of their bizarre "scientific method." This is what an ex-expert has to say:

"I have been an expert," reports Sidney J. Slomich, in an excerpt from his book, *The American Nightmare,* "have lived among them in their anticommunities—could have rested among them. I hope I have left them well behind me. An expert sees his small piece of reality and little else. He confuses understanding with control and makes of the latter his single virtue. One of our leading social scientists has said that the chief accomplishment of this age is to have changed so many political problems into technical ones. . . .

"I have been an expert, I hold a bachelor's, master's, and Ph.D.

in political science from Harvard University, where I studied federal and municipal government in America, political philosophy, international law, Russian history, the Soviet economy, and international relations.

"I've done research for the Army on Czechoslovakia; I spent a number of years as an officer of the CIA; I worked on strategic problems including Vietnam, in Army think tanks—among them the Research Analysis Corporation; for similar private companies I've done research on communications satellites, on China, and on arms control. . . . I was senior scientist, then director of the Arms Control and Disarmament Study Group at Cal Tech's Jet Propulsion Laboratory. . . . I have studied and published on advanced technological applications to urban affairs; I have taught political theory and foreign policy at various California universities. . . . recently I have been serving as consultant on social goals, urban and suburban affairs, and the sources of aberrant social behavior, for a variety of private clients. . . .

"So I have been an expert, and I'm not bragging about it. I accepted the necessity of working within the system, believed that it was possible in that way both to affect the system itself constructively and to accomplish something. Only in the late '60s did I come to understand that government, business, and what is correctly called 'the Establishment,' were too inert, too committed to the shape of things as they have been to inaugurate human policies, that for change the people had to take government back to themselves. Only the people awakened and grasping power from these mindless mega-institutions can effect change. . . .

"The entire system of expertise . . . is basically a fake. . . ."

One might be encouraged by the fact that this is a *man* speaking, a former *expert.* So, one might think, there is hope, these people *can* see through the veil, the blindfold *can* fall from their eyes. But Slomich's is an isolated case, sure *not* to be emulated by more than a handful of men. The reason is not only that the experts are too arrogant in their thinking and too wedded to their methods to see the light, but also that in the age of propaganda, self-deception, and public relations they rarely come into conflict with reality, or, more precisely, do not see or acknowledge it when it occurs. But the most important reason most experts will not follow Slomich's example is that they are nurtured and reaffirmed in their actions by the adulation of most people. Intellectual woman power will curb the experts to a considerable extent in the 1980s, though most women, just as much as men, have so far engaged in expert idolatry.

16

WOMAN POWER AND THE FUTURE OF HEALTH

AMERICANS are quite unhealthy even though most of them have brainwashed themselves into believing that our health and health care are, like everything else, the "best in the world." But at least a half dozen countries are ahead of the United States in life expectancy, particularly that of its males, and have a better record of decreased infant mortality. In fact, in certain underprivileged areas, like the Chicago slums, infant mortality is as high as it is in India.[1] And what is bad elsewhere must be regarded as doubly bad in the United States, with its superior resources. But the average citizen, who after all does not live in slums, is not very well either. He annually swallows, it has been estimated, over twenty billion pills. Most of those pills, it might be noted, are swallowed by people who are "well" rather than "sick" in the statistics on illnesses.

No statistics can give us any insight into how poor American health really is, for "health," physical or mental, is a matter of standards and definitions. Clearly, there are millions of Americans who consider themselves, and are considered by the statisticians, to be well merely because the standards for what is called "well" are low and arbitrary. As long as people are at all able—

despite back pains, Excedrin headaches, nervousness, heartburn, and so on—to crawl out of bed in the morning and do their jobs no matter how rotten they feel, we call them well. Perhaps a better way of counting the nonwell would be to count those who will admit they do not feel well; or perhaps even to count those who need one deodorant or the other, since unpleasant body odors are generally a sign of impaired health. On that scale almost the entire nation would qualify as unhealthy.*

When a person is really sick and needs a doctor and a hospital to get "well again," he or she is faced with a quadruple threat. First, there is the cost of the services. True, much of those are often absorbed by some expensive insurance schemes, but good care, or what goes by that description, will always cost more than what a person is insured for. Second, there is the service itself. Hospitals are crowded and often inhumanely run: people, especially the very ill, are exposed to frightful and frightening conditions. The doctor is busier than a flight captain landing a disabled 747 in a hailstorm, which makes a leisurely doctor-patient search for causes and remedies difficult. Third, there is the threat of losing time and with it a hold on one's job or business or profession. Fourth, there is the actual poor quality of the services even the affluent can expect.

"It's now come to the point," says Dr. D.S., "where my patients pay a hundred dollars a day in the hospital. Yet when I go on my daily—or shall I say nightly?—round in the hospital after a long day of seeing patients in my office, the nurses, who used to have all the information ready about every patient when costs were half as high, no longer even know who is in which room.

---

* It is always claimed that Americans are such gluttons for deodorants of every conceivable sort because they are so squeamish about their bodies. Actually it is more probable that Americans have become so sensitive to body odors because most body odors they emit really are "offensive" since so many people are not well. Theodore H. Rosebury, in *Life on Man*,[2] presents much convincing information on this subject.

Yet their demands rise constantly. I don't say they shouldn't, because demands on them rise too. I just say it is a miserable situation." How about the good doctor himself? Medical statistics have shown that more than half of all surgery in the United States is undertaken to correct mistakes made during earlier surgery. And many reports have shown that there is an enormous amount of needless surgery; it has been estimated, for example, that nine out of ten (!) hysterectomies are unnecessary.

The reason for such excessive zeal is not just that doctors operate to make money, though with doctors today seeming almost to be test drivers for the latest-model expensive cars, many a uterus will have to be sacrificed to the last installment. Perhaps a greater cause of unnecessary operations, however, is the fear of malpractice suits. The increasing indemnity payments awarded to patients for malpractice—a boon at first—eventually led to doctors' raising of their fees (to pay for the high insurance against possible suits) *and* to their doing more rather than less than necessary. For in line with the general machismo posture in the male world, nonaction is more readily interpreted as malpractice than dubious action. Like soldiers, doctors are trained always to do something rather than nothing.

But all the inadequacies and costs of health care in America are only a minor reason for the general health's being so poor. Even if every person had a personal surgeon and a fully equipped hospital room at home, people would not be much healthier, for good medical care really has very little to do with good health. The problem is to be well, stay well, not to get sick, rather than find good medical care when the damage is already done. Why are people so unwell?

There are many reasons. Most important, perhaps, is their basic attitude to their bodies, which they regard as something separate from their souls, even though the psychosomatic approach has now made considerable inroads into medicine. The untenable separation of body from soul was not made only by finicky Christians—the ancient Greeks distinguished rigorously between the body (*soma*) and the soul (*psyche*)—but the matter was aggravated by Christian views and later by the materialist orientation by which most contemporary societies live. Yet soul and body are one, and to harm the soul-body "system" even in the most unphysical way is to provoke what the medieval saints and physicians called *rebellio carnis*—the rebellion of the flesh.

The blows to the less carnal areas of the body-soul system in our society are many and we need name but a few, in cursory fashion. There is the "rat race," which takes a toll. There is the attitude to old age that makes people engage in futile and unhealthy efforts to stay young, or at least to seem to stay young. There is the dissatisfaction in their work which wears most people down, mainly because the daily tasks demand from them that they stifle rather than stimulate their creativity. (Curiously, while it is advantageous to live below one's means economically, it seems to be pernicious to live below one's means as far as one's natural gifts are concerned: they come to plague us if we do not use them.)

Then there is dissatisfaction with play. Play is generally not, as it should be, *re-creation,* but a mad expenditure of energy. The person who "works hard" is, as everyone knows, a likely candidate for serious illness; but the person who on top of that "plays hard" will surely not be long for this world. People who cannot quite make it to their heart attacks in their offices generally try the gym or the tennis court. Or they go to the other extreme and slump down in their chairs in front of the TV, letting painful cacophonies be rammed into their skulls (have you ever listened to TV without viewing the picture?) in a state of complete and debilitating lethargy.

In particular, fear makes people ill—fear of losing their jobs, of running out of money, of losing love, of a million things. People are perhaps less aware that in an age in which such a premium is placed upon flawless and protean sexual performance, fear of sexual inadequacy can add mightily to all the fears already gnawing at them. Here is a passage from a *Playboy* story about a man speaking to himself on the way to the bedroom with the young lady of his keenest desires: ". . . as we walked I prayed: Please God, please, let me do all right and not puke or be impotent or forget what part goes where, please let me fuck this child, please just let me [detail, detail, detail] . . . and please let me do all right and then, after that, you can do anything you want with me—but please, God, don't let me come this close to ecstasy without letting me have it." [3]

The teller of the tale is a thirty-year-old (!) man in rather relaxed and favorable circumstances. The reader may want to know whether things worked, and in fact they did ("I don't think my performance was anything more than competent . . . but it wasn't too bad, either. . . ."). Still, such anticipatory fear must be traumatic, and the story must be fairly typical, else *Playboy*'s editors would hardly have chosen to present it to their millions of readers. Many, then, seem to live with such fears in our age in which superhe-manism takes its toll by striking back at man in the most sensitive department, making a fool of the he-man. How can he live with such fears and not become ill? The removal of these and other fears would do more for the nation's health than the most elaborate health services could.

In the field of "health" the he-manesque, machismoesque, "no-nonsense" aspects of our society show up in almost caricaturelike condensation. Man, the atavistic hunter and killer and slave-driver, makes himself and everyone else sick with his violent, competitive approaches, first to life itself, and then to illness. He drives fear into himself and others. Then, when the fear has made people sick, they are kept sick by being afraid to reveal their sickness. For the person who finally cracks under the strain of the executive suite or the rush-hour traffic on the subway or freeway will quickly be regarded as finished, ready to be thrown out, devoured, treated as schools of fish and groups of other animals treat those who show signs of illness.

Some very recent surveys indicate that people suffer less from anxiety than they used to, and more from depression, which is also sickness-inducing. According to a poll reported in the *Los Angeles Times,* "some psychiatrists are calling [our age] the age of depression in contrast to the age of anxiety a generation ago." Dr. Harold Visotsky, Chairman of the Department of Psychiatry of Northwestern Medical School, is quoted in the article as saying, "Today's depression is becoming epidemic in our part of the world. The age of anxiety described by Camus and Auden in the late '40s is passing and we are now entering what may be the decades of depression and apathy." The reasons given for the state of the depression by the doctors polled are "urban tensions, racial tensions, crime on the streets, rampant pollution, Vietnam, inflation." Against this background "personal events, such as an argument with a spouse, a change in working conditions" apparently trigger depression and often illness.[4]

It is doubtful whether the distinction made by the doctors between anxiety and depression is valid, because anxiety and depression often go together. What seems certain, however, is that current living conditions as a whole adversely affect the body-soul systems of a very large number of people—not just a small number of "malcontents"—and that additional billions of dollars for better medical care, even if they were to become available, which they never will, might not do much to improve public health substantially. A different atmosphere seems needed; one in which demands on the individual and by the individual on others are not necessarily lighter, but different, less harsh, and more in keeping with the individual's intrinsic capabilities. Can an infusion of woman power into the workings of society help bring this about? Can woman power help liberate people from the health-harming American "pace"?

One further reason why so many are sick is people's faith in doctors, hospitals, medications, operations, and their concomitant low confidence in their own ability to keep or make themselves well by their own efforts. This orientation is undergoing a change at present, with an interest in health foods and an increasing variety of practices designed to engender and maintain health. But most people, though they may be disappointed with a particular doctor or drug or operation or hospital, remain believers in modern medical science and especially in drugs and in surgery. Dr. W.T. says, "It is almost unthinkable to send a patient on his way without giving him or her a prescription for some drug or other unless, in serious cases, one were to recommend surgery. But it has got to be the one or the other. A person who comes with a complaint—not just for a checkup—would feel that he or she have wasted their money if they did not walk out with a prescription." This belief in medical mechanics, in cure rather than prevention, and rather mechanical cure at that, is very much in keeping with the spirit of the times. It can only aggravate the state of health in this country.

What, then, can alleviate the health situation? Better medical care, as we have already said, can be of only marginal value in a sick-prone society. It is one important answer, however. But how can health services be improved? Men automatically take the posture: more money, more organization, more bureaucracy, more government, more doctors, more hospitals, more machines. Yet even though quantities of money and doctors and nurses and hospitals may be needed, it is not so much the quantity of the services as the quality that would make a difference. Woman power will do a lot here, first by better comprehending the nature of illness, which is easier for women than for men, who are particularly dense where human frailties are concerned, and quickly transform the entire health matter into a business, a racket, a political thing. Woman power, in general, will know what to do to keep the healthy well and take better care of the sick. But what is actually needed?

How about leisure? Will the coming decade provide so much leisure that people will be able to endure the rigors of the pressure cooker in which they work and live? Will people have the four-day work week and benefit from the expanded leisure time? Trend studies produced by routine futurology conclude that this will be the case, but it is improbable. Expanded leisure time, even if it were forthcoming, would not necessarily provide better health, partly because people would still worry and fret—as they do now on weekends—over the hazards and insecurities of their lives, partly because they would not know what to do with the time unless society changed a great deal. In fact, the thought of an American population under roughly current conditions "playing hard" three days of every week conjures up some apocalyptic visions, with millions of hunters roaming the woods and destroying animals if not shooting at each other, golf courses resembling trenches under enemy fire, a thousand fatalities occurring from drowning and car accidents as a matter of weekend routine, and a prize being awarded the lucky angler pulling the very last fish out of America's waters.

In a saner society, civilized by woman power, it is actually far more likely that the now sacrosanct institutions of the weekend and the vacation will come more or less to an end. Weekends and vacations are essentially symptoms of a regimented, immature society: one needs such devices for children. People who work truly well and creatively, and do things to their liking and do them well, generally follow no such rigid schedules. They work when they feel like it and rest when they need it. Einstein or Leonardo or even Henry Ford did not knock off at five P.M. every day for that first martini or prepare all year for that one vacation. In a society in which nearly everyone works "only" for money and in a huge organization, resembling in appearance and customs an army more than anything else, people must have furloughs, like soldiers. But once under the influence of woman power, the fever for competition and growth will give way to a different form of economy and society, people will become less regimented and will have more true leisure than they do today. They will work when they can and rest when they must, which will do more for their health than superweekends.

To speculate about transplants is one of the futurologist's and the fool's favorite pastimes: they see cyborgs everywhere, brain banks, heart banks, what-have-you banks. How will all this work? Will the rich be able to obtain new hearts on command after overindulging during a bender in Acapulco? Will Joe Namath, once he gets older, have enough pull to get himself a new pair of legs from some powerful young fellow? Will there be a black market in extra-large something-or-others? Will grafters and extortionists in and out of government occasionally take limbs and organs in lieu of cash? Will the Mafia move in? Will the powerful everywhere be able to commandeer healthy organs from dead, sick, or even healthy people if they need them?

It is not likely that transplants will have much of a future, though this seems to be opening spectacular horizons. It probably simply represents a false start, and in the 1980s is likely to be all but forgotten. It cannot be the answer to better health anyway, if only because of the scarcity of donors. The true answer can only be a healthier life in a kinder environment, the avoiding of illness, natural aging and dying—not ever more radical and desperate medical devices and innovations. Transplants are just health mechanics. Nothing of importance will come of it.

The current transplant madness will end also because of a saner and more mature approach to death which, under the influence of woman power, may finally be adopted. Once death is accepted as part of human life, people will refrain from prolonging death (rather than life) by all the obnoxious methods and devices now in use. Doctors and relatives ask, "But where do we draw the line? What rules must we establish and follow?" That is a male-formalistic approach to the matter. Once there is no chance left of recuperation, death should be allowed to follow.

Unbelievably, however, modern medicine not only prolongs death, creating lasting agonies for patient and family alike, but even in ordinary cases of approaching death is unequipped, medically, technically, and emotionally, to deal with it. Once a person is beyond the hope of recuperation, doctors and families tend to be utterly perplexed as to what to do with him or her. The hospitals do not want such a person, for they feel they are in the business of curing people, and space is scarce. The nursing homes are expensive and abominable. To take the dying person home is regarded as a nuisance in our fun-oriented world, and as unwise by physician and family members alike.

How about psychiatry? A.H., an analyst of Jungian orientation, says, "People show the full nature of their unreasonableness in what they expect from psychiatry. Either they feel it has nothing to offer, or they take it for a cure-all. Under current social and psychological conditions the capabilities of psychiatry, though quite real, are strictly limited. Psychiatry can help certain individuals in special cases. But the vast mass of half-sick, anxiety-ridden, driven people, whose inability to cope with life as it now is makes them ill in one way or another, can only be helped by a change in the cultural and emotional climate in which we live. The true future of psychiatry as an aid to the truly ill is yet to come—but only in an age of conditions more conducive to general mental and physical health."

In a more feminized society a reduction in the hatred and hopelessness that now make people sick will help them stay well. Conversely, an increase in truly healthful and pleasurable activities—and they really are identical—will follow in the wake of a progressive feminization of society. This in turn will lead to different forms of health-preserving recreation. It can confidently be predicted that the cruel and unusual self-torture of jogging will end. While running is natural for children, it is unnatural for adults. Anyone who has seen paunchy or skinny men of various ages drag their recalcitrant bodies awkwardly along San Vicente Boulevard in Santa Monica or around the Pentagon during lunchtime, hollow-eyed, pale, panting, and sweating, can only feel compassion for their plight and take heart from the hope that they will soon be liberated from their dangerous exertions.

One cannot leave the subject of health without venturing the guess that a more feminized, rational, de-he-manized society will probably take up yoga on a large scale. It is no accident that some, dissatisfied with the value structure and life style of our society, have looked into the past and to the East for something else. To the extent that they have brought back karate, this is perhaps just one more manifestation of the he-man reflex (except where women learn it for self-defense). The East has better things to offer to those seeking mental and physical health than karate. Yoga is a prime example. Many Americans have already discovered that yoga is better for their health than doctors, drugs, or operations, and enhances the practitioner's well-being because it simultaneously strengthens and relaxes all features of the body-soul system. It is no accident that more American women than men have so far taken up yoga, because of their better instinct as to what is needed for good health.

The influence of woman power on society in the coming decade will nowhere be more dramatic than in the area of health. Women have from the beginning of time had more respect than men for the human body-soul system, more intuition in dealing with that system when it is well, and more empathy and patience with it when it is not. Free also from the male compulsion to throw out billions of dollars, or to rake in hundreds of thousands of dollars annually as "successful" doctors now believe they must, woman power will bring about a genuine improvement in the national health, including mental health.

Humankind is intrinsically enormously healthy—people individually and collectively survive incredible blows, physical and mental, and endure incredible stresses and deprivations for very long times. But they have now maneuvered themselves into a style of life in which they are reaching the limit of that endurance and, perhaps even worse, are living physically in a marginal way —that is, they hardly ever feel really well and vigorous and full of *joie de vivre.* Here as elsewhere woman power is likely to come to the rescue in the coming decade—directly, by helping the sick get better, and indirectly, by helping make society more salubrious for us all.

Conclusion (I)

ONCE MORE: A WOMAN IN THE WHITE HOUSE?

It is always entertaining to speculate about whether there ever will be a woman President in the United States, and when. And also about what that would do to the country, or what kind of a country the United States would have to become in the first place in order to elect a woman President.

It is likely that under the growing influence of woman power in American politics the nature of and public response to the Presidential office will change. The job is now blown up by increasing layers of propaganda. "The most powerful man in the world," "the leader of the free world," "the hardest job in the world," "the most responsible job in the world," "the loneliest job in the world." Actually, the President has little power in many realms, though considerable power in others. He is the most important job-dispenser in the country, the greatest dispenser of patronage, and he has power over immense sums of money. He also is constantly followed by that inconspicuous little man with the black football who enables him to launch a worldwide nuclear war without consulting anybody. Still, that power to launch war is not "really real"—not as long as there is some strategic balance in the world, which there is and which is likely to remain.

But the President has, or so it seems, the power to devalue the dollar. Or to make war or peace in Southeast Asia. Or to go to China. Or to make an alliance with France. Or to make those Zambians shape up or those Russians to invite him to visit. But all that power is not real either, because it cannot be used arbitrarily. The constraints are always greater than the power, as John Kennedy found to his amazement. In *The Political Illusion* political philosopher Jacques Ellul demonstrates that political leaders in our day can make only two kinds of decisions: they decide on what *has* to be decided anyway, whether or not they create the impression that their decision is freely arrived at; or they decide on trivia. The President can decide that his party's convention should take place in Miami or San Diego (though innumerable factors may lead him so forcefully into selecting one city over another that the decision is quite automatic). Still, he can decide some things. He can decide to release James Hoffa. He can decide to negotiate with Hanoi. But all these decisions are trivial, unimportant; they are big perhaps when viewed from the perspective of an assistant postal inspector, but trivial in terms of constructive solutions.

On the big issues, on war or peace, on a sound economy, on civil rights, on matters that really affect the quality of life of the nation or its citizens and follow a certain dynamic, the President can only be his own rubber stamp, so to speak, no matter how he furrows his brow on TV and suggests how heavy is the burden of his office. The President is his own premier *propagandist* and as such wields a certain amount of power: if he can sell the American people something out of the ordinary, something they would not otherwise do, then he can go ahead and do it, thanks to the support he has obtained from them. Which is why Presidents are now so concerned about the "credibility gap."

With greater sobriety in the political arena, which can be expected to be one result of woman power in politics, the credibility gap will widen further: the Presidency will soon have the fire-water squeezed out of it, and then shrink to its truer proportions. The power of the Presidency will further decline with more people—again under the influence of woman power in politics—being able to stand on their own emotional feet instead of selling out totally to their leader. People will then not overthrow him or malign or impeach or assassinate him. They simply will *withdraw* from him some of the followership and adulation they now lavish upon him, and this will diminish his power.

The power of the Presidency will further decline because of the changing emotional, political, economic situation in the world around us. The rather arrogant claim to American leadership of the free world has always been a myth in any event, even after World War II (except perhaps for a year or so), and is now increasingly revealing itself as a myth. The President of the United States is, and more and more will be, "merely" the chief administrator of his country, not of the Western world. Consequently, the American people will have a more sober view of what the Presidency is, so that they will no longer go around believing that only a supersuperman can carry the job (a belief our ancestors surely did not share). And its waning power in the world will finally bring America home from the worst ego trip in its history and make it turn from foreign to domestic affairs. Women will also force their President increasingly to deal with the concerns that *are* his principal business—domestic affairs.

It will then become quite possible, indeed likely, that a woman will become President of the United States. For it will then dawn on people that the job of being President cannot possibly require a supersuperman; if it did, it would simply be a monstrosity, there not being a supersuperman in the country. Americans will give up the idea, their unconscious underlying fantasy, that the job requires the supersuperman, that their leader must be one, because they are such a supernation. These ballooning fantasies are likely to recede.

A woman may not have the qualifications the American people, in the tin age of propaganda, have come to believe their leaders must have—but neither, surely, have Johnson, Nixon, Humphrey, Agnew. And one can think of many women who could do as well as or better than these men. But the real point is whether the American people would elect a woman to the job; for the job, by definition, can be done (for better or worse) by virtually anyone who is elected. Under female prodding, it probably will become clear to the American people that the job, if done responsibly, is mainly domestic; that the job, if done properly, is not just an electioneering and ward-heeling activity of heroic proportions; that the job requires true and genuine concern with domestic affairs; and that the basic womanly qualities—such as compassion, skepticism, prudence, realism, and a finer sense of justice—do indeed qualify a woman well to do the job as it ought to be done in the interest of the American people. Once the electorate recognizes this, it probably will then elect a woman President—and it would be surprising if they did not do it in the 1980s.

What will a woman President do? It would be fatuous to predict in detail what measures she would take or what policies she would set. She would have a different approach to situations, a different way of thinking about them. She would also, like the women who will be active in politics, government, industry or unions, have different reflexes.

There are two contemporary forms of thinking and reacting in conflict with each other: the *social conscience* and the *power reflex.* Men, by and large, are conditioned to respond to almost any problem, situation, occurrence with the power reflex, which is handed down from father to son. The power, the prestige, the unity of the tribe (nation or organization) is what counts. And that power reflex is often a harsh, partisan, unfair, destructive response. Social conscience, on the other hand, is the very opposite, a humanized way of looking at the world; it demands justice, fairness, and a different priority of values. The large nations, and all large organizations are today ruled by men who give priority to the power reflex over the social conscience and what, if they had one, it would dictate, at home or abroad. Revolutions have never changed that, least of all the Communist revolution: in the Soviet Union or China or North Vietnam or North Korea the same power reflex prevails and cavalierly takes precedence over the dictates of social conscience, as it does everywhere else and as it did before the revolutions. Though they love their country just as much as men, in fact often more, women are more conditioned to respond in terms of social conscience. Should such genuine social conscience be brought to bear on government and politics from the Presidential level, there will be great and beneficial changes for the nation and all its citizens.

Conclusion (II)

A TELLING SURVEY

THE critical question for the future will be how women set their sights, and that is hard to predict, for that will depend on the degree of self-confidence they can muster. If they merely try to be "as good as men," they will put themselves down from the beginning and will not even reach that overly modest aim. A recent Harris Poll [1] shows that, on the whole, women have not advanced very far in that department.

On the subject of woman power the pollsters play the same role they do on most other subjects, which is to prevent those questioned, and later those reading the results, from breaking out of the narrow and arbitrary confines of their initial postulate. What the pollsters invariably do—and it has made them formidable integration propagandists in our day—is what the representatives of the (male) political establishment do: they pose most questions in terms of limited, wrong choices. They polarize the public mind where *other* and entirely different answers are indicated. For very few people have the courage or intellectual stamina to say to the pollster: "The choices you are offering are all unacceptable, and besides, there are entirely different choices that exist in reality and that *I* am making." Naturally that would make no sense in connection with the selection of a candidate: when asked whether I favor Nixon or Ted Kennedy, if those two are already the nominees, it would make no sense for me to say I favor my brother-in-law or Ti-Grace Atkinson.

But where issues are involved it would make sense. If I am asked whether I am for stricter punishment of criminals or a more humane treatment, I can say that this is not the question, for many professional criminals are treated too leniently while many nonprofessional first offenders are treated too harshly. Similarly, if women are asked (as they were by the aforementioned Harris Poll) whether they think that "women in public office, including the Presidency, can be as logical and rational as men," the women are intellectually cowed into saying either "yes" or "no." The question whether they might be *better* than men in public offices, including the Presidency, is never asked; and women, given only the limited choice presented by male chauvinist Harris, cannot break out of the box and say, "Listen, are you asking me whether a woman in the White House can do as well as some imaginary superman, or as well as Nixon or Johnson? If that is your question, then let me tell you that if she cannot do *better* than Nixon or Johnson, the whole women's effort is for the birds!"

Will women be able to liberate their minds from the propaganda poured out by the (male) establishment? Gloria Steinem says women have been brainwashed in different ways than men. This is true in some areas, such as woman's role in society, but it is not true in others. In almost all areas of what is now called "public policy" (itself a propaganda screen) women have been brainwashed just the same as men, and except for a few independent thinkers, have shown no sign of being better able than men to throw off the entire propaganda network strangling the contemporary mind.

In the aforementioned Harris Poll "55% of the women (and 62% of the men) agreed" (why "agreed"? Did Harris "suggest" it?) "that to be really active in politics women would have to neglect their husbands and children." A beautiful example of insidious distortion, invisible establishment propaganda. What is "politics"? What does it mean to be "really active"? To be really active in the kind of politics the (male) establishment engages in is indeed very time-consuming and requires the constant performance of odd tasks at odd hours. But who says that "politics" itself should not be the first thing to go, that it doesn't impede rather than promote good order, decent administration, progress, the solution of problems? A woman who would take up the standard political career and be "really active" at it would have to neglect her husband and children. But why should she? Why should anyone? Why should anyone, man *or* woman, be "really active" in the kind of "politics" that now plague our country? What does the Harris Poll envisage women as doing when they begin to exert woman power? How does he expect them to go about it? How do the respondents to his poll expect women to go about it?

There is no reason a woman "really active" in what needs to be done in a thousand areas of public life should not do a splendid job in the course of a perfectly smooth, unhectic working day *and* engage in as much domesticity as she needs or wants to. Why should she chase around the country ward-heeling, fence-mending, propaganda-dispensing, deal-making? Politics is not the same as working on the issues or even providing decent administration—it is the opposite.

To return once more to the Harris Poll. Most important, "the survey showed ["curiously"] more sympathy among men than women for women's liberation groups. Women rejected such groups by 49% to 39%, but men split 42% to 42%." Aside from the fact that, as Gloria Steinem remarks, many women are not honest when questioned on the subject, whether by friends or pollsters, so that we do not really know how many women approve, it is significant to see how many men approve. Do women recognize that such vast approval is really a cry for help? That it is the expression of a hope that the women will *get going* and *come to the aid* of our society and put an end to, rather than rescue, "civilization as we have known it," and help, if not lead, men in creating a new civilization worthy of the name?

Conclusion (III)

A DESIRE TO AVOID SUCCESS?

DESPITE all efforts to see into the future, the future remains unclear. It isn't yet, it can develop in various ways; the reason we cannot know it is not that man or woman lacks the gift of seeing through the veil; it is that in the infinitely complicated play of impulses and forces all outcomes are forever in the balance. Besides, our ignorance of the future cuts across several levels: suppose we knew how many women would be in Congress, in the labor unions, in the corporations, in other organizations, suppose we knew what jobs they would occupy—we still would not know what kind of world it would be, how such a physical invasion of men's bastions on the part of women would affect society, or what it would do to the women taking on such a large share or to the men yielding it to them. We still wouldn't know whether people would lead happy, bored, peaceful, or miserable lives.

The matter is further complicated because the battle for a greater and different participation by women has so many fronts, all of them fluid. After all, we are not facing a situation in which all the men and all the women struggle in two opposite armies over a piece of the action, over control, over policies. There is a difference with regard to all this between the generations. Even the most modest beginnings of equality between the sexes or the image thereof might induce panic in many older men *and* women (an elderly man who must undress before a twenty-eight-year-old female urologist built like Raquel Welch comes to mind). On the other hand, the "issues" that have loomed so large to Bella Abzug, Betty Friedan, or Gloria Steinem may no longer seem revolutionary, in fact may seem passé, to many of the young, both male and female. Many a young girl studying the law or whatever has no fear today that she will be especially inhibited in the exercise of her profession when she is ready for it, and many a young man not only fails to fear female competition but, as evidenced by the growing number of male liberation groups, is ready and eager to shed the image and reality of male domination.

If one were merely to look at the younger generation, one could say the battle, for all intents and purposes, is already over, and the Abzugs, the Friedans, the Steinems, despite their intellectually and personally heroic and monumental past accomplishments, are now the John L. Lewises, the Walter Reuthers, the George Meanys of the movement; that the ice has been broken, the job been done, that from here on we will be moving on the wings of the growing younger generation into a future in which the partnership society will be a reality and a boon for everybody in it; that because the old grow older and the young take their place, the partnership society is already a *fait accompli.*

There appear to be enough individuals, male and female, in the younger age group to whom the thought of a bona-fide partnership society is a natural, acceptable, indeed preferred life style to make it a truly self-fulfilling prophecy. Looked at this way, the society seems to be divided into three parts: 1. the liberation forces, 2. the antiliberation forces, 3. the young, who on the whole, including most males, seem to be in tune with the liberation forces. The success for woman power would seem assured.

But nothing is decided. The (male) establishment is only beginning to dig in; until now it hadn't because it was very slow to grasp the true dimensions of the challenge. Once it began to understand—and it still has only begun to understand—it responded with its conditioned reflex: tokenism. The dispassionate analyst must understand that tokenism is a formidable weapon, more powerful than it would appear to be, considering that it is recognized by almost everybody for what it is, and even widely ridiculed. But tokenism is a very effective defense weapon.

The strength of tokenism as a social device can be seen in the universal way in which it is, and in fact *must* be, practiced. It would simply be impossible for a national magazine today not to have a few blacks in its ads or its stories; it would be impossible for an airline today not to show blacks relaxing in its airplane lounges (though seldom close to single white women or vice versa). A publicity or advertising director in any enterprise who did not practice tokenism would be fired, as would any magazine editor or any personnel director.

The same is true for women today. The (male) establishment, aware that something is afoot and fearing for its position, has resorted to tokenism. The (male) establishment is not truly perceptive when there are changes, but it is sensitive to the vibrations and it responds. Very much contrary to what they did without a thought only a few years ago, men will not ask their secretaries today to clean out their ashtrays or run for the coffee, at least not without some hesitation, some uneasiness, some awareness of the fact that while it would not be inequitable, it might be unwise. A sprinkling of women everywhere, on the bench and in the crane cab, in the executive dining room and in the saddle of a race horse, is evidence of something. But of what? Tokenism, as the beginning of a trend?

Presumably, if only for simple reasons of momentum, many more women will be in many more professions at much better pay a decade from now than today (though, as has already been pointed out, even that is not certain, for a general political and social backlash may engulf us all at any time). What effect will that have on the women who succeed? Will they, like the suffragettes before them, be content to participate in life as it is? Will they adapt and adjust to the male environment, the male establishment, become Mr. and Mrs. Executive or Mr. and Mrs. Lawyer, or Mr. and Mrs. Colonel?

Women to whom we have talked say that that is not possible, but they may underrate the hazards of success. They may be especially unaware that the "liberated" young may have lost, or have begun to lose, the reforming impetus just because they have never lived in the old climate.

What women will ultimately attain, and what effect it will all have, will depend on the aims they choose for themselves and the ways and the stamina with which they will pursue them, all of which will in turn be a function of their self-confidence and will to succeed. And strangely enough, if we can believe the interesting conclusions by Matina Horner, a Harvard psychologist, "women actively fear success." In the first issue of *Ms.*, Vivian Gornick reported on her interview with Dr. Horner and on the findings the latter had made as a result of her research into the motivation of women.[1]

Dr. Horner's working hypothesis at the beginning of her seven-year study and her conclusion at its end, confirming the original hypothesis, is that women experience an "anxious, active desire to *avoid success*" in *competitive* situations. Women, concluded Dr. Horner, are not "as Freud said, and Erikson said, and the whole Western culture repeats" repelled by competition; and do not, as some psychologists thought, suffer from a "hopeless will to fail"; rather, says Dr. Horner, the idea of success creates conflict, ambivalence, anxiety, and a desire to avoid it. Ingeniously adjusting the widely applied so-called TAT (Thematic Apperception Test) to test groups of young women and men, Miss Horner found that while the boys associated positive ideas with success, the girls often associated negative and self-destructive fantasies with success.

For example: "We asked Phil, a bright young student to tell us a story based on the following clue: After first term finals, John (an imaginary person) finds himself at the top of his medical school class. Phil puts down the following associations: John worked hard . . . he always wanted to go into medicine and is very dedicated . . . he continues working and graduates at the top of his class." "Now," says Dr. Horner, "consider Monica, another honor student. She too has always done well and she too has visions of a flourishing career. We gave her the same story to think about, as we had given to Phil, but with 'Anne' as the imaginary person and successful student. Instead of identifying with Anne's triumph as Phil had with John's, Monica had this association: 'Anne starts proclaiming her surprise and joy. Her classmates are so disgusted with her that they jump on her in a body and beat her. She is maimed for life.' "

Dr. Horner continued the experiment and found that "in response to the successful-male cue (after first term finals John finds himself at the top of his class . . .") more than 90% of the men showed strong positive associations. . . . On the other hand, in response to the successful-female cue, 65% of the girls were disconcerted, troubled or confused." In other words, when told about the success of other boys, boys expected that success would bring rewards; when told about the success of other girls, girls expected, at least unconsciously, that such success would bring calamities. Dr. Horner concluded: "Unusual excellence in women was clearly associated in the girls' minds with loss of femininity, social rejection, personal or societal destruction . . . their responses were filled with negative consequences and affect, righteous indignation, withdrawal rather than enhanced striving." And Dr. Horner found, further, that fear of success manifested itself mainly in women of demonstrably high intelligence.

One big question, then, is whether women will be able to generate the self-confidence, the desire to obtain rather than avoid success. This will largely determine whether the partnership society will become a reality, whether woman power will permeate and transform society to bring it more in line with human needs and make it more suited as a framework for a civilized and fulfilled life for women and men. That is one of the big "ifs" discussed at the beginning of this book.

There is no reason that women, if Dr. Horner is right and if they do have an unconscious conflict with regard to attaining success and a self-defeating attitude toward it, should not manage to shed this inhibition, especially in a situation that is already changing and in which the social consequences for the successful female are less dire than in earlier situations. The women, once they gather more confidence, will probably find themselves in an upward spiral of ever-increasing self-confidence when they discover that the self-confidence of the he-man, of the entire (male) establishment, is not what it pretends to be. The he-man may want success: he does not unconsciously wish to fail, as the tested girls did. But his self-confidence is shaky, partly because of the defeats he was recently suffered.

So whether women will succeed will depend on their will to succeed, the breadth of vision they dare to behold, and the elimination of unconscious quirks that turn their conscious desire to succeed into an unconscious one to fail. This may seem to be a more careful prediction than was made in the Introduction, in which the third part of the twentieth century was flatly depicted as the period of the transformation of society into a more civilized, enlightened, livable one. But there really is no contradiction: all things considered, women will shed the desire to avoid success; they will gain the necessary self-confidence and, to the extent that they may now lack it, acquire it in the evolving situation. Besides, Dr. Horner may not have tested "liberated" girls. Perhaps they have it already.

Will the women have the stamina? A beautiful blonde, when asked what had become of her antiwar activities, replied, "I gave those up years ago. Why, I can't spend my entire life on a thing like that when nothing is happening. I've taken up the ballet instead." This seeming flightiness is not an isolated instance. In conversations with other young women, and young men as well, much of what appears to be flightiness, inability to stick with something, a nervous inclination to shift continuously, has appeared in conversation as well as in actual life, from one issue to another. Ultimately this may not matter. The changes required in society are greater than the individual issues in the news at any given moment, and while woman power sometimes seems flighty in regard to its foci of interest, its underlying attitudes appear strong and stable. If this diagnosis is right, the prognosis is that woman power will bring about, in the coming decade, the foundations of the partnership society in which we will all be able to live and let live in saner and more civilized ways.

WHAT ABOUT THE REST OF THE WORLD?

WHEN the coming age of woman power is discussed and it is predicted that the influx of woman power into the (male) establishment in the coming decade will have a decisive impact on all aspects of society and on what people's life styles will be, is the discussion about the United States, the West, or the entire world? Are the Communist countries included or excluded?

The focus of this book has been the United States because woman power seems to be gathering momentum here at a much faster rate and on a much larger scale than elsewhere. However, this does not mean that woman power will not enter the stage and reshape the drama played out in all other areas of the world as well, as a *dea ex machina.* In fact, a global wave of reciprocity and interaction is clearly indicated: as woman power makes great and visible strides in the United States, it will encourage woman power elsewhere to make greater efforts, which in turn will broaden the worldwide base for its effectiveness. Moreover, the (male) establishments elsewhere are likely to see that the growing influence of woman power will ultimately work to their benefit too, and become less inclined to fight it tooth and nail.

Let us examine quickly some other countries. In Germany

male chauvinism has always been particularly fierce, with wifey having to run like mad for her pork-bellied husband's slippers and prepare his sausage and draw his beer and serve him like a scullerymaid from altar to grave. And the rigid German male establishment has been particularly successful in brainwashing their women, who are thus fiercely antilib in that medieval land, except for the very young. But underneath his conservatism the German burgher—male or female—is a radical, an explosive creature; and repression of women has been on such a grand scale for so long that under the influence of reports from the United States (with which the Germans have a hate-love relationship) a social explosion is likely. In Italy and France men have always been more chivalrous to their women, but quite repressive nevertheless. The women will liberate themselves and enter the stage in their own right in those countries as well in the coming decade. The Italians and French are less tyrannical, and their own he-manism is less compulsive, hence the change will probably be smoother and less cataclysmic than in Germany, but it will be equally profound.

In the Communist countries, particularly in the Soviet Union, woman power also is likely to go through a decisive stage in the coming decade. In Communism's early days women were rated more or less like men, as "comrades," but they really had to become men, in fact robots: Communism, after all, tends to be a somber, joyless, unfair, and unproductive way of life and looking at things for the individual. Once Communism was a going concern, life went from bad to worse, and while most men were badly off, most women comrades were more so. It often is reported that most doctors in the Soviet Union are women, as though that were something great for the women, but in reality the medical profession was severely downgraded in Communist society. Still, if we disregard that in Communist countries nobody is "ahead" in the way we think of being and like to be "ahead," women may, in the area of work, actually be better off than in the

West, in the sense that they are less *discriminated* against. Their lot, however, is unenviable.

There are some indications in the Communist world, and especially in the Soviet Union, that women will come to the fore and put an end to the domestic and foreign, military and political hemanism there. Should that come about, the relations between the two "superpowers" would improve, belligerency would decline, and the détente of which the (male) establishments on both sides of the Iron Curtain always talk, but which they do little to bring about, might then really occur. This would make a more peaceful orientation of the two countries toward each other a possibility, and also allow for the further feminization of both societies.

In India progress has been very rapid in the area of woman power, and is continuing. As for China, with its billion population, we must plead ignorance. Once woman power becomes effective in the United States, in other Western countries, and in the Communist world, China's role—which is now seen by (male) establishments merely as an ascendant nuclear power and new mortal enemy for all the others—is bound to change. China will probably benefit by, and then also contribute to, the world détente that the rise of woman power will bring with it indirectly and directly, inside countries and among them.

AN HISTORICAL VIEWPOINT

IT ALWAYS helps one's perspective to roam through time and space and learn how others have seen things in ages that are now as irretrievably past as our own age soon will be. The following observations made by a Swiss traveler in the United States just a little over a hundred years ago are therefore presented to the reader. In 1866 Joseph Joachim—after having emigrated to the United States—wrote the following impression about women in this country:

> If one looks at American culture and society in general, the superiority of American women, as far as esprit and education and manners are concerned, is striking and commands admiration. Whereas boys often must leave school before they are fourteen years old and go to work, the young miss continues her education and rounds it out at one of the many girls' colleges. These institutions, always directed by women, provide an excellent curriculum, far better than most men's colleges. . . . Many women even acquire a classic education, and American women authors and poets are no rarity. . . . Two-thirds of all primary schools are headed by women, and women give

public lectures, are telegraph and postal clerks, acquire medical degrees and even (according to the newspapers) occasionally become preachers.

This explains why women here, thanks to their intellectual superiority, exercise an influence on men and the social and even political situation that would be impossible and unthinkable in the old world. It also explains that they are aiming at the highest goal and demand "emancipation." [Joachim then reports on the program and activities of Lucretia Mott.]

In fact the women here are already emancipated. They accompany men at meetings and political travels, engage in political intrigue and write pamphlets on the subject of public elections. . . . Some bluestockings even have tried to give public political speeches and aroused the enthusiasm of their listeners.

American women are usually of the Anglo-Saxon type, with regular and fine features and svelte figures. When young they are very beautiful, but they age early and then turn into the very opposite. They marry early; those still unmarried at twenty-two are regarded as old maids. In Cincinnati a sixteen-year-old lady declared herself in court a widow and mother of two children!

American women are vain, interested in fashion; they love to go for drives and to the opera. They make men wait on them and light the fire for them in the morning. Women shining their men's boots or laying out their clothes do not exist in America. They have nothing in common with the good-natured little German *Hausfrau.* As soon as the man makes money, the woman spends it lavishly. If he makes no money, however, or if he falls upon hard times, the American woman reveals innate energy and heroic readiness for sacrifice. Without complaint she accepts the greatest privations, and while her husband may be far away looking for gold or to earn money in some other fashion, she works and battles in order to live and bring up her children; she would regard it as shameful to ask for help. I have seen frail women plough the fields or take fruit to a marketplace thirty miles distant.

The position of women in the United States is a sign of the state of the society in general and its state of civilization. In the streets, in public meetings, at the theater, in church, on the railroads there is no man who fails to give a woman precedence in the most civil fashion or to offer her his seat. This is the case just as much in states like Minnesota, Texas, or California, as in New York or Georgia, and is practiced by the bearded woodsman just as diligently as by the gentleman. A woman, whether married or not, can make even the longest journey, from one border of the Union to the other, without having to suffer insults or humiliations on railroads or steamboats.[1]

These excerpts from Joachim's notes are interesting because they reflect, not so much the American woman's emancipation at the time, which must have seemed far greater to a conservative Swiss observer than it actually was, but because of the impression they convey of spunk and incipient independence on the part of the woman. They also reflect an early willingness on the part of American men to accept women's assertion of their rights—a willingness American men may still have, despite their he-manism, to a greater degree than women at present perceive; this willingness may become an important complementary factor in the rapid transformation of our society in the 1980s.

Appendix

PEOPLE SPEAKING (Interviews)

These excerpts from interviews with men and women, mostly ages 16 to 24, were conducted by Margaret Carpenter (M.C.), except for two, which were conducted by her brother, Edward Carpenter (E.C.). Several interviewees requested that their actual names not be used, a request gladly granted because it indicated candor in their statements. The decision was thus made to change all interviewees' names (except those of the first two, who are public figures).

THE following excerpts are from interviews with about eighty people, mostly young women, but also some men of varying ages, some older women, and a few children. The focus of the interviews was the future, on what those interviewed expected to happen and what they hoped would happen, which was not always the same thing. There is a serious limit as to what people can or will say with regard to the future, which often turns their thinking off rather than on. They find it easier to talk about the present and also about the subjective and objective experiences that made them what they are on the contemporary scene. This does not detract from prognosticating on the basis of what they said—on the contrary. As pointed out in Chapter 2, the most important element in a good prognosis is a good diagnosis.

The reader may initially find little in these excerpts to support the book's cautiously and conditionally optimistic prognosis for the future, for this seems to be at variance with the excerpts' many negative statements and apprehensions, their expressions of disillusionment and concern. It may seem like a contradiction to say that it was precisely the interviewees' worries, concerns, restiveness, desire and demand for change that led to the optimistic analyis. Widespread optimism or satisfaction or unconcern with an existing situation is not necessarily reason for optimism on the observer's part. On the contrary, if everyone is optimistic and unconcerned in a situation rife with dangers and negative elements, that is reason for a *pessimistic* prognosis. When people in such a critical situation show a certain amount of awareness and concern, reject certain policies and philosophies that have led to undesirable results, and, above all, exhibit a certain vigor and independence of thought, a willingness to think in new terms, and a capacity to react sensitively while the majority may still be numbed by custom and propaganda, then—if there are other factors to support it—there is a basis for optimistic conclusions.

The interviews reveal that many people, primarily young women, are now viewing their worlds with increasing realism and intellectual awareness, and that they appear to have the drive and fortitude to help bring social and political matters into greater harmony with people's needs in the technological age that is just beginning.

Ilona Hancock, thirty-one, gives some indications of how the "Renaissance women," whom Jack Smith mentions in the next interview, might want to restructure politics, work, and personal relations. As well as being a faculty wife and a mother, Loni is a member of the Berkeley City Council, one of four radicals elected in April 1971.

LONI: One reason I would like to see women enter politics is that I think they can redefine the personal relationships which are now prevalent in the political game, the whole life style that being politically active has tended to mean. Being a politician, a person holding an elective office, means for most people—mostly men—that they work twenty-four hours a day, they do not see their children, they have inhuman lives that are justified only if the person is a real crusader or a person who will do anything for the ego-satisfaction and the prestige and the power that come with holding a political office. I think that we will get a very different kind of politics if we can structure it so that political people have a chance to—well, I call it remaining fully human, like relaxing and watching flowers grow in the backyard and reading a novel from time to time.

M.C.: Do you think these changes will come about only because women will have entered politics, or would men eventually get their lives so fouled up that they would have to make those changes themselves?

LONI: No, I think that men have been living that way for generations and generations. Perhaps the mess the world is in is predicated on something as simple as the fact that most decisions are made by harassed, unhappy, overtired men.

M.C.: But will women be immune to the pressures that make men that way?

LONI: I think we necessarily have to be talking about women with a *new feminist consciousness.* I have a feeling that many women who entered all-male fields, say, the generation before us, were put in untenable psychological positions where they had to be as aggressive and manipulative as their male colleagues in order to get their respect. Those women made certain sacrifices that we do not want to make, although I don't think we want to berate them for having made those sacrifices. I have had to resist the feeling that I had to outmale the male politicians in order to have their respect. When I was first on the City Council, there were dinner meetings called all the time. When the pattern became clear to me, I explained that I wasn't going to come to them—I wanted to have dinner with my family. They don't have them any more, but at the time the comment was made, "If you can't play by the rules, you shouldn't be in politics." It is not only unfair but makes an interesting assumption, which is that men have no obligation to be home with their families at dinnertime or any other time. That's where I feel the women's movement has the seed of being the truly revolutionary movement of our time. It will humanize professions, politics, by liberating both men and women to use their talents and also have a meaningful personal life. Sex-role segregation has required mostly men and the few women who have tried to enter professions to work ten hours a day, fifty weeks a year. That is unproductive on many levels, while many people stayed home underutilizing their talents.

I have a hard time, because coming from a radical position necessitates attacking many things in the city. Now attack is not a feminine method of operation. It's very difficult to do, and yet you just have to do it sometimes, or simply allow things to happen that are unconscionable. I also see the ego-battling and tearing at each other that goes on among the men on the Council, and I think it's because of the way that they have been socialized. Women have a much more nurturing attitude, which could do a lot for politics. A female friend gave me a Chinese proverb during the campaign about the different kinds of leadership. There is one kind where you say, "Thank you, thank you—look what you have done for us." It goes on down from there to the best kind of leadership, which is when everybody says, "Look what we did for ourselves." That is what Left politics is about, and certainly the women's movement is needed for that kind of politics.

When I think about the women's movement, the really long-term thing I see happening is a restructuring of work. This is one thing we're attacking in our Affirmative Action Program—I'm really excited about it. I really question whether the economic system as we know it can survive. Large numbers of minorities are entering the job market at a time when there is constant danger of recession, and obviously technology is cutting down on jobs. I think the result of the women's movement, insisting on job equality at the same time that minority groups are, is going to necessitate cutting jobs in half, or something like that. One thing we have written into our Affirmative Action Program is that as many jobs as possible will be cut in half—six months on and six months off, or five hours a day, two and a half days a week. This will structure a situation where both adult members of a family can work and also have time to spend with each other and their children. That would make an enormous difference in society right there.

Jack Smith, columnist with the Los Angeles Times-Washington Post News Service, often writes about the concerns and proposals of feminist organizations, especially the National Organization for Women (NOW).

JACK: I write about language, and if NOW wants to give me a subject, I'll write about it, although I'm not making fun of them. Except that I think that women really have a gift for comedy, in the sense of the court jester. They have more wit than men in general. It's a profession of theirs—they need it. They've been oppressed and have to be funny to survive in all kinds of situations. They risk danger all the time like the court jester. Women always say things that a man can't get away with. That's why I've always liked the company of women better than men. I can't stand stag parties, and the last all-male organization I belonged to was the U.S. Marine Corps, and I vowed never again.

I can't believe that women would bring about a utopia any more than men, because I feel that way about *people.* If women are very different from men, they can be very different in an *adverse* way too. If women don't want to be thought of as that different from men, in the physical sense, I don't know how they can be thought of as being that much better. There is nothing in women's record to suggest that they would keep the peace if they were in power any better than men do.

M.C.: So you think that women would be as corrupted by the system as men?

JACK: The oldest profession in the world suggests that women will sell what they have to sell—the same as men. I think that most men are corrupted because of their responsibilities to their families.

It sounds kind of pompous for me to sit here in this big green chair talking about oppressing women, but I've got one woman I can liberate, and I've liberated her. It's interesting to watch a woman become liberated. It's partly because my wife is working and I'm working so much that I can't dominate her the way I used to! But there are a lot of resources and creativity in women. My feeling is that women don't have a chance to express themselves and flower or to use anything that's inside them. I know many newspapermen's wives—they're about the only women I know—all of them pretty remarkable women. They are bright and interested in things, and they all want to do more than life lets them do.

On the other side, the big myth of women's liberation is that there is a marvelous man's world, and if women could only get into that, they would be happy. Well, there isn't. Ninety-nine percent of the things that men do are terribly dull and banal and imprisoning. Maybe not if a guy makes shoes and really likes making shoes—but does his wife want to be liberated to make shoes? They want to be liberated to be doctors and lawyers, but who doesn't? I think that the line between men's activities and women's activities has got to break all the way, but I would like to see women *invent* something besides what they've done. NOW has said, I think, that they are against volunteer work for women, that volunteers are just being exploited as unpaid labor. Maybe so; maybe they shouldn't be unpaid. But the kind of things that women are able to do after they are out of school and have their children seems to me to be a step in the right direction. Isn't somebody going to stay out of the factory and do something creative? Isn't there something that we can do with ourselves as human beings besides what we have always done in the past? I don't look to women as superior beings, but I think that they can create new ways of using themselves with their spare time. I don't want them to put on overalls and be other men.

M.C.: Have you ever felt threatened by the idea that women might be getting rights that were once the prerogative of men?

JACK: No, it comes as a surprise to me that they don't have equal rights. They have to point out to us where they don't. I do wonder if we would ever get to the point where there aren't some divisions between roles and activities. I suspect that the differences between men and women—besides the obvious physical and sexual differences—may be very complex and deep. I not only feel that it is true, but also that it is one of the great wonders and joys of life. I have a horror of men and women being exactly alike except sexually, which would reduce a male-female relationship *absolutely* to a sexual relationship.

M.C.: Do you have the feeling from observing young women that they are changing in their expectations of their own lives and that they are really doing things very differently from their mothers? Or are they are just *talking* more about *universal* problems?

JACK: I have seen a lot of women who move with a lot more ease in what used to be the man's world. The women are that much more interesting. I'm sorry to say that I never stop thinking of them as sex objects —the older I get, the worse it gets! Anyone who denies that is not telling the truth. There is something heartening about talking to a whole person, and then you realize that it hasn't always been that way. Anything that means making them Renaissance women I'm for.

M.C.: You mentioned earlier that you hoped women would do something new with their talents and energies that would not be just repeating men's mistakes. I wonder if you see much value in the youth culture emphasis on women going back to crafts: weaving and baking bread, doing macramé?

JACK: The primitive crafts, the homespun things, seem to me to be things that women have always done in the home, if they could find time. To do it out on the sidewalk isn't any different. What I was thinking is that women could really be innovators in the coming thing of what to do with leisure. That is why I think it's a great mistake for women, either individually or generally, to be guided by a "me-too" philosophy when we seem to be on the verge of searching for new ways to engage ourselves. The reason we have a youth culture is that we have a lot of youth, a lot of ferment, and a static quality about society that just couldn't last. They are shouting for change, but I don't see that they are making any changes that will make life that much more beautiful or wonderful in the future. They certainly fill the air with music, questions, slogans, bumper stickers. I feel that nothing happens too fast in life but disaster. But in the historic sense, I feel we have got to be on the verge of something. And I would look for it to come from women.

Pam is one of many women concerned with helping people discover or create alternatives to institutions that may no longer suit their needs and aspirations. She was very active in campus politics at the midwestern university where she served as student-body president. Following the Kent State riots in 1970, she was asked to participate in a major investigation of campus unrest. At the present time she is developing a program to help high-school students organize for greater self-representation.

PAM: [The ACLU's attempt to organize high-school students in the San Francisco Bay Area] is based on a lot of assumptions. One is that a lot of groups are pushing for their rights, groups that never had been seen as groups before, like black people, women, and now students. Mainly it had been seen as a college-student-rights movement, but it's been moving down into the high schools. We publish little cards for young people on what to do if you're arrested, so the police can't run a game with you because you can say, "I know legally you have to do this and this." That's powerful, because it stops the police from faking you out and making you do things you don't have to do.

So this project is an education project to educate people as to what their rights are. Another assumption the project is working under is that the United States says that it's operating in a democratic way. Yet in reality it works in an authoritarian way—people at the top making decisions and then going to the people for reaffirmation of those decisions. They're not saying, "What should we do?" and then acting out the policy that the people want. The most tragic thing about it is that the people of the United States seem to accept this, because we're so used to the fact that someone over us is going to make the decisions. It's the feeling of the people who wrote this proposal that one of the reasons is the way the school system is set up. We socialize people in the schools to fit into the society. If you examine the schools, you see that they *perfectly* train people to fit into an authoritarian system—the principals make the decisions and the kids carry them out. Little things like getting a few students on the curriculum committee are a change, and that's good because it points to the fact that people are thinking about who's making decisions. But in a sense it's tokenism. So this project is to help kids who see that they should have a role in how their schools are run, to help them come up with ways of doing it. That could be getting a bill of rights in the school, which for example might outline the procedures for which a person would be suspended or expelled. It happens that kids are suspended for things that bother the principal—the arbitrary use of power that you see over and over in our society. That's one of the things that any rights movement tries to stop. Kids might want to do something like have an open campus, which means that they can leave the campus at lunchtime and eat at McDonald's, if they want. When I was in high school, you just didn't even think of doing that—the kids were just too afraid. Kids are realizing that it's silly to have to stay on campus.

That's the theoretical explanation of the project. The thing I've been finding is that in every school there are only two or three kids who are turned on to the fact that there should be changes. Another thing that's surprising here is that the kids who realize how messed up education is go to alternative schools. The ones who would be potential radicals have moved on to alternate structures instead of trying to change this one. I'm not saying that's not bad or good—it's just a problem. The kids who do want to change can't find any supporters for a couple of reasons. The students feel the schools are all right because they've never had anything else—this is just the way school is. Then there's another group of kids who realize that something is wrong but they don't want to get into trouble; they don't want to make waves. Then there are the schools where—I guess I'm being picky—they make *token* changes.

M.C.: You mean the administration makes small changes in anticipation of trouble?

PAM: Right. For example, at Balboa High School in San Francisco there are lots of "troublemakers." So they formed an alternative school within the school and put all the troublemakers into it. It's like sending the "bad" prisoners to Vacaville. You give the "troublemakers" more freedom to leave campus and to rap with the teachers, while the greater institution isn't changed at all.

M.C.: It doesn't sound as if you're terribly optimistic about the project at this point if there are so few people interested in change. Do you expect that a lot of momentum will build up eventually?

PAM: Saul Alinsky said something about organizing, that always it's going to be 1 per cent of the people who bring about the change. I'm still kind of a Pollyanna sometimes—I think that the masses are going to rise up. But realistically, that's not the way it's going to happen. I think the function of the project is to provide moral and legal support for these kids. One thing is that I keep getting the feeling that they have never been taken as seriously before. And I can provide a lot of resources, give them ten bills of rights from across the country and say, "Take what you want from them," then talk about how to get it through the local school board.

M.C.: Do you find that the kids take the initiative easily or do they need a lot of prodding?

PAM: You find both kinds of kids. You have the kids who have been working on this for a long time, and I'm just more information. Then you meet the kids who are interested and would push it if I did the work for them. But I refuse, because that's not any good when I'm just a benevolent authoritarian person. I've had a couple of workshops. There are all kinds of kids at the first meeting, say thirty, who are all enthusiastic and want a follow-up. But then only eight show up at the second meeting. I'm down and up about the whole thing, but I basically think it's a good idea.

M.C.: How do high-school women react to the project? Is the conference on women's studies the first thing specifically for women?

PAM: Organizing high-school women is just one component of it. What I tried to do was find issues that are common to a lot of high-school students by going around and talking. The first thing I found was that there's a lot of apathy. The first conference I had was on underground newspapers, how to get them going, how you can use them to educate people. Another thing I was interested in was high-school women and what happens to them, because that's one of the roots of the problem—the whole mess of men and women and oppression. I'll try to help organize anything I think kids are interested in.

M.C.: Do you see the women's movement as a distraction from more essential racial problems?

PAM: Someone once said, "A revolution is a symphony of many liberations." I really like that because people over the last few years have been realizing the totality of the problem. It's not just racism, or capitalism, or sexism—it's *all* of it. So everything has got to change. But what hangs me up is determining priorities. Do I say, "I see all black people, and their priorities are this and this" or "I see myself, my interests and skills, and so the priorities are this and this"? I have a whole guilt thing about not identifying more strongly with the black movement, because I don't.

M.C.: Do you think that's because you were often apart from blacks and moved around a lot when you were growing up?

PAM: I have always been in white communities. In a big group there might be five black people, and two of them were my brothers. I went through a period where I said, "Fuck white people!" That was back in '68, when that whole thing was going strong. But it didn't ring true and my heart wasn't in it. My head *was*—I could intellectually say that I must divorce myself from white people, but I didn't feel it. I wonder how many black people are in that position—where the rhetoric that's put forth in the media is separatism, but the reality of what I see is that society is *so* slowly moving closer to integration. But it's just *so* slow! It puts me through weird changes.

M.C.: I think it's healthy to have groups forming, just to emphasize the possibility of alternatives. For instance, a lot of people seem to think that the war cry of women's liberation is "Get out of your kitchen, lady!" It's more like "If you get tired of your kitchen once in a while —and you're normal if you do—there are the following things you can do." But as far as black women are concerned, I've heard that many feel that they can't identify with white middle-class surburban women who say they want to be liberated from their kitchens, because black women have generally been working all their lives and want to be liberated back to their kitchens. Do you think that's a representative view?

PAM: You get that. I read somewhere that that's bullshit—that black women aren't saying that, black *men* are saying it for black women. The thing that we have to keep remembering is what you said, that women's liberation is not "You get out of your kitchen." It means all kinds of liberation. It means liberation that stops black women from being the lowest-paid people in the society. There's a lot of macho stuff going down with black men, and that's a whole cultural thing that's got to start stopping to be truly free. Black men are at the bottom of the totem pole everywhere, so they get their feeling of superiority from dumping on their women and making her the lowest. It's got to come. As we deal with black liberation, we must deal with women's liberation too.

M.C.: What about Shirley Chisholm and Angela Davis? Do black women look at them as symbols of liberated women or just as black women?

PAM: The thing that I'm always struck by is that Angela Davis and Shirley Chisholm are good, but they're also media stars. I wonder how many people can relate to Angela Davis on a day-to-day basis. Her life is so removed—she's a professor! That's very far from being a domestic or my mother. The leaders of black working-class women are going to have to come from black working-class women, women who can say, "I come from the same background, and I see that we're being messed over, and this has got to stop." It's not going to come from Angela Davis or Shirley Chisholm, although they will be helpful.

M.C.: Have you noticed any real changes in racial attitudes among high-school kids you've come in contact with?

PAM: A couple of trends in some of the urban high schools. It's very factionalized—black students here, *chicano* students here, whites here. There are a few people who are crossing the lines and interacting. But for the most part it seems like a very tight segregation. I think this has a lot to do with housing patterns, because black people live together, white people live together. Until we break down that housing pattern, the totally free interacting society isn't going to come. But then you have the kind of people who are in the position I was in when I was in school. Their parents have moved into predominantly white communities, and they're like one in five black people in their school. There seems to be a lot more interaction this way. But with only five out of a school of two thousand, that means messing their minds over too. Like I said, it's coming so slowly. People are fighting busing, which is one way to start breaking it down. The racism is just—wow!

Every once in a while I go through this thing of thinking that I must hate black people because all my friends are white. I have a few black friends, but that's the same thing most white people would say. It puts me through weird changes, but I've pretty much come to accept it. I love these people very much, and I can't say that I consciously hate black people. All I can do is try. I have this fear that one day I'm going to wake up and realize that my whole life has been bullshit. So sometimes I think I shouldn't be friends with these people, I should leave them and go to Howard University. It's hard on me, but I'm sure that there are other people in my position.

M.C.: What kind of living situation can you see for yourself in ten years?

PAM: I see two things. If things work out with a man I'm close to, I will probably be living with him in a communal setting, having lots of people coming down to visit and stay. The thing that got us going was visiting the farm of some radical Catholics up in Michigan—they're wonderful. They ripped off the draft boards in Evanston. They are living in Uptown [a poor section of Chicago], and they also have a farm in Michigan. Their idea is to make it so people can come see what it's like to be in a commune, to get back to the land, to be with people who really love them. We saw that, and it just blew all of our minds. So I want to have our land like that, so people can know there's a place where they can always feel at home and relax. I want to be a lawyer. I want to be doing something I think is useful, working with people a lot, working for change. I'd like to still be able to travel occasionally, because I guess that's just in my blood. I don't like to feel that I have to stay in one place. Eventually at some time I would like to be part of a community that has kids. I think I would like to have *a* kid, just to do it! In ten years I'll probably be ready to handle that responsibility—right now there's no way.

M.C.: Do you think that human relationships are changing because women are thinking about themselves a lot more, and that in, say, ten years relationships will be radically different?

PAM: One of the most beautiful things I see coming out of this is that, while women feel that they can be more assertive and career-oriented, men are starting to be more emotional, more giving, more loving, more vulnerable. I think that's really beautiful, because the hardness that many men have grown up with is responsible in some part for the way the world runs—you know, with wars and a society that could allow someone to starve because he's not working. Humanism is not there, and if anything, that's going to be developed in more men. The men I'm close with are beginning to break down the idea that women's place is in the home and men must do certain things outside the home.

M.C.: If you see this kind of change already, do you think that women are not going to have to resort to the kind of violence the suffragettes did to get what they wanted?

PAM: I'm schizophrenic on that, because I don't want to participate in any violence, partly philosophically, partly I'm scared! The other part of me is realistic enough to know that violence precipitates change and that society most times does not move unless it feels threatened—very seriously threatened. That might have to be a part of it. I *wish* we were hip enough not to have to be that way. But I'm very afraid that people don't want to give up their power.

M.C.: You said that violence precipitates change, and you made a very eloquent defense of the students who resorted to violence at Kent State in your television debate with Agnew last year. Do you think that Kent State, for instance, really changed anything?

PAM: It was a springboard for a tremendous educational drive about the war. There was a certain stratum of people who realized that the war was wrong. Out of our strike at Northwestern the most positive thing I saw was that we could educate people about what was going on with the war, and it made more people realize what the state will do to protect itself. It's just another part of the process of radicalizing more and more people.

M.C.: What happens when you run up against people like Agnew, though?

PAM: We can't get to him, but we can get to his daughter. You write off people like Tricia Nixon as being just lost. Maybe I've mellowed out —or copped out, or compromised or whatever—but I just think that whatever is going to come is going to take a while—*years* of changing people. And Kent State is just another part of the process of turning people around. All I know is that it did alter people's consciousness. One beautiful thing at Northwestern was that the students closed down the university in spite of what the administration said—*that* was people taking power and "determining how their institutions are to be run."

M.C.: Some people say that if women only knew what is going on in power circles, they would be horrified to see that men sit around trying to think of ways to perpetuate their own power. You have had a taste of involvement in campus and national politics. Do you think there is anything to that idea?

PAM: I've heard a lot of people answer that question, and the answer I like best is that it's not a conscious conspiracy—that the Male Conspiracy Club will meet on Tuesdays at four—but an unconscious thing. When you see the Attorney General of the United States quitting to become a campaign manager—to me, that says it all. When you read *The Selling of the President* and find out how much energy—conscious energy—is spent on getting power! Power is as highly seen a value as the changes you can bring about with the power. People seem to think it's good just to get power. Power over other people is bad for its own sake.

Ellen describes how she became a radical feminist during her freshman year at a small liberal arts college. Now a sophomore at a state university, she is preparing for a career in law. At 18 ½ she has done much reading and thinking about the potential influence of feminism on society and the direction of her own life.

ELLEN: It's funny that when I was in high school, when I was fifteen or sixteen, all my friends were guys. I had one good girlfriend and about five good male friends. It wasn't until I got to college and I could not get close to any of the men there—I got really close to about five women—that I began to see the whole reason why this had happened. In me there was a whole thing like, "I don't want to be associated with those flighty girls. I want to be associated with stable men. I'm strong and I can go hiking and do all the things they can do." It wasn't until that year that I saw the value of women in their own right. I got to the point where I was able to go out to dinner with just women without thinking it was second best and wishing I were with a guy.

M.C.: But you didn't necessarily exclude men from your life—you just opened up to women more than before?

ELLEN: Right. I didn't purposely do that. There were just no men.

M.C.: When you were with guys your age, did you talk about your ideas?

ELLEN: Oh, yeah.

M.C.: How did they react?

ELLEN: Radical men are some of the worst men I've had to deal with. In a discussion they'd say, "You're not oppressed. What are you giving me this shit for? Fight for the brothers!" They don't listen. They would ridicule me, like they'd turn it into a big joke. Nothing can make me angrier than somebody turning something I consider serious into a joke. Two other women and I went to see Gloria Steinem speak. When we came back and walked into the coffee shop, a big chorus of men called out, "Are you liberated now?"

M.D.: Do you think they joke about it because they're afraid of it?

ELLEN: Yeah, that's the only assumption I can come to. It's been so drummed into men that they are supposed to be in control, from the time they're little boys sitting at the table telling their mother to bring them a sandwich. Also that men are so needed. I would say, "Look, if you can't respond to me as a whole person, then you're not needed as far as I'm concerned." It was scary for them, I think. At this point in my life I am very against marriage as an institution, both for the legal barriers it creates for women and the psychological ones. There are very few men I know who would say sincerely, not just to get out of marriage, "Look, I really don't want to get married—I don't want to take away your full personhood." Most men think only of being benevolent dictators and being "nice" to the woman, but what does that matter?

M.C.: Even if the women you went to high school with lose interest in the movement per se, do you think they will still try to carry out the goals of the movement in their lives?

ELLEN: Yes. In a sense the movement is not petering out, because I discover women every day who are coming to an awareness. My eleven-year-old sister is a feminist to the greatest degree. One day she told me a story confidentially about how the boys at school wouldn't let her play basketball because she was a girl. She said, "I was so good. I gave them a whole talk about giving me a chance because girls can do anything boys can do. Then you know what I said? I said 'Fuck off!' " That was great! She's reading the books and everything, buying feminist buttons. She has a knowledge at eleven that I never had. My seventeen-year-old sister is getting into it too, but she's never been in a relationship where she's been dominated.

People who have been into the movement I don't think are getting out of it. Once you taste it, you hold on all the tighter. But I'm not sure how much political awareness there is, and it's hard to reach some women. Single university women are the easiest to reach, but they have less at stake. Whereas working women and solid upper-middle-class women have more to lose. My aunt lives in a ritzy suburb, is married to a dentist, has two sons, a Mercedes, and a live-in maid. She says, "Why should I want to get up at eight to go to work when I already have a maid?" And yet she tells me that something within her is not fulfilled; she doesn't feel she's contributing to anything. It's very hard to reach her.

I want to be at the top so I can create the most change. I could see sitting on the Supreme Court. My ambition is to be President. But on the other hand, I can't envision it because I'm not sure I would want to be President of this particular government. The first thing I would do would be to say, "Let's change everything."

M.C.: How would you change things?

ELLEN: From an economic point of view, I believe this country could provide all the material needs to its people. We're rich enough to provide food, beds without rats, and even TVs if people want them—that can't be contingent upon the work of the society, because work of society is based on the idea that dirty work gets paid less. The ego-fulfilling prestige jobs get paid the most, so you have double benefits at that level. I would switch to a system where the dirty jobs with no intrinsic satisfaction would have higher pay, and a ditchdigger would only have to work a few hours to gain the same kind of monetary rewards that, say, a brain surgeon gets in eight hours. I can't see letting people starve and go without medical care. Changing the education system would be the second priority. There would be a more flexible structure in terms of age—kids who are just eating up knowledge would push ahead until they learned what they need to know. I'd provide much more vocational training, that wouldn't be put down as less desirable. Also, kids would be provided with subsidies through a certain age so they could do what they wanted without parental pressure—until society changed enough so that parents wouldn't have an urge to control their kids.

M.C.: It sounds as if there would also be less emphasis on degrees in your system. What will this do to competition in the job market?

ELLEN: First, the job market will be more equaled out, and it will no longer be such a disgrace to do vocational work. People would choose it because then they would work fewer hours, and men would no longer need such high-paying jobs because they were no longer the sole support of families. As for degrees, the system would be designed to let people learn what they wanted to do. By the time you got to university level and wanted to be a doctor, you would learn to be a doctor without feeling compelled to cheat and convince other people you knew more than you really did. Degrees reinforce deception. You should work until you master a task, and if you don't master it, you just say, "That isn't for me" without being disgraced.

M.C.: You have been talking about how you would change the economic and education systems once you got to the top of the political system. Do you expect any changes in the political system itself?

ELLEN: My hope is that people would learn a basic concern for each other in their upbringing and education so that we wouldn't need the kind of government we have now. We might need a body to organize the distribution of wealth, but we wouldn't need the kind of government that is interested in securing power for itself. People would become the most important priority.

M.C.: Do you think that the very presence of more women in politics will change our goals?

ELLEN: No. Maybe for the first couple of years women will be a little timid because they're not used to having control over the situation. But I don't see that the women heads of government we have now are any less aggressive than the men.

M.C.: How do you think change will come about if it's not because women have something different to offer the system?

ELLEN: Just through the awareness . . . I mean, I'm not sure that change is going to come about. But if it does, it will be through women, oppressed people, who have had to fight so much harder to overcome oppression. If I got in power, I could do it by taking people with me who agreed with my ideas.

M.C.: What do you see as the main obstacles to change?

ELLEN: People's unwillingness to change. My generation is supposed to save the world with their peace and love and understanding. They may be able to spout words about peace and love, but they go home and scream at each other and their parents. The external facets of these kids—their hair, their drugs—have changed, and that's what scares older people. But their basic values aren't any different. They're interested in getting powerful and having the glory, but not caring too much about the next person and not understanding his point of view. I don't see what all these older people are complaining about when they've just produced carbon copies of themselves!

M.C.: Will these kids continue to use drugs?

ELLEN: Yes, it's an easy way to put up a barrier between you and the next person. It removes the hardness of trying to get to know a person. It's hard to sit and try to understand someone sometimes. I think clothes are used as another barrier. If you have people running around naked, you have less of a conception of their role and status in society than when they're wearing their mink coats or Cardin suits or whatever. I think people are becoming much freer about nudity and bodies.

M.C.: If women are more casual about displaying their bodies, do you think men will change their attitudes toward women?

ELLEN: Oh, yeah. If men saw all kinds of women running around nude, I can't see the whole fascination with breasts and behinds continuing.

M.C.: Do you find the male body attractive?

ELLEN: Oh, yeah. I like bodies, all bodies.

M.C.: How do you react when you're wearing a short skirt, say, and a man makes a comment?

ELLEN: Well, on the one hand, I feel I asked for it. But on the other hand, I feel why should that be so, since men don't get comments no matter what they're wearing?

M.C.: Do you think women worry about their appearance only because they want approval from men?

ELLEN: No, I have to look at myself in the mirror too. It's a question of personal esthetics—I feel better when I know I don't look like a slob. On the other hand, I object to the idea that women have to resort to exaggerated makeup and other kinds of trickery to be noticed and be attractive. If nudity becomes an accepted way of life, I think there will be less emphasis on whether you're skinny or fat. The more of your body you display, the more ridiculous it becomes to worry about how a particular area looks, like your face or your breasts. I know a lot of men who are no longer looking at women's bodies just in terms of whether they have the "perfect figure."

Like many women in their mid- and late-twenties, Sally initially became interested in the women's movement in the 1960s, when everyone seemed to be searching for a cause to champion. In her case religious conviction strengthened her feeling that women's liberation is more than just another here-today-gone-tomorrow social movement. After receiving a B.A. and a Master of Library Science degree from a Catholic women's college, she became a reference librarian at a research corporation, where she has been instrumental in organizing a "women's lobby" to improve the status of female employees. She is also very active in NOW.

M.C.: Do you think a lot about the future?

SALLY: Not as much as I do about the past.

M.C.: In what terms do you think about the future when you do?

SALLY: Long range, I'd say. "It's a bad century" type of thought, and this century will yield to another century. I guess it's partly because I'm Catholic, when you actually get to it. I mean Catholic background and Catholic training. I've been from the background of the eternal, so to speak. And then you march on through history. Being brought up in Augustine's City of God, the whole thing is planned, everything is set. It inclines me to see monumental patterns and to see an individual life as both negligible in the human realm and important as an individual, more important than the human pattern.

When I was in high school I read about the feminist movement, and wow! In the sixties everybody had their own movement, and there I was with no movement. And I had a sort of religious experience when I was in college that gave me a very firm notion that you have to perform. It confirmed most of my Catholic thoughts that you have to perform—not serve for humanity's sake, but for your own sake, for the sake of the service as an individual, between you and God. And therefore I am more inclined to do something more grandiose, at least in my own mind, than I am to do some little thing like hospital work.

And then when the movement really started to get going, suddenly the logic of it impelled me. I realize this sounds weird considering the tenor of modern times, everybody knowing the odds and playing it close to their vest. But death has always seemed to me a very real thing, very imminent, and the secret to me is to be willing to die, or be ready to die, not having any fear of it. And the only way to do that is being involved with a life. Suddenly I got hooked onto the movement and hooked up into it. It was a sort of a burst of energy, the bursting of a dam that had finally overflowed. I knew that I had got to make a commitment in my life, in the movement. When the opportunity came, I said, "At last, something to do."

The cause is manifestly just. It's one of the most obvious causes I've ever seen—I mean, it doesn't even require any stretching. You don't even have to make that little jump over the hump. Suddenly you just stand there, gaping at the fact that people are still at this level. You read the speeches from 1848 and 1860 and 1910, and they're completely relevant to today. You think that those women were brilliant or we are slow—or both. Most people don't know what's right to do, apparently, or they're not willing to do what's right to do. Now, I happen to see what's right to do. If I think something is logical, intellectually right, there is no question—I'll kowtow to anybody on the basis of a loose social interaction, but if it's a matter of *principle,* I can break up cocktail parties.

Part of my business lies in being able to be friendly, or at least keep an illusion of affability. I'm not a person who dislikes people. And I have a rule of thumb that people do what you tell them to, what you expect them to do. You can get away with a lot by just playing on the better side of people and giving them their cue. You walk up to them with your eyes wide open, naïve, and say, "But you believe in *rights,* don't you?" They say, "But of course I do," and march along with you. Frankly, there's nothing that will change relationships, for women, as much as a little power. In many respects: the confidence it gives them, the respect it gives others, the worry it gives some men. That kind of thing cannot fail to create more respect, at least regard, even if it is a relationship based on fear. On an individual basis there will be worry for jobs, advancement, promotions. But as more women get into it, more women will have more respect for the movement. Scratch a woman and you find a feminist. Suddenly they are going to realize that it's personal profit and not just a group of nincompoops. They are going to keep their eyes on it. And a woman who keeps her eyes on women's liberation, sooner or later finds out exactly how bad it has been. I'm not saying you're going to get moral rearmament, but gradually you're going to get the "Watch it, buster—don't tread on me" kind of attitude.

M.C.: Do you think that once women are in a position to say "Don't tread on me" they will change their basic values?

SALLY: I sure as hell hope so. Women have been trained to be self-created losers, they have been trained in the slave morality, which is practically no morality at all. They have been trained to believe that the valuable traits to have are deceit, cunning, debasement, humiliation, bootlicking, flattery—that stupidity constitutes a value for a woman. The dumber you are, the smarter you are. That using people and having to use personal relationships with men is an item of barter for money, for hard cold cash, either in a job advancement or a marital thing. It's every woman having the morality of a harlot.

M.C.: If we could ever get to the point where because we no longer have these economic relationships of dependency we could wipe the morality of harlots, what kind of natural virtues could women develop?

SALLY: Who will know?

M.C.: You don't have any feelings about innate characteristics?

SALLY: I think that there are probably only a handful of innate characteristics, and most of them can probably be trained out. Most are not innate characteristics but innate *conditionings*. Like a woman has got to bear children, and bearing children may produce certain characteristics. Innate characteristics certainly have been trained out of men. The idea being promulgated by movies and television now is of the woman as nothing but a sex object and the man as the "*real* man"—who probably has never had any real relationships with human beings. He's some kind of a petrified *dog*. Men have been conditioned to be hard and unemotional.

M.C.: What has been your experience with black women as they are touched by feminism?

SALLY: Black women I've met aren't as touched by feminism. It's just another thing they have to worry about. In a way, the fact that they have had the other burden too gives them a style which can throw off sexist burdens as well. Since the prejudice is unnamed, they can say, "Aha—you're prejudiced," because everybody knows that it's not good to be prejudiced against blacks, when it may actually be sexist prejudice. A lot of black women won't know who cleared the way, they won't know that the foliage is down—or that the bush was ever there. When you clear the way for women, there is no way the fall-out can't be complimentary to *every* woman.

M.C.: Do you see this "fallout" in terms of men as well, or is your primary sight just on women?

SALLY: Well, I have ambivalent feelings there. Women in NOW, which is one of the few feminist groups that accepts men, see things two ways. Some women at the meetings see them pass papers out and say with love and gratitude, "They are *so* good at detail work!" But then they'll say, "But we do love them." A lot of men will allow themselves to be used as part of the consciousness-raising, in the sense of "Look, a man is serving me for once in my mortal life," or "Look, a man is with me, therefore the power group says it's okay and it must be okay. At least there are some of the *Herrenvolk* in there." To prove that it's not a women's club. As far as I am concerned, we're doing this for both of us and it's good for public relations. Men have behaved in a sexist fashion, they have driven women under since the beginning. It has been to their profit, but in the long run nobody is going to profit more for this.

M.C.: How are men specifically going to profit from the movement?

SALLY: Because it's not good to be mean and vicious. It's immoral. It has completely dulled their moral sensibilities. Half the human race they perceive as some kind of amorphous lump designed for their own personal gratification, and then they wonder why marriages break up and they die at fifty. There's one thing: they'll live longer once some of this pressure is off. I mean *I* can fix tires and little things like that Outside of the question of being morally right, there are better relationships, truer relationships, less demanding roleplaying. As far as men being bosses and managers, they'll be able to draw on all of America instead of just fifty percent of it. It will affect the entire economy. Eventually women will become bolder about claiming their rights. It's funny how weird people are about advancement, people who have been down for a long time. They play it cool, they say they don't care about it, because they're waiting for the other shoe to drop. But once you get through the notion that you can make it, you can really make it, you can be alive, then they care. But usually it takes that kind of attention from one of the master race, the *Herrenvolk*. The most successful women are the ones who have been encouraged by a man, usually in the early part of their careers—which is why we need so many men in the movement. Men have always been the boss people, and women just can't get over that fact. If women ever stop thinking like that, they suddenly realize how bad off they are. For a lot of men it's not going to be to their profit at all—they've already got nice convenient slaves at home, and they are suddenly going to find themselves carrying the laundry in and out and taking care of the kids. They're not going to like it. But neither did their wives. There's not going to be much fun. There's going to be profit, but there will probably be a tradeoff. When the dust clears, what they have lost will probably be less worthy than what they have gained. But the one thing they will have gained about which there is no question is moral righteousness.

M.C.: And how do you think this moral righteousness might affect politics or big business?

SALLY: The whole effect of the movement, along with all the other movements, will be to humanize things a great deal, and idealize things. I don't think it will bring an end to the war. That whole business about women being pacifists is a lot of hooey. The female of the species is deadlier than the male. Most women could plan a battle and carry it out as well as the men from an emotional standpoint, if trained to.

M.C.: But is that the point? Is there going to continue to be that kind of training, for men or women?

SALLY: Probably not, because it is happening in conjunction with a lot of other movements. You tend to find allies everywhere, and pretty soon your allies' philosophies permeate yours. I've got to say it about the quality of the people in the movement, I have never met such open, kind, sensitive, reaching-out people as the women and men I've met in NOW. Even the women who were glory-hunting, their style is so open. For the first time the sense of sisterhood is real, like the early Christians.

M.C.: Do you find that involvement in the movement gives you different attitudes toward people, and women specifically?

SALLY: I feel it more with feminists. I think it's actually stiffened my attitude toward other women—I tend to expect more of them. And if they don't yield it, I tend to not respect them as much. I make judgments of them more than I used to. The more you get into an idealistic group, the less and less you tend to go along with the one aspect of "cheapo" ethics, namely, "everybody does their own thing." When women tell me their own thing is taking care of their husband, not trying to get ahead on the job, bootlicking, seeing themselves entirely as an adjunct to him—the great amorphous Him—I say it stinks. I'm not saying that every woman should be working, but they should be doing something as themselves, not just being somebody's foot or somebody's dog. I don't care how nice the person who owns you—nobody *should* own you. So it hardens my relationships with many women because they know that I don't respect them. Not for not being feminists, but for not being *people.*

M.C.: What is this attitude of women becoming people going to do to the family?

SALLY: Ooh, that stings. Well, there are going to be some changes made. First, it would be very nice if we could get everybody to share: let the men take half and the women take half and let society figure it out. That sort of thing will probably require a phased, organized change. Fifty or a hundred years from now somebody may look back and say that was Phase I. But it doesn't look that planned now. It will undoubtedly cause a lot of breakups between husband and wife, and it will cause a lot of new pressures to build up between parent and child. No longer will the child have his own private tutor, babysitter, etc. There is something illogical about a child having his own person. Women devote their entire lives to producing more human beings. But who is going to *do* something, to make it worthwhile to live? It's going to hurt. This notion that the child is sacrosanct is false. If you don't want to bring a child into the world, that is one thing. But on the other hand, just because you bring a child into the world doesn't mean you have to give him your own life! There are some adjustments that the child, the family, and society are supposed to make. When the dust clears, I don't think it's going to be all that bad. First, children are resilient as hell. And nine times out of ten the kid ends up the opposite of his parents anyway.

M.C.: What about overall trouble in society? Do you think that feminists will have to resort to extreme measures such as violence?

SALLY: With my love for drama, I've been looking for the first bomb that's thrown. I keep thinking of the Pankhurstians in England. Unfortunately, in their case it was one of them that died. You do feel that boost when you're in the movement and you hear that two sisters have been killed sniping in the IRA. "You think we're nothing, huh? You'll get a bullet between your ears." There is a certain impulse because the weapon used against us has been mostly ridicule. The emotion that has been aroused is rage, and rage breeds violence. The interesting thing about the women's movement is that it's all *yeast.*

There is the publicity we get, but it's like Barnum—"There is no such thing as bad publicity." Society is so antifeminine in its orientation that the most dyed-in-the-wool Aunt Tom will realize that prejudice is against her too. Women will say, "I'm not for women's lib, but. . . ." And that "but . . ." will rule the world.

M.C.: What do you think about the idea that the woman's place is in volunteer work? Is that going to die off, or is that to provide a basis for a new revolution?

SALLY: You've got two things going there. Again, the economic situation stifles that, the good aspect of voluntarism. The short-range aspect of voluntarism is to discourage women from achieving on an open competitive basis. One thing I think women will do is help to destroy the value of competition as a principle. Instead they can set up the value of achievement; let's just get the job done. I hope women will not have to pass through the phase of *fierce* competition, except on an individual basis. We'll teach them that working together for accomplishment is more important. For our society, that kind of competition is wasteful and behind the times. But as far as voluntarism goes, I agree with the finding of the NOW committee in the recent annual convention that it is dangerous in the short run because it promotes professional amateurism. But in the long range there is too little for people to do in society. We've got to start to become involved in the world and *demand* to be active in that world. Not just be child-breeders. Maybe the value of voluntarism will go up when both men and women engage in it. But in the interim we should steer clear of it as a solution. The women's movement itself is entirely voluntary, even though most women don't think of it as voluntarism. Doing a job for nothing is being an Indian instead of a chief. Not that this movement is to make chiefs of everybody. The opportunity to be either an Indian or a chief is constitutional, although not actual. I hope the cumulative social effect of the movement will be to make everybody no longer think of himself as big or little, winner or loser, but people. To make every boss a little more sympathetic to the problems of his—or her—underlings, and to think of them as people he works *with,* not people who work *for* him.

M.C.: Do you think that the new humanism and lack of competitive roleplaying will come out soon in education?

SALLY: Well, the ultimate effect will be ten decades. I'd give it a maximum of five years and you're going to see some real pressure and some real results in the sphere of education. That's the next coming area for women's liberation. You're getting more women knowing you're in for a long haul. They may not want to fight for themselves, but they'll fight for their daughters. From that standpoint, schools are extremely susceptible to political pressure, and they're going to get it.

M.C.: What's going to happen to the girls who are perhaps ten years younger than you and I, in high school now, and growing up in a period when there is a lot of awareness of discrimination and women's problems? Are they starting a step ahead of us, or are they going to have to bumble around for themselves, going through the same process?

SALLY: Clarify one thing: the problem is not *ours,* it is *theirs.* Technically, the problem belongs to our opposition. Our problem is one of *solution.* There is no question at all that these women who are coming up will have been sensitized to the possibility of problems, they will be ready—the same way you and I had to be sensitized to racism. We said to our parents, "Of course racism is wrong—it's like anti-Semitism," while they were going through mind-blowing sessions trying to shake racism. And these women will be saying "of course sexism is wrong—it stinks!"

M.C.: Another thing you were saying before is that the way people react toward you depends to a certain extent on how you expect them to react. Maybe these kids, girls in particular, will take it for granted that they will be treated decently, they'll expect certain opportunities.

SALLY: Oh, yeah. They'll be quicker to scratch.

M.C.: Have you had any experience with girls of this age in NOW, or through church? Do you have any feelings for their attitudes?

SALLY: Somewhat deplorable.

M.C.: In what sense? Because they don't care? Or because it's something they haven't discovered themselves?

SALLY: Yes. They don't care. A lot of them are going through the full flow of adolescence, and nine-tenths of adolescence lies in trying to adjust to social relationships, which are tinged by both sex and sexism. A lot of them have no sense of commitment to society and its established norms. They say, "Sure there's sexism in the establishment—I'm not going to go the establishment route anyway!" And of course a lot of them are simply sexist trained. They're more sensitized to it in a public-relations sense. They'll buck big sexism, but sometimes they will treat little sexism as a joke. But little sexism is where the actual life impact ultimately lies—that gradual deterioration of self-respect. You wonder why they aren't out in the streets, but combat is a very special style that not everybody possesses.

M.C.: Some people have looked ahead to see what is sometimes called "post-scarcity society," a society in which people are no longer tied to each other out of economic necessity. Can you make a jump into a situation where there wouldn't be this kind of economic necessity, to imagine what it might be like?

SALLY: Yes. There are a lot of women who have been living in a "post-scarcity society" all their lives, and it has done very ugly things to them. The tone that *we're* hoping to set with women, my secret hope for moral rearmament—that sort of changing of ethical values—depends on a tone of rigidity and sternness, even a touch of harshness. "You will stand ramrod straight on the line and you will die for the cause." That sort of thing is not the ultimate, but there must be a period of that before you get any kind of structure to your character, some sort of passing through the fire. Necessity is the mother of virtue in this case, some sort of harsh necessity.

M.C.: Maybe it's not necessarily a question of not *having* to work past a certain point, but finding other means of occupation.

SALLY: That would be great, but you have to build up a moral core to do that. Inertia is the nature of man, as it is of all objects. Unless you build up some sort of moral imperative, even in a handful of people. . . . Religion usually supports ethics in a vast social sense, and ethics always supports religion even in a very personal sense. But society and individuals must operate with some ethics regardless of whether they have some religious life. There are two ways of having ethics. One is to think it out clearly—that is the "I saw what was right and I did it" idea, which I partially share. But it's heavily influenced by the other method: "You will be taught what is correct, you will follow the teachings." And the majority of humanity has got to be taught. You've got to have some sort of legal standards despite the compulsive aspects. I'll use the law for women's liberation, but in this case I feel the aversion to law much less because we *are* the majority, the government was made to support us. It hasn't known it up to now, but it will soon learn.

Many young women today have quietly incorporated into their lives the changes that older or more militant feminists seem to spend most of their time discussing. Audrey is a calm and independent 18-year-old who decided to try out a new way of life when the traditional high school-college-marriage route lost its appeal for her. On her own initiative, she spent her senior year at a high school in Norway and the following summer in Sweden. She is now working at a pet shop to finance weaving lessons and her eventual return to Sweden for further training in weaving and textiles.

AUDREY: Actually, the reason I wanted to spend my senior year in Norway wasn't so much that I was infatuated with Norway, but that it was the only way my high school would give me a diploma at my age without my spending another year there.

M.C.: Did you go on the American Field Service exchange program?

AAUDREY: I went on my own. I just wrote to the Ministry of Education, Oslo, Norway. With one letter my application was accepted. They said they needed an American student. I found that people are more dependent on each other in Norway, perhaps because I was in a town. Instead of going to a movie, they would just go visit relatives. There were always cousins and grandparents around.

M.C.: Do you like the idea of an extended family?

AUDREY: It's fine, but I don't need it. I think it was a little bit too much with relatives around *all* the time. I wasn't brought up with that.

M.C.: Did you feel that Norwegian women are more liberated than American women?

AUDREY: From the Norwegian women I knew, I would say there are two kinds: either they stay at home, marry a boy from the same town, and stay there all their lives; or they're very radical and go off to protest against everything, disown their family.

M.C.: Which group did you feel more at ease with? Did you find your particular friends were the radicals?

AUDREY: For the most part they were. I had kind of a hard time fitting in because I wasn't one way or the other that much. I went to Sweden on my own in the summer. It was funny, but the people there were much more like me. Instead of just protesting against things which they didn't like, they did what they wanted. I would like to do it that way, even if I don't always. Just to protest makes me sad. I really had a much easier time in Sweden, and I'm much closer to them.

M.C.: Do you think the kind of society we are moving toward in the United States is eventually going to be somewhat like what you found in Sweden as far as family structure, sexual mores, and value systems are concerned?

AUDREY: I think it is going to take time. Things have to become more natural here.

M.C.: Do you get the impression that Americans are just testing out these roles and making a lot of noise, instead of just going out and doing what they are talking about?

AUDREY: To some extent, yes, although there are exceptions.

M.C.: Do you sense any change in the year you have been away?

AUDREY: A really big change. For one thing, people are starting to do things with their hands, being happy and creating things for themselves. They are being more dependent on themselves. I would be so bored if I didn't have something to do, while everyone in Norway would get up and crochet or macramé.

M.C.: What can you imagine yourself doing in ten or fifteen years?

AUDREY: I hope to have a home and a family and I want to go on with my weaving. I know when I finish with this textile course at the school in Sweden I can go on and take an extra course to be accredited as a weaving teacher, so I have that to look forward to, plus this other program in occupational therapy, which is what I am really interested in. If I ever needed money, I could go commercial, either work in a weaving shop or sell my own things. That's why I am so happy—because there are so many possibilities.

M.C.: Is it really important to you to know that you have a way of being independent?

AUDREY: Yes. I've never thought of marriage as a way out. I am working now in order to pay my way over to Sweden. I know my parents would support me, but it makes me feel better to contribute something.

M.C.: Would you want to raise your children differently from the way your parents raised you?

AUDREY: No, not really. I only hope I can have as much patience as my mother had. The only thing I might try, although it is not a fault of my parents, is to teach my children to use their hands more. I would want them to know they could have a good time by themselves and could teach others too.

M.C.: Do you consider yourself as part of the counterculture?

AUDREY: I don't know. Most of my friends seem to be in the middle road. They are going ahead and doing what they want, but they try to explain what they are doing to their parents in order not to hurt them. I think most of them want a good relationship with their parents.

Women who are active in the feminist movement usually develop such an awareness of the inequalities and injustices of our social system that they are not content merely to make changes in their own lives. Spreading the word on the need for reexamination and reform has become a way of life for 23-year-old Maryann. After discovering the women's movement through radical politics, she organized and participated in women's groups, taught and lectured on self-defense for women, contributed articles to several women's publications, and encouraged the formation of men's groups and a men's liberation paper called Brother. *She is now working on a master's degree in journalism and rewriting a sexual autobiography.*

M.C.: How did you become interested in the women's movement? You seem to have been into this for a long time. When did you actually begin?

MARYANN: I had my first opportunity to be in it around the time of the People's Park incident in Berkeley, about May '69, when a few women asked me if I wanted to go to a women's meeting. I elaborately declined at the time, inwardly thinking, "Well, I really don't want another meeting a week and it probably won't be interesting." I was not ready for women's liberation. I turned them down because I was oppressed and biased, and nine months went by before I had another chance.

M.C.: Was it just because you didn't want to get involved with groups of women?

MARYANN: I think it was because I was male dominated. I had been going to mixed meetings and it was just an unconscious reaction to say no. I've thought about it a lot since, and what must have been behind it was a feeling that it was going to be irrelevant. After the People's Park I began to feel kind of oppressed. Then the Tenants' Union was another male-female organization; we organized for a rent strike and it was pretty grueling work, six months of organizing. When we saw the rent strike was going to happen, there was a desire among men and women for more of an encounter, because we had worked together but didn't really know each other. We had a couple of meetings, then the women expressed the desire to have one just for women, and I thought that would be a great idea too. That was December '69. We got together and it was everything that we'd hoped it would be.

M.C.: Was it a kind of "flash" experience for you?

MARYANN: No, it was just a warm gratifying experience. I had already begun to do a lot of thinking about my past life and how I was always harassed in the street. I was beginning to put things together and hearing other women talk about their experiences helped multiply the knowledge. *It Ain't Me Babe* [underground feminist paper in Berkeley] had been started and I wrote an article on women's shoes, relating to self-defense, and this was even before I was taking karate. I had hiking shoes—not many women were wearing them—and I loved them so much! They really had given me the nerve to stand up to guys on the street.

Then around March '70 the Berkeley police wanted to buy two helicopters. Our small group, which had been working in political stuff for some months, decided to try and get the helicopter money for child care. We got back into organizing around what was strictly a women's issue; well, not really, because the helicopters would have affected the whole community's rights. We had an Easter egg roll at Provo Park for women and children and explained the issue. That got the mothers out, then by the time the City Council meeting came up, we got two thousand people there, so we had done our work well. Almost all the public speakers were against the helicopters. It was defeated, and the women got about thirty thousand dollars for child care.

That group began to call itself Women of the Free Future. Then we got into rape because one of the women in our group was raped in her house, and she wanted us to go to the City Council. We spent a lot of time preparing about nine demands that the City Council could implement, such as free public transportation for everyone from dawn to dusk, better lighting around apartments, making landlords responsible for putting locks on windows, and we asked them to put out a circular to everyone in Berkeley about how to defend yourself—just common-sense things.

When I came back to Berkeley in the fall of 1970, I was working on a book. It had two names—first *Don't Call Me Chick or I'll Bite*

Your Balls Off, then it was changed to *The Land of the Biggest Bully*. It was just a funny narrative of how a nice middle-class girl gets into the movement and then realizes that women's liberation is where it's at. It happens to be all true, but it sounds like a novel. I wrote a lot about my sexual life because I thought this was what was lacking. Just little tips in there, like how much fun it is to be on top—things that would significantly change people's relationships because they would go home and try something out. Women need this frankness. The book was rejected as too risky [risqué?].

Later I found out about a free karate class by a guy named Doug, the husband of a woman in the small group. The longer I stuck with it, the stronger I got—my diet tended to become better and it helped organize my life. It was a big commitment, ten hours a week, but I liked being there with the women—it was very friendly. Doug taught it with the idea in mind that eventually the women would take over. I think he knew that even though he didn't want a hierarchy, eventually there would be one, and the women would turn on him. And he had other interests—he began to get into videotape. So, after about three eight-week sessions a number of us really knew karate, and Doug asked us to start teaching. We weren't really quite ready, but we did. That was in the fall of 1971. It was nice because of the combination of the philosophy: of women teaching other women self-defense, because we would provide a good example for them not to drop out. Also we wanted to perpetuate the philosophy that Doug had taught the course free in the hopes that we would teach others. Especially here in Berkeley, where people are so transient—so if you left in six months and went somewhere else and taught, that was fine.

I want to see one hundred million women know self-defense: all the women in America, especially the younger women, so that you can have a sort of front so that each one of them can suppress the person harassing them. Then there won't be any ambiguity at all, about which women are provoking things, which women are letting it go by, which women actually like it or claim to. But all women have to participate in a discussion about the different forms of rape—what starts it out and how the whole psychology can be destroyed.

M.C.: Do you think the situation will get very much worse before it gets better—men hassling women and the whole social setup that makes men want to oppress other people?

MARYANN: I imagine so, because of the economy. The more people suffer, the more they turn on each other—you see this in the movement all the time. We see this even in a class analysis, no matter what people believe; when they're unhappy their frustrations boil over on who's closest. Even in a relationship where there should be respect and understanding and restraint, there's often anger, violence, and betrayal. And men who lose their jobs or are afraid of losing their jobs, who are coerced in their jobs, often turn right around in a pecking order, and instead of assassinating their boss, they go out and they beat up some woman. As long as men are sexually insecure, and believe in a Christian notion of purity for the women they possess, they are going to engage in a conspiracy whereby even on the street they allow men to harass their own girlfriends, when the girlfriends go out without the men. Often single men are so disillusioned, have lost all hope of making love, so are content to take it out in wisecracks. That's a futile negative way, like children, to get love. So they get their petty kicks this way and the women rush home, relieved at the lesser of two evils: "Gee honey, I'm glad to see you, let's go out together." I don't see how to break that except by eliminating the men on the street. They can stand there, but if they open their mouths, the women should attack them—any sort of attack. I remember the precipitating incident for my first attack, which made me think I ought to get some self-defense fast, was in the spring of 1970. I was walking down the street with my boyfriend, drinking a milkshake. It was a great day and I was really feeling good. Some guys outside the Forum made a crack about me having nice tits. I turned round, took a few steps back up to them, and *wham!* I threw the milkshake all over one guy's shirt. It was great! I threw it on the wrong guy, but he had been encouraging his buddy. I said, "That doesn't matter. Now maybe you'll confront your friend and ask him why he was saying what he said to me." And I never saw those guys bothering women again.

I can't tell you what a great feeling of satisfaction it was. It was risky—I tended not to do these risky things after I knew self-defense. I tend to be more verbal and maybe just push a guy instead of such an aggressive action. Because you realize that in a fight you'll probably get hurt to some extent, even if you know self-defense—just one contact with a big fist can leave a big bruise. So the main attitude I have is to educate them. The more self-defense you know, the more restrained you tend to be: you understand where it's coming from and try to respond in a mature fashion. If the guy is still really abusive, I try to call a crowd around me so they can witness what is going on. Usually, in the last year or two, there has been social pressure. People will side with the woman. There'll be men from men's liberation who'll try to deal with the brother and women will be willing to help you. So in the daytime when someone harasses you, you can actually utilize it to make it an educational situation. At night it's completely different: it's really difficult to rally support, so you're really on your own. I would advocate avoiding going out by oneself on foot almost at all costs. I think that women have to develop the attitude that they're good enough to have a car, even if it's a used hundred-dollar one, even if they have to go to Movement Motors and learn to work on it themselves—God forbid!—some form of transportation. My motorcycle was under a hundred dollars, it's two and a half years old, and I just have to be careful getting off and on and where I park it. If I didn't have it, I would have a car and a big dog. Women should also not live on ground floors—almost all rapes in houses occur on the ground floor.

M.C.: Do you think the women's movement can succeed, given the nature of women's problems, their social and economic backgrounds?

MARYANN: Unfortunately, most women still have children, and once they have a kid, they must be deaf, dumb, and blind if they are relatively poor and don't feel terrifically oppressed by having that child. I think it will need the biggest political movement anyone can imagine to just get child care, a basic demand. I'm shocked that so little headway has been made on child care, such intransigence by the government. The big movement will form because the counterrevolution against women's rights is already mobilizing, like the antiabortion thing: abortions are so important, yet people are mobilizing against it. It shows that even though women tend to be natural anarchists, and don't perpetuate forms because they tend to become boring, they have power problems and even seem ineffective because of the tremendous outlay of energy. We'll all be forced to support whatever umbrella organization comes out. And there's no reason to think other women wouldn't betray us. There was a great deal of concern some years ago whether the exceptional women would continue or betray us. Will there be prison guards in the women's movement?

M.C.: Do you think there's already too much elitism in the movement?

MARYANN: No, I tend to think elitist women tend to work in the male movement. Like, my first reaction of it being irrelevant when I was a sexist, they tend to denounce the women's movement and weed themselves out . . . which is fine. I'm not sure where the women's movement is: I think it's on the lips of most white women in households. People like my mother have gone even further in making jokes about it. They treat it more seriously than ecology; they begin to incorporate it into their lives a little. They begin to nudge their husbands to do a little more work. They begin to just feel better. The women's movement has contributed to a large number of women in their fifties no longer suffering from the menopausal feeling that their life is over. They actually have a new lease on life. They even take off their makeup; they get a more natural look, they let their hair grow long or they wear it in a shag; they get a more androgynous look and this makes them bloom again. It stimulates them, and they can feel closer to their daughters too. I think it's very important to cater to all the different types of women, women that aren't young. I think the black women are coming to terms with it a little. At certain conferences you go to you do find black women who get up who do endorse women's liberation, and I think that within five or ten years, for their own survival, they'll have to get with it a little more and rebuke their men, that kind of thing.

M.C.: How do you see the women's movement within the framework of radical politics?

MARYANN: Well, I think it's revitalized radical politics by stimulating a very strong men's movement. I think that Weathermen started in around us, following 1970, right about when I withdrew from the heterosexual movement. I think that the [anti-war] movement began to get destroyed by Weathermen, people from upper-class backgrounds, men and women, who came into the movement with the idea of emulating other revolutionary struggles, misinterpreting them, wanting to be macho to prove themselves, to go underground, wanting to do violence to sacrifice mass organization with the attitude that workers were pigs. I think that they effectively, along with police infiltration, destroyed the movement. Nobody wanted the old movement. I don't blame them. Many were disillusioned because the women had left it and had valid criticisms. And so the white male identity began to decompose, and this was a good thing. The white male identity has to be destroyed all over. Actually the women's movement helped the male identity to crumble, and from the ashes of that crumbled male identity, they began to get together in small groups and see that they were being so competitive toward each other and being so hate-filled that they couldn't have a decent movement, that there were little kingdoms. Berkeley was divided into little kingdoms, each run by a different male with his little coterie of women and weaker, smaller guys. One big movement guy and a bunch of smaller guys doing his work. It wasn't good. The "gay" movement also helped to challenge that identity and say, "Men, you'd better at least learn to face each other, to explore each other's sexuality, to get an idea of what it's about, to reform yourselves."

M.C.: Do you think the hope for the movement is in young women? Or do you think that more and more older women will be drawn in eventually?

MARYANN: Well, I guess older women who get divorced—and, like, three out of five people do get divorced—their economics are such that they tend to become more militant. They have to—they're fighting for their children, they become the head of the household. Now, I think in situations where women are not the head of the household, they don't really become militant. Like my mother—she's not really fighting sexism on her job, although she might be aware of the sexism. Her responses have always been very overtly the responses of an oppressed person: she comes home with migraine headaches. I don't see her changing that. So again, some older women will; but some won't, they'll just be timid about it. Now the thing is that young women are already ruined by the time they are fifteen. They are socialized and timid, they're still going through the ritual of dressing up or seeking male approval. This is the most corrosive element. Puberty is the time that has to be focused on. I don't see most women as being any different at all, even if they're hippie young women. I happen to know a lot of young people, say from about ten to sixteen or seventeen, and I don't see them as liberated at all. They get knocked up, they cater to men, they dress up for approval, they're not inner-directed. Maybe they're just young.

M.C.: You don't think that they gain from our experiences at all, at least to the extent that they're aware of problems as we were when we were in high school or junior high school?

MARYANN: They're a little more aggressive in dealing with things; they're quicker to say "Fuck you." They're able to reject. The secret of preserving one's own identity in the face of sexism is to reject the person who is delivering the sexism. If you can reject that person, then you have turned the approval game around: "I don't need your approval; now you'd better start seeking mine." So unfortunately women still exhibit submission gestures instead of fighting at those times, sort of insisting that they don't be called "chicks." So what I would like to see is to have self-defense taught to women in the secondary schools, before they drop out of school, because once you go through these militant body attitudes, you do incorporate something into your personality. That's what's really needed. I would really like to see a heavy women's consciousness program starting around sixth or seventh grade, where they would think about what they wanted to call themselves: do they want to call themselves "women" or "girls," this kind of thing.

M.C.: Do you think that women have any innate qualities to offer politics?

MARYANN: Yeah, I think women are much less likely to continue the pretensions in much of modern politics. I think that again and again you find women want to get down to brass tacks, and they do want to be democratic about things. They don't want to just go on talking for the sake of talking. They are action-oriented. They're not crazy about backroom politics; it's a male form. So I think that's a good source of hope. However, oftentimes if you go to work within something thinking that you're going to change it, it's actually stronger in the long run, and it will assimilate *you.* I think that will probably happen to women in politics—that the types who will stay in will be types who are more like male politicians.

M.C.: Does that mean then that you're not really optimistic about the possibility of change in the long run?

MARYANN: No, I think that they'll have the right line. It will be some change, but not the real fundamental *feminist* change that we'd like. In other words, the substance of things, the demands will be the literal correct demands, but these women's methods will be traditional methods, and they will have the traditional ego problems. Or in other words, women like Betty Friedan, Bella Abzug, Shirley Chisholm, Gloria Steinem are ambitious. There's nothing wrong with being ambitious per se. It's just that they're going to end up furthering their own careers, you know. They're going to fight for women, but the American political system forces them to concentrate on their own careers. Any time they're working together in a coalition, that's really good. That shows that they're willing to sacrifice some of that egoism.

M.C.: How do you see personal relationships changing in the next ten years?

MARYANN: Well, I think that right now you have a phenomenon similar to what happened ten years ago in the black ghettos. Most women can find some kind of part-time gig, but the men can't find any kind of work at all, so there are so many situations where the women are supporting the men. It's a pretty demoralizing situation. It is hard to be the head of the household. What happens is that women end up feeling the same oppressions that men used to feel—feeling sterile, feeling alienated from their spouse, feeling that the spouse is getting dull or something, feeling that they're drifting apart. And the spouse begins to feel sexually insecure, feels that woman is getting all sorts of male approval out in the world, but that he himself is becoming isolated the way women used to feel isolated in the house and would go out and have an affair or whatever. When the men want to have an affair, it's just that much more difficult because of the conventional nature, the fact that women are not yet nearly as aggressive sexually as they must become to have equality. The women have to become sexual equals. Otherwise there is less sexual contact than there should be, and everybody suffers. That's one of the big things that has to change. Especially as women earn a little more income, as they get cars, there's no reason why they can't invent new social forms and be much more direct, in taking men out for coffee, in bringing them home if they want to, in expressing affection, not forcing the men to go through some ritual. I think that's really important. As a Jewish person I actually feel a little isolated, like from the working class. People who are from some sort of Christian background, they've got a little more sexual repression. The Jewish women are usually a little more sexually liberated. They don't have guilt about sex because they've never had a Virgin Mary-image setup. You find that in general more Christian women have never had orgasms, and this is a very important part of feeling that you deserve to have something in life, getting some sexual pleasure, you know. So we recommend that they just read about it and learn how to masturbate. Again this is the whole thing of finding one's voice. They can't tell the men what they like sexually, and therefore the men can't give it because the men are very ignorant. And I really think it's up to women to lead the men sexually, so first they have to find out what gives them pleasure, and so this where understanding your own body will become a liberating thing. The shame has to be taken away. People have to spend all that time being nude with the lights on, taking baths together, giving each other massages, doing sensual things. Wherever the movement concentrates on that, I think it's a good movement. Where the movement just talks about strict political issues, I find it very dull. Like I found that one of the best experiences in this small group is when we all took off our clothes and sat nude, and saw the differences in each body, how much diversity there is in bodies, breaking down that standardization. That really did break down the competition between women. Like for me, the nicest thing about the women's movement has been just being able to *like* women, probably for the first time, en masse. I think I really did have problems in resenting women before, being jealous of them, being afraid they were going to take away my man, and do things behind my back. And really that's all gone. Mostly, I guess what it is is that I no longer feel insecure, I feel like a woman amongst women, and this is beautiful, because it was a bitterness before, and it's drained from me. It just affects your whole life. If you're spending a lot of time on negative energy, resenting women or having paranoid suspicions—and I think I was paranoid, definitely—that's no good, you're really isolated. You are forced to depend much too much on men for approval, and if you're without men, you don't think of turning to women, so that you're just out in a limbo. Well, for me, that limbo has been eliminated.

M.C.: How do you see the family structure changing?

MARYANN: Well, I'd like to see the family totally abolished. I think that it's just a sin for children to live with parents under any circumstances at all. In every instance children have a counterrevolutionary effect on the parents. It's very oppressive to the parents, it's very oppressive to the children.

M.C.: Well, who's going to raise kids if parents don't?

MARYANN: Well, I think that they should be in child-care centers, and that all adults and older children should rotate taking care of them. People should get paid to go in there once a month, something like that, and take a turn. I wouldn't mind that. Like I'm not going to have children, but I'd like to do my part, I like children. But I also don't like getting them on a one-to-one level. It's just like you're a parent, it becomes just as oppressive within five minutes. But if I could go into an enjoyable environment and teach a few of them at a time whatever skill I possess, relate to them that way, I think it would be the absence of neurosis. And I've had a chance to think about the differences in children who leave their parents at an early age and children who stay. Now I left my parents when I was fifteen, and I think this is one of the biggest factors in my personality, why I'm a freer person, why I'm not married, why I don't have children. I was able to start creating an identity of my own away from their cautious concern and their projection of values. I mean, I love my parents—I'm hung up on my parents, my parents write to me more regularly than anybody else.

This is again especially the Jewish family, the children are wedded to the Jewish family in a way that even your own boyfriends and girlfriends become insignificant. When my boyfriend and I went to see my parents, they didn't really accept him. Now, you see, if they hadn't raised me. . . . But they never even really accepted my *Jewish* boyfriends. It was always "We make exceptions for our children," and everybody else gets judged as dirty hippies. Now this is just a source of constant bitterness, because if they try to divide me from my friends, I have to choose between them. You never can outrun that guilt: you're a child, you owe your life to your parents, they gave you life, they spent the money on you. Like you're supposed to lay down your life for them.

M.C.: Do you see the institution of marriage continuing if parents don't keep their children? Or do you think that's going to be abolished, too?

MARYANN: I hope it's abolished. I mean, the fact of women taking on a different name is so ridiculous, taking on the name of the person that they live with, becoming chattel. Women have to notice the freedoms that they have in being single before they're married. But the nuclear family is the source of the lack of freedom. It's also the cornerstone of America. And when you hear Nixon expressing that, you know it's gotta go. People aren't free when they have to come back to that family, when they slave for that family. That makes them conservative, you know, when they have to make the payments on their houses. A really free people would be people who could rely on all elements of the community to help them as they get older instead of feeling that they have to rely on this one monogamous unit, even as an economic unit too. That's why it still is perpetuated, people need it to survive right now, and I want to see alternate forms of survival. But I'm against communes, because I think that they tend to lead to elimination of a mass movement. Because if they solve the people's needs, they tend to become inactive, they stay in their commune, they have a good time, they have twelve friends, they pool their resources.

M.C.: How do you see education changing?

MARYANN: Well, I think schools have to be abolished also. I think that cable TV and TV and the use of computers can make home learning a possibility for everyone. I think it's also desirable because it's more in the spirit of true learning, going at your own pace, doing it in a pleasant environment where you can turn on.

M.C.: Doesn't it bother you that there will be fewer personal contacts that way?

MARYANN: I haven't noticed much personal contact now, and I'm not really crazy about having personal contact with those teachers. No, I wouldn't miss going up to the campus at all. I think there's too many people there, it promotes schizophrenia. The ideal group is ten people, so you might want to supplement home learning with getting the children into group processes where they learn democracy. But as it is now, where the teacher is with thirty kids, that's not democracy, that's fascism. In fact, there have been studies done of psychiatric residents, and they learn better from television because there is an invariable antiauthoritarian response to any person standing up there if you're there in person. I know I have that in all cases. I probably would have even if there were a woman up there too. You know, you just don't like somebody dominating.

As Maryann and Sally point out, many women of high-school age are more concerned with liberating themselves from their parents and the pressures of adolescence than they are from male dominance and restricting stereotypes of a woman's role in a man's world. The contradictions and confusion that emerge in the following discussion with 16-year-old Debbie suggest that although young people seem to take freedom and change quite for granted, they are caught short by the lack of opportunity to exercise their freedom in constructive ways, especially in small towns like the ones where Debbie has lived. Since the only apparent alternatives to doing what one's parents expect are self-destructive pastimes like taking drugs or drinking, traditional solutions (marriage and child-rearing as an escape from boring education and employment) eventually regain some appeal as a way to combine independence and security.

E.C.: How would you describe the major changes that you've gone through in the last three to four years?

DEBBIE: In moving from school to school, I changed a lot. Going from a little community to a bigger school, I changed for the better in the way I thought about things. I had a wider view of things, I took more things in and considered more, but yet I went down a lot because I started taking drugs and drinking and skipping and doing a lot of things I shouldn't. Then I moved on to another school and things are better right now than they ever were before. I don't take drugs. I do smoke pot when I can. I drink now and then. I don't skip school, my grades are pretty good. But I still haven't changed my ideas; I'm just sort of maintaining for a while.

There are good and bad people, and it was the bad people who made me change. I started to smoke dope and drink. That caused problems at home with my parents. My mother couldn't handle it to the point where she was becoming a total wreck. I'd made my dad a total wreck when he came home on weekends. So last summer I decided to go spend a couple of weeks with my brother. I found what I wanted there. I could do whatever I wanted, I could go wherever I wanted—with limitations. But I couldn't do it here, where I was always having pressures and pressuring other people. I didn't find one person at the high school I went to before that was totally straight. Everybody either smoked or drank or did something. I found myself skipping classes and skipping school with my closest friends, getting in trouble, and my grades weren't good. I'd go out real late on Fridays and Saturdays and not come back until the next morning. They weren't bad influences—I helped. I went right along with everything they did. I don't know how to describe it, good or bad. They just sat around all day smoking pot and dropping acid, the way kids are doing now. I don't think many kids care about school now, except for the kids that don't do that. They pull through with passing grades. Everybody was constantly stoned or drunk at school. One of the main reasons is that they're rebelling against their parents. The only way they can do it is by drugs, by drinking, skipping school, dropping out, running away.

E.C.: Do you think this generation gap is partially a result of parents not considering their kids as responsible as the kids do?

DEBBIE: Yeah. Kids don't think they're getting enough credit. Kids think they're big and can take anything that you dish out to them, but you can tell underneath they're really scared and don't want to go out by themselves and take on all those problems. The result is that they finally are aware of this and go home to their parents because they know they're not ready to go out on their own. They're really not ready for anything. Like living with my brother and his wife—they give me a lot of responsibility and put a lot of trust in me. For the first few minutes I wasn't sure if I could handle it, because it was pretty big. Their letting me do almost anything I wanted was a lot of responsibility for me because I can't break their trust, and I can't break what they've put up for me. But there is definitely a gap between kids and their parents. Things happen to kids that they don't tell their parents. There are some things no one knows about me. That upsets parents because they want to know everything about what happens to their kids, but they just wouldn't understand some of the things that happen. I have more trouble when my parents try to find out what I'm doing. I want to be myself and I don't want anyone to bother me about what happens in my life.

E.C.: What kind of rewards do you get from drugs?

DEBBIE: Actually none at all. When I get upset and smoke or something, I feel good and have visions and I'm really happy, but afterwards I'm depressed and come back down again. The kids I know who have talked to me about drugs take mescalin and acid. They just love it—they touch and see things, not even being themselves. Most of them sell it or push it, some grow it. They get a lot out of it, I guess. I don't know if they're just putting people on or if they really do enjoy it.

E.C.: Do you think the relationships among your friends are any different from, say, your parents' thirty years ago?

DEBBIE: Yeah. Definitely they're different. The drinking has something to do with it. Kids go out, get drunk, and make it in somebody's bed or the back of a car—that goes on all the time, every day you hear about somebody. Everybody accepts it because everybody's doing it or at least has tried it . . . you don't criticize, you just take it for granted and don't think anything of it. From what I know our parents didn't do that, though I have had girlfriends say that their mothers got around a lot.

E.C.: Why do you think things are freer now?

DEBBIE: People are just moving on to other things. Everything is coming at us at a fast pace: dresses are changing, clothes, hairdos, drugs, alcohol. Everything is changing at once, people are going into different fields.

E.C.: What kinds of things give you the most pleasure now?

DEBBIE: Being with people I like, having a lot of fun. Not getting in anything involved, like whenever you go out, you have to have a drink or you have to smoke—just having fun. I like being with a lot of people. I hate basketball games, but I go because there are lots of people, all free and at ease. You be yourself, whatever you want.

E.C.: Do you think there's a big difference between your attitudes and your older sister's?

DEBBIE: Nope. Well, yeah, she's been around a lot longer than I have. I'm still a dumpy little kid. She cares more about politics—I'm really not interested in that.

E.C.: What's the most common form of birth control used by girls at your school? The Pill? Would you say that most girls are on the Pill?

DEBBIE: Oh, sixty percent, I'd say, of what I know. I'd say they start taking it when they are fourteen or fifteen probably. My brother's daughter comes home and tells me about kids that are making it at twelve and thirteen. And that kind of upsets you. Because, like, *I'm* young, I'm sixteen, but they're *really* young, looking back. But mostly I'd say they get the Pill at fourteen and fifteen and start doing things to need it. I've heard of girls going out and just seducing guys —ripping them off. Of course, the guys don't care and do it right back, but most of the girls go right along with it. If a guy makes a move, they'll let him, unless they're really really up on their reputation at school or something.

E.C.: Do girls talk much about marriage?

DEBBIE: No. If they do, they say, "I'm not ready for it for a long time" and "How can anybody settle down with one man?" They just don't want to get married. A couple of girls are thinking about it because they've been going with a guy for two years or something and know it's serious.

E.C.: How do you feel personally about that?

DEBBIE: It's not for me. For one thing, I want to go to college. My life is just ahead of me and there are a lot of things I haven't done—I want to travel, meet people, do interesting things. And if I get married, it'll put me down. Most of the kids I know don't have any plans to go to college, because they don't want to go to school another four or five years. And when I say, "You have to have a college education, or you'll just get the little things and won't get any of the good jobs," they say, "Well, if I get married I'm not going to have a job anyway. I'll have kids and I don't want to work."

E.C.: Do you think there are certain jobs within a marriage, like child-raising, doing dishes, cleaning house, bringing home money, fixing cars that should be allocated to one person or the other? Men's jobs or women's jobs?

DEBBIE: No. I think that if a woman wants to do the things a man does, that's fine, she ought to do it. Though if a woman does have children, she ought to stay at home and raise them, at least till they're nine or ten or in school or something. Those are the years its personality grows and it shouldn't be jeopardized. A child should have all the attention it needs.

E.C.: Are women better at raising children than men?

DEBBIE: I wouldn't know. I guess there must be some men around that would be a lot better; I can't think of any.

E.C.: Would you think that in your marriage the major share of child-rearing would fall to you rather than your husband?

DEBBIE: Yes. I definitely do. The husband's got to make a living, and I would think that my whole time would be for the child and to the house. When he came home, he'd be the center of it, and he'd have a lot of time for the child. But in the daytime, he should be working and the woman should be at home with her kids.

E.C.: Do you expect marriage to be like your parents' relationship, or are there some changes you'd make?

DEBBIE: I don't think I would want the kind of relationship my mom and dad have. My dad is so set in his ways, and I wouldn't want my husband not to take into consideration things I wanted or wanted to do. I'd want to marry a guy that's gentle and kind and would give the loving. But what comes along with marriage is fighting, and I would want a lot of fun and to be happy.

E.C.: Do you think that things will be substantially different in fifteen years? Let's say you get married at about twenty-five. Do you think your marriage will be different because of the rapidity of social and technological change?

DEBBIE: Yeah, it will be different. I have visions of everything being electric, everything being in the walls. When I'm thirty and have a child, it will just be double what it is now. Younger people are getting pregnant younger—like nine- and ten-year-olds are getting pregnant now, so I don't know what it will be like then.

E.C.: Do you think things will be better for the housewife in fifteen years?

DEBBIE: Yeah, it will be easier. Everything will be automatic. But things will be more expensive. I don't know what it's going to be like in the future.

E.C.: If everything is automatic, you'd have more time to spend on things other than housework, right? How do you think you might spend that time?

DEBBIE: Oh, I don't know. Just doing things that women do, like go out and date, have social gatherings and parties. I really like to entertain. You'd go more places, do more things.

E.C.: If machines get into every other area of the house, do you think that machines will be involved in sex?

DEBBIE: I don't think sex will change that much. Everybody now is trying for a new way in their sex life. I don't think they'll get anywhere—everything has been tried now. Now you can plant sperm in woman so she can have a baby if she couldn't otherwise. I'm sure that scientists will come up with something different, but I don't think the basic sex life will be different.

E.C.: Do you think that group sex and group marriages will be big in the future?

DEBBIE: I definitely think group sex will be as big as it is now. People are living with each other in communes and stuff and having sex with everyone in the household.

E.C.: Can you see yourself ever involved in group sex?

DEBBIE: No. I don't think that's right. If you are going to have sex with someone, it should be someone you care about deeply. I just couldn't have that many feelings to have sex with six or seven people.

E.C.: How do your friends feel about it?

DEBBIE: I don't think they approve of it. A lot of them don't even approve of sex between just two people, even though they do it themselves.

E.C.: What do you see as the future for nudity?

DEBBIE: It's big, and it probably will continue to be. In 1985 there will be space outfits and hardly any clothing at all. Right now people go around at home with nothing on. Eventually I think that people will walk around outside and not care.

E.C.: Do your friends ever have parties where everyone is nude?

DEBBIE: No, never. That would get into the group sex thing.

E.C.: What other changes do you expect in 1985? What will the world be like then?

DEBBIE: Screwed up more than it is now.

E.C.: In what ways?

DEBBIE: Politically, everything is changing. Things are changing sexually. People will be more free in years to come. People are moving around more and trying different things.

E.C.: Do you have an image of what Portland will look like in 1985?

DEBBIE: Supercity—just huge, like Los Angeles. There will be more people, freeways, smog, polluted rivers.

E.C.: Where do you think you'll be in 1985?

DEBBIE: I'm going to try to be in the country, if there's any more country. Everyone is moving from the cities now. I want to be somewhere where I can be partially alone, where I can do the things I want without lots of people around.

E.C.: Do you think we're going to be able to solve our problems as we go along, or are things going to come to a head and start deteriorating?

DEBBIE: Yeah, I think everything will come to a head at once. We'll have a big mess. More people will die from diseases and things. There will be so many of us that people will just start dying. Population is the thing, also water supply.

E.C.: When do you think this catastrophe might start to happen?

DEBBIE: Probably close to 2000.

E.C.: Does that affect your ideas about childraising?

DEBBIE: Yeah, it really does, because you've got to take into consideration that we're already overpopulated now. Anyone or any family that doesn't want a child shouldn't have it. I don't think families should have more than two or three kids—they can get their happiness from just a few kids instead of a whole bunch.

E.C.: Are there special things you'd teach your kids so they could handle this catastrophe?

DEBBIE: Yeah, I'd just play it along. I wouldn't know how to go about raising a child, but I'd just teach them the good things in life so they'd be good people. With the way things and kids are changing now, I'd have to look and see how kids are then and take it from there.

Abigail, 23, has found that the best-organized women's groups often defeat their original purpose when they become rigidified and self-serving. Since feminism is predicated on choice and growth, the process of consciousness-raising may involve outgrowing one group after another in order to find individual solutions to changing problems. Abigail "resigned from women's liberation" after realizing that NOW and campus women's groups at UCLA did not suit her concept of feminism. Nonetheless, she still considers herself an ardent feminist, and she is currently working part-time at Everywoman, a combined women's center and feminist bookstore in Los Angeles which also publishes a women's paper called Everywoman *and has just started the first feminist book club.*

M.C.: What made you look into feminism?

ABIGAIL: When I was at UCLA, I was very unhappy. All my friends were getting married and having children and I really did not want to get married until I was at least thirty. Then I would go home and my father worried about whether I would lose my virginity or what he would do with a thirty-year-old unmarried daughter and all the other worries that society pushes on you. At that time, I wanted to go ahead and get a Ph.D. because I thought that that much education would enable me to survive without a man, at least until I found the right man. I guess my idea was eventually to get married but not right away. I had never had much contact with professional women because I came from a poor immigrant background, but it made me really angry when people would tell me that when Mr. Right came along I would give up my studies. I knew I had a problem and I found out that National Organization for Women existed and that it was composed mostly of professional women. I wanted to find out what their problems were both professionally and personally, so I joined. I was a somewhat inactive member, just going to occasional meetings, but I learned that this was not what I wanted. My aim then was not just to hang up my own shingle. I wanted to be superfeminine and supersuccessful, a superwoman.

The problem with professional women is that they are still emulating the male style. Many of the women in NOW, for example, rented their own luxury apartment, bought their own Cadillac, and hired their own secretaries. I personally feel that many of the women in the power structure of NOW are more interested in their own political gain than in women. NOW has done some very effective things—abortion legislation, child-care centers. And those women work their rears off, they put all their money into it, they work until twelve at night. Although I am down on NOW as a political organization, on individual projects they have been great. I am not with them now because I just was not interested in demonstrating.

Another big problem in NOW, and in the movement in general, concerns class differences. It is very easy for a middle-class woman to understand the oppression of a poor woman, but it is very difficult for a poor woman to understand the oppression of a middle-class woman. It is very difficult for a poor black woman or a poor woman from Appalachia to understand that the middle-class woman who lives in a fifty-thousand-dollar home, who has her hair done once a week, who has an outstanding wardrobe is also oppressed, that she is living in a gold cage instead of an iron one. Many poor women are alienated from middle-class women because of this. There is also the problem of intimidation. The middle-class women are generally more highly educated, more articulate, more poised, and in general have the advantages the society admires. Although *we* don't value these advantages, they are initially an alienation point for the poor women. The latter have a feeling of inadequacy. They are accustomed to kowtow to the former, who are accustomed to push. It is hard to find an equalization.

I personally have resigned from the women's liberation movement.

M.C.: Why did you resign?

ABIGAIL: I feel that the general impetus of the movement is very negative in that there is a tendency to deal with the individual situation in such a general way, *i.e.,* the oppression of women in dealing with all women, that they are not really dealing with individual problems and their needs. For example, a woman who, after ten years of marriage, suddenly becomes a feminist does not want to get divorced. She wants to work out that problem with her husband. She is put down by the group because she is just a housewife.

There is an extreme stress on conformity. I hate conformity in the system and I hate it here at *Everywoman.* I went to certain groups at

UCLA, and they all looked the same. Everyone had the same jeans on, the same boots, the same long hair, and the same shirt. I used to sit there and say to myself that this is not what I want. This to me is not feminism. Everything is dealt with with a rhetoric. "I don't feel good about my relationship with a man." "Well, you're male-defined. What you really need is approval." This is not the real thing.

I am technically no longer part of the women's liberation movement but I am part of *Everywoman.* We are not interested in producing a great paper in terms of literary achievement, with great layout, with incredible photography, so that everyone will say what a fantastic paper this is in terms of quality. We *are* interested in that, but we are more interested in how we get the quality. If we have to sacrifice individual right, if we have to put down another person, if we have to get a certain layout by having meetings and political intrigue, then we don't give a damn. *New Women*, for example, has a hell of a good layout but they are trying still to sell: "Women, be ultrafeminine. Go out and get your hair done. Have your own secretary and have fourteen lovers." And that's called women's liberation!

M.C.: How has working for *Everywoman* changed your life?

ABIGAIL: First of all, through the movement and through NOW as well I have met a lot of women for whom I have respect, even if I do not agree with them, because they are fighting. I have seen a lot of goodness, a lot of commitment and a lot of struggle, which I have tried to emulate. I was about nineteen when I joined the movement, and I am twenty-two now. I think I have acquired a much greater feeling of self because I know now that I can make it without a man. That is not an antimale statement, but I do not have to have a man around me to have a feeling of worth. I think I am able to stand up against male intimidation much better than I could before, and the reason for that is because I saw other women doing this, women who were older than I was. Sometimes you feel as though you were the only "weirdy," the only woman who does not want to get married and have three kids. And then, when you join the movement, you realize there are a lot of women like you. It really is an encouraging kind of feeling. Of course, you must watch out for this tendency to use group support as a crutch—your self only comes out in the group and you fall apart the rest of the time. You have to learn to incorporate this into everything you do. I feel that I have become a stronger human being because I got involved in issues that deal with my own personal feelings. You have to learn to stand up for what you believe in, and that is a very tough order.

M.C.: What are your goals now?

ABIGAIL: I don't have any goals now. I don't think about the future much. When I got out of college, I went into the business world, where I was discriminated against and yet was not able to identify myself as a feminist for fear of getting fired. I saw women dying on the vine, hitting a typewriter with a master's degree. It drove me out of my mind, almost to the verge of suicide, and this was even after I had joined the movement. I can understand wanting to get married after working in the business world, working very hard and not being compensated, dead-ending month after month. You say, "I've got to get married, because at least I don't have to get up every day and face work."

M.C.: But you've got to get up and face the laundry.

ABIGAIL: Right, but right now, to be perfectly honest—and you're hearing this from an ardent feminist—I would rather get up to face the Kellogg's cornflakes than face the shit of that job. I would still have some time to myself, which is not true on a job. Housewives have a tremendous amount of power when they're supported by their husbands, because then they're free to come do their work at *Everywoman* without worrying about the money. On the other hand, this is oppressive to the male too. It would be ideal to have both work if they like their jobs.

M.C.: Do you see the possibility of change in the business world too, so that being a female executive may not be such a horrible thing?

ABIGAIL: Any company in which there is hierarchy or titles is going to be corrupt. Even if I am just sitting at my desk, a maid, a female maid, came in the night before and cleaned off my desk so that I can work at it. Some receptionist answered the phone for me to get the call through. Someone took a meager salary and did a lot of shitwork so that I could make a lot of money. Therefore, I could not be committed to companies like that.

M.C.: What kind of change do you foresee? Do you think that there will be change so that everyone will participate on a rotation basis?

ABIGAIL: Yes. I think that there will be a tendency to do that more and more in the system. The first thing that I think will happen is that there is going to be a desexualization of society, and this is the now. Some people think that once fifty percent of the working force is comprised of women, there will be a change, but I don't believe that this kind of osmosis is going to occur. In order to reach that level women will have to compromise. Business will change only when women have had a chance to prove themselves first by setting up their own, successful, feminist corporations, making the existing system obsolete. Then the companies are going to have to have training programs. They are going to have to insist upon competency rather than on a pretty face, and that will take time and money. Eventually it will maximize their profits, but they must be willing to lose money temporarily.

Ron enjoys fantasying about the future and foresees a world of strange machines, asphalt-paved oceans, and people who aren't afraid to try anything. Contrary to his final statement, he is a 29-year-old industrial engineer with a penchant for very old clothes.

RON: This is about Sylvia Plath. It's in *Life* [November 12, 1971] and it says:

"*The Bell Jar* is a major text for women's liberation. Writing in the early '60s about the cosseted, conventional '50s, Sylvia seems like a kind of naïve prophet who knew instinctively what Kate Millett had to write a doctoral dissertation to discover. All the characters—most of them remorselessly lampooned—try to force Esther into a subservient role. Buddy and her mother assure her that if she has sex before marriage to a "clean" boy, she will be lost beyond redemption. In those pre-Pill days she believes them, but at the price of furious resentment. Though the book is written in an offhand, often funny style, an undertow of implacable demand and unappeasable anger moves just below the surface."

That makes me think about what it was like for me during the pre-Pill days. I became aware that a lot of people were working on the Pill, it was going to happen, and sexual freedom was going to reign. Now that it's here and realized, I don't think that I'm as much impressed with it as before. There's what's known as the "epidemic," an epidemic of venereal disease. It obviously has been encouraged by the fact that making love to people doesn't represent the threat of pregnancy, so that there are many fewer inhibitions and a lot more communication of disease. I was talking to a girl who used to work at a free clinic, and most of the cases they treated were for venereal disease. To me, one problem has replaced another.

M.C.: Do you think that kids in high school now, who are benefiting from a more open attitude toward sex—premarital, marital, or extramarital—are going to have fewer inhibitions about sex? Or will sex always retain the aura of the untried, the unknown, another novelty?

RON: It's universal. To me it's like the sun coming up in the morning—the same problems are going to happen a million years from now.

M.C.: Then you don't think that it's going to make any difference if kids know more about sex before they try it themselves?

RON: No. As a matter of fact, if you wind the clock to the time when *1984* was written, they had the "feelies" in *1984*. Orwell knew that nervous synapses have to do with electrochemical change in the body, and electrochemical changes can be simulated in the laboratory. It's possible to hallucinate with artificial drugs like LSD, and it's possible theoretically to recreate an entire sexual experience electronically and electrochemically. It might be possible to take all thirteen-year-old kids into a laboratory, apply the electrodes, and they would all have these fantastic orgasms. But I don't think that that would take the place of Saturday at the movies as the most innocent stage of sex. It just isn't the same thing. You can't relate to a machine. Even if by some miracle of technology you get some emotions plugged into it, it's going to be like listening to a phonograph record—it's just delightful listening to a record, but there is no mistaking that and being at the concert.

M.C.: But do you think this kind of mechanical masturbation could have some kind of therapeutic value for people who for one reason or another don't have access to the real thing?

RON: I think it's very valuable. It will create an entire new industry, for example. There will be the General Motors of Masturbation, Chrysler Masturbation, American Masturbation, fortunes will be made, the French will be jealous as hell, the United States's technology will again sweep the world, the Japanese won't have a thing on us.

M.C.: No, but they'll try hard to imitate us. Can you imagine that this would be used instead of group therapy for businessmen to get over their personal hangups?

RON: Yeah. I think all kinds of tools will be invented in the future, no matter what kind you're talking about. Somehow pencils are going to be different two thousand years from now, and it will be more fun to write with pencils than it is now. I don't think you'll get "feelies" from a pencil, but I just think everything is going to continue to get better. You can't imagine it now, how the light bulb and the clock will be better.

M.C.: Do you think people are going to continue to want a better and better light bulb and clock or whatever?

RON: Yeah—they always have.

M.C.: What about what's happening now with the hippie groups, rejection of technology and material values?

Ron: They want better and better health foods. The health food industry is going to develop into a big thing. Right now Orowheat is making delicious bread. A couple of years ago you couldn't even buy bread like that, but now I buy it at the supermarket. That's a good thing that has developed. Is it going to stay good? Yes, because people want it that way. There is more Orowheat bread on the shelves now than six months ago, and maybe Wonder Bread will be wiped off the earth—I hope it is, and I think it will be, because people like Orowheat better. There is a constant desire for improvement. At the time when Wonder Bread makes its resurgence twenty years from now, it will be regarded as an improvement over that nasty old health food bread that doesn't melt in your mouth—you have to chew it. People will probably go through a phase where they decide that they don't like chewing any more. You can't restrict change.

M.C.: Do you think that man himself is going to change, or that just the things he creates will change?

Ron: I don't think the fundamental man will change. I think the emphasis will become different, just the way the emphasis has switched from Wonder Bread to the new kind of bread, which is really only the old kind of bread. People will change their attitudes, and it won't be as necessary to fight territorial wars as it used to be. It won't be as necessary to conquer technological barriers as it once was. I imagine that the intensity of the Industrial Revolution has abated, at least in the United States, Japan, and some other highly industrialized countries. Chances are there'll be new communities. But I just think that the new ones won't be that different, they aren't going to be revolutionary. Hippie communities now are no different from "bohemian" groups. I used to hear this term "bohemian life," but I didn't know what it meant, except that they did it in Paris. People who weren't married lived with each other, they cooked funny food, they were artists, but fundamentally there was no difference between them and the hippies today. It's leaping from one escape to another. It's like people wanting to go back to the land. They've never been to the country in their lives, so what do they do when they get there—escape. Not that there's anything wrong with escaping from prison to the country and living fruitfully there. But you can't let yourself get caught again.

M.C.: What happens to the girl who grows up in a sexist society? Do you think there is any parallel with the hippie who grows up in the city who wants to escape?

Ron: Yeah. If I know what you mean, which is that women grow up in a society that forces them into things that they wouldn't naturally want to be in and then suddenly they realize that they want to get away from that. Yes, I think that's perfectly natural. They should get away from their restrictions and find out what life is really like. I have no quarrel with that, except that I hope that they don't beat down somebody else in finding out what life is like. I feel the same way about hippies: there is no reason why you should want to kill your parents. You don't have to kill them—all you have to do is go away. The same thing is true about women in a sexist society—you don't actually have to tear it all down. Something that comes to mind is that if you really want to tear down society, you'd have women's lib, gay lib, and all the others plugging *for* the nuclear holocaust instead of against it.

M.C.: Do you think that the goal of women's liberation is to destroy society?

Ron: No. I just think that there are a lot of sensibilities that have to be dealt with. Sexist society didn't develop just because of somebody's evil plot. It has to do with immutable human emotions and psychological requirements. Men have to have a certain feeling about the women that they are with and women have to have a feeling about men.

M.C.: They *have* to?

Ron: I think so. I'm talking about on a societal level, vast numbers of people. I'm not talking about individuals. Males and females make couples and they get together for certain reasons. Human beings are animals, and on a simple level the men have to like the women, and the women have to like the men.

M.C.: You don't think they will by themselves?

Ron: Yes, I certainly do. But I don't think we have to go around the barn about it. I don't think women have to hate men before they can love them or vice versa. That's like everybody's zigzagging and they happen to meet at odd times in the middle. You'd never produce anything—like kids, as the most obvious example. The emotional impact of male-female coupling is much more important than kids. Why do you want kids to exist? Basically because you like life, it's a reaffirmation of life. That's the only sense that you can make out of it. If you didn't like life, you wouldn't have kids. There are a lot of other things involved: you like to see this little image of yourself, you want him to become a genius and get rich. But basically it's because you enjoy the possibilities of life.

M.C.: Do you know any liberated women?

RON: I don't know what that means. I don't have that figured out at all. The impression you get from the press is that a liberated woman is somebody who doesn't worry. Well, I haven't found anybody who doesn't worry.

M.C.: What do *you* see a liberated woman as?

RON: I think a liberated woman is a woman who isn't afraid to do what she feels like doing. That's "not worrying" in a way, but to me it has a different implication, because I worry about everything I do, but I'm not afraid to try certain kinds of things. If a liberated woman wants to wear a certain kind of clothes, she does. If she wants to work at a certain job, she does. I don't like to hear women use bad language much, but I don't think they should be afraid to. I'm rather uninterested in the idea of spending a lot of time trying to keep up appearances, and I think liberated women don't worry about keeping up appearances.

M.C.: Would it surprise you if one of your sisters announced that she wanted to go into the family business?

RON: My father has been encouraging at least one of my sisters to do that, and maybe the other. One is very good in economics and has worked with our computer people, and my father thinks that she would be a very good businesswoman.

M.C.: What kind of position can you see her taking over?

RON: President! Why not? One of our major competitors is run by a woman.

M.C.: How would you feel about that?

RON: I'd feel all right. But *I* expect to be president! She's not in the business now, but I think I'd rather have her be president than a lot of men I can think of. She's more sensible. One of the problems in business is that you're running into people's egos. They want to be a big deal—they talk that way, they dress that way. They get unlisted telephone numbers, not because they don't want anybody to call them up, but because an unlisted number has status. Well, my sister isn't like that, she doesn't like stupidities. She likes a certain kind of efficiency in whatever she does.

M.C.: Do you think these qualities of efficiency and common sense are particularly female?

RON: As a matter of fact, from my family experience, yes. There is more efficiency and common sense in evidence among the female members of the family than there is among the men. As a matter of fact, that's a good example. I think my mother and my aunt were more liberated than most of the girls I know now—they weren't afraid to do things. I don't know what they did about sex, but I know what they did about getting jobs. My aunt was a fighter pilot, she ferried fighter planes from coast to coast. When I first remember her, she had a reputation for being avant garde in that she smoked cigarettes and swore like a trooper, also bursting into tears at odd intervals. In terms of making their way through life, they were less afraid of discrimination—maybe they just took it for granted and so they didn't worry about it.

M.C.: Do you have any fantasies of the future to bring this to a close?

RON: Yeah. Everyone is going to lie on moving sidewalks and straws will come down and feed you milkshakes and carrot juice and alimentary paste. My real feeling about the future is that there's going to be a huge number of people, there are going to be some laws that are unthinkable now—for example, enforced population control by fining.

M.C.: Do you think that's going to be effective—fining?

RON: Yes, because they're going to fine by chopping off joints, one joint at a time, for every suspective copulatory movement. They'll put sensors on people's pelvises—they'll use a piezoelectric cell which will give off electrical impulses upon an acceleration. This will be monitored by some giant computer in Copulation Central. And then they'll have commando teams in helicopters that will descend on the area where the person is and they'll chop off fingers.

M.C.: Fingers?

RON: Well, of course they'll get down to more useful appendages later on.

M.C.: But who's going to run this system, who's going to decide when to give alimentary paste?

RON: Well, that's the big problem. It will be done by achievements of some kind or other, or tests, or maybe people will fight it out. I don't know. Maybe they'll be nepotistic, family inheritance, a caste system will grow up. Managing mass unemployment would be a very difficult thing to do. I hope it doesn't get that way, but I don't see how the development of leisure time is going to lead us to anything but that point. The four-day week, the three-day week, the one-day week, the one-hour week.

M.C.: But isn't leisure itself going to be a big business? You've got to keep all these people occupied.

Ron: I forgot to say that you have to give them drugs because you *can't* keep them occupied. We can't give them all motorcycles and let them ride rampaging over the sand dunes or the Santa Monica Mountains, which would be covered with Astroturf so they won't burn up. You'll have to preserve green belts. Everything will be a park. There's going to be the industrial park, the recreational park, the governmental-educational-social service type of park. That's all there will be, except for the oceans. But the oceans will be covered with asphalt—that's from the Solid Ocean Collaborative, of which I'm president. "Sack the oceans." I applaud Standard Oil in San Francisco, and they shouldn't have been fined for their oil spill, because that was the first effort in paving over the oceans, which will be a great boon to mankind, because you will be able to drive to Japan. There will be no speed limits on the ocean, and I'll be able to go as fast as I want. The California Highway Patrol will have to stop at the twelve-mile limit, then I'll be able to take off. Think I'll drive down to New Zealand. I don't know what the future is going to be like.

M.C.: Do you want to state your disclaimer about the future?

Ron: Here's my disclaimer about the entire interview: everything I said is a pack of lies. I would like to be described as being a seventy-eight-year-old man with a large paunch. And please tell everyone concerned that I am dressed immaculately in shiny black acrylic paint with no other obvious clothing.

Anne is a 39-year-old suburban housewife and part-time office worker who found that it was an easy and exciting transition from "the straight scene" to women's liberation. She describes consciousness-raising techniques, such as guerrilla and elevator theater, as well as the ways in which increased consciousness has changed her attitudes about herself and other women. She is currently very active at a women's center and is writing articles for publication in feminist periodicals.

M.C.: Do you want to start by telling me how you got into women's liberation?

ANNE: I was very concerned about ecology and pollution. On Earth Day last year in April I went down to a place where Zero Population Growth had a booth. I was thinking that ecology isn't the nitty-gritty anyhow, you've got to reduce the population. The booth was manned—or womaned—by two kids who said that the group wasn't any good and wasn't doing anything. I thought that it doesn't look like they're going to be really into this for very long, and then they're going to go off and have six kids a piece. So then I began to think that wasn't it either; women are the nitty-gritty of the population in terms of causing all the pollution. So then I got into women's liberation, and I haven't done anything for ecology.

M.C.: What led you to the Women's Center?

ANNE: An article in the newspaper. I went down there and I was dressed very straight. Being from the suburbs, I thought it was going to be a lot of matrons and housewives. I went to a consciousness-raising group, and there were all these way-out types in their jeans and amulets and all the stuff that they wear. But I felt right with it immediately.

M.C.: So you weren't put off by them?

ANNE: No, I thought it was great! I've always wanted to be involved in something like this. I didn't particularly like the straight scene, I just felt that it was my lot in life. The consciousness-raising in that first group was really group, and I even commented to them that "Isn't this great? Here is a group of *women,* sitting around talking about significant things, not talking about their wash or their kids!" I really thought it was marvelous.

Then I got into women's theater. We had rehearsals in the park. We were going to do a guerrilla theater thing for the Fourth of July. We were going to auction off all the types of women—there was the housewife type, a nurse, teacher, hippie, and a couple of others. We had to have guys for it, unfortunately. They would be in the audience and bid for the women. Like "I bid an all-electric kitchen for the housewife." "For the hippie living in a commune I bid a butter churn." They would be competing with each other trying to offer this woman whatever she is supposed to want. We worked and worked, but it didn't gel. Somehow it got dropped and we went into this Nixon Family skit, which we put on for the Women's March [August 26, 1970] at the Department of Unemployment [*sic*]. There were five of us: Richard, Pat, Julie, Tricia, and David. I was Pat because everybody thinks I'm so prim. We had big papier mâché masks that we had made ourselves during long sessions. We had a puppeteer to help us. Just to digress, women are so funny. Some woman came in to help while we were all working. She goes right to the only man in the room to ask what to do. He didn't know—he was just making masks. Anyway, we held the masks above our faces so that they wouldn't muffle our voices, because in guerrilla theater you have to holler. No one expects you to be there, you just appear among the people.

M.C.: You didn't have a stage set up?

ANNE: No, we just walked right in and—*pow!*—laid it on them. That's guerrilla theater. Like at the Music Center they did something just when all the shows were breaking, when there were huge hordes of people on the plaza. Somebody pretended to have a heart attack or something. You can create an area by how you stand. We did the Nixon skit at the Music Center too.

M.C.: What were the reactions?

ANNE: It was so funny! There is a huge room at the Department of Unemployment [*sic*], and all these people were waiting in lines to get their unemployment checks. We went marching in through the middle door by all these lines of people, and all the heads turned and everybody stopped working. Then the gal who was Richard suddenly stopped and we all bumped into her. Then she made a noble gesture and we all tittered, being real nicety-nice. Then she said, "I'd like to make one thing perfectly clear—I am the President of the United States." And we all go "Oooh-eee!" She said "I'm not here to talk about pollution, or Vietnam, or the alleged Charles Manson." It was just after he said he thought Manson was guilty. "I am here to thank you all for being unemployed. By being unemployed, you're helping me in my fight against inflation." And then she led into the women's thing by saying, "I especially want to thank you women, not only for being unemployed but also for taking low wages when you do work." At the end we passed little thank-you notes and some people were scared to take them. They had a lot of statistics on them about how many women are working and how their wages are less. When we did it at the Music Center, we had a good group of people watching. There was one woman who kept saying, "For shame, for shame."

M.C.: How effective do you think techniques like this are?

ANNE: I don't know if we changed anyone's mind or raised anyone's consciousness. Another girl and I started doing elevator theater for a while.

M.C.: What's that?

ANNE: Well, an elevator is a great place to put on guerrilla theater. What I wanted to do was get one of these big high-rise buildings and try to make it appear as though there was a mass exodus of secretaries out of the building. We would plant women in the building and have one or two get on at each floor at lunchtime. We cased all the buildings on Wilshire. We were going up and down elevators for days! The women would march on with their coffee cup and steno pad and say, "I've had it! I'm not going to take it any longer!" By the time they got down to the lobby, there might be fifteen or twenty women saying they were quitting. I thought if we could just find a spot to burn the steno pads, it would be groovy. But we never did get enough people together, so we just did it in twos and threes. One girl said, "I'm a secretary, but my boss thinks I'm a waitress." Another said, "My boss just thinks I'm an attachment to my typewriter." And a man turned to her and said, "Yes, but you're a pretty attachment!" We got one woman going one time when we were in the elevator. We were standing in the back, bitching about our jobs, and one woman turned to another and said, "Yeah, that's right." I thought if there's one consciousness we've raised, then the whole thing may be worth it.

M.C.: Do you think that this finally is the way that women's liberation is going to have an effect, through little things mushrooming and influencing women where they work and where they are discriminated against?

ANNE: I doubt it. It's very inefficient because you're putting out a lot of effort to reach just a couple of people. The elevator business was really a waste of time, because it never got any kind of publicity. We more or less have to get into the media to make it.

M.C.: How do you feel about using the media? The media are so often accused of distorting the issues.

ANNE: They misrepresent and distort so fantastically! I think these publications might help; there are lots of feminist publications. But I'm afraid that they are just being read by the same people.

M.C.: Do you think that there is going to be a real change in the position of women in society in the next ten or twenty years?

ANNE: Oh yes. I don't see how it can be avoided.

M.C.: What areas do you think will be most affected?

ANNE: Employment, the home structure. My personal feeling is that men have a deep resentment of women, and this is why they are putting them down all the time. One of the reasons that they have this resentment is that men are always under the thumb of women. First it's their mother, then their women teachers. By the time they grow up, they have been dominated by some woman for so long that they just want to get even, even though it may be subconscious.

M.C.: Do you think that women contribute to this?

ANNE: I think so. The reason they contribute to it is that they don't have any other areas in which they can branch out. What they are trying to do now is get fathers more involved with raising children. I think that if the male child is more in contact with his father, he will not be so resentful of his mother, because the mother doesn't have the whole burden of controlling him. Then men won't feel that their balls are going to fall off, if you will pardon the expression, if they don't go out and dominate some woman! And the women won't put *everything* into their children if they have some other way they can go. They won't be so dominating perhaps.

M.C.: How do you think this process is going to take place? Do you think there is going to be clash, conflict, even violence? Or do you think it's going to be a slow penetration?

ANNE: I don't think there will be too much of a clash. I don't think women are violent by nature. They have more sense than to be violent.

M.C.: Some people have said that the only way to make a dent is to hit hard.

ANNE: This is true, but we can make our influence known without actually going out and socking somebody in the head. Women are conditioned not to use violence, and they have to get over this. If you're attacked, hit to hurt.

M.C.: What do you think femininity is?

ANNE: I really don't know because it's always so mixed up with so many negative things, like being helpless, passive. I've seen vulnerability and femininity put together so many times. Katherine Hepburn said in an article that she was vulnerable and feminine, like it was great to be vulnerable. It's *not* great to be vulnerable! It's horrible! It puts you in a terrible bag. Why should all the good things about a woman, like her sensitivity, her regard for life, be distorted into vulnerability? Women have more regard for life because they know what it takes to create one. If you think about man's contribution to the creation of life, it's an orgasm, which is the ultimate of pleasure. Woman's contribution is labor pains. What a fantastic contrast! They say that you appreciate the things that you have to work for. Men just have an orgasm and then split. So naturally they are not as concerned with overpopulating the world. They think about *re*populating the world after we blow it up. They think about all the orgasms they'll have, and women think about the realities.

M.C.: How do you feel about lesbians in the movement?

ANNE: Down at the Women's Center there are all these women I have known for months and I am just finding out that they are lesbians. I was never bothered by them. I get the feeling that we are conditioned to believe that a lesbian is someone who is going to try to rape you, and this just isn't true at all. Some of them are beautiful women—you would never know. I am constantly brought up short by my own conditioning. I always thought that a lesbian was probably an unattractive woman who couldn't get a man, and if they can't get a man, they'll settle for a woman. But this obviously isn't true because they are beautiful, intelligent, articulate, charming personalities, many of them are well educated, gifted writers or painters or potters. Some of them have children, so obviously they've had heterosexual experiences, but they prefer the other.

M.C.: Do you think that the fact that there is less hushing up of lesbianism will be beneficial in the long run?

ANNE: Oh, yes, very definitely. I think gay liberation is great, for men and for women. I think everybody should be more tolerant of different life styles because it doesn't hurt anybody. And of course they're not contributing to the population explosion.

M.C.: Are the lesbians very active at the Women's Center?

ANNE: Yes. One girl said that the lesbians are freer because they aren't hung up about always thinking about men and trapping a man. Women spend a huge amount of time thinking about men, dressing for men, orienting themselves around a man or the possibility of a man. Simone de Beauvoir really brought that out in *The Second Sex*. She said that women are so divided all their lives because they have to think about education and careers on the one hand, and getting a man on the other hand. A man can go full steam ahead on his career, and he doesn't worry about getting a woman. And she said that the ease with which women drop their education or their careers shows how little they were dedicated to them in the first place. It would be so great to be committed to something rather than a man, some worthwhile thing—not office work. If I could just publish something so I could feel good about my writing. I have an article which I first called "The Happy Shitworkers," but I got nothing but hostility about that. I know so many women who are passively happy with their office work—I could just strangle them.

M.C.: Have you had a lot of experience with office work yourself?

ANNE: Oh, God, yes. It is horrible!

M.C.: Do you think that it is going to take being in a flunky position—that men are going to have to be secretaries for a day—to understand what it's like? Maybe on national Secretary's Day all the male bosses would take over their secretaries' jobs.

ANNE: That's what we were trying to do last August, have all the women not work for one day so the men would have to do everything. But of course nobody did it.

M.C.: Perhaps you would really have to switch roles rather than striking, and have the men take orders instead of giving them. The secretaries would probably have a better understanding of their bosses too.

ANNE: Office work is so confining and so immobilizing. I hate that phrase, "I just couldn't sit at home all day." What does she think she's doing all day long in that office? She's sitting on her can. Office work is very broadening, and I don't mean of your head! At least if you're home, you could go from one room to another. If you get rid of the shit jobs, probably more than half the population will be out of work. I think a lot of this could be automated and the pay could be better. What we should do to take care of all the people who are out of shit jobs is bring back the crafts. Seriously—not just calling them hobbies. That makes me cringe.

M.C.: Has being active in the women's movement brought about any radical changes in your own life and attitudes?

ANNE: Oh, yes, it's helped me fantastically. I feel better about being a woman, I feel better about other women. I used to think that women were a poor substitute for a man. I don't feel that way at all any more. Now I know what women can do—we can do anything, really. Before I thought I could do something in spite of being a woman, but now I know it's not a handicap.

M.C.: What about this sense of power from knowing you're able to do things? Do you think that women in the movement are going to become more and more political?

ANNE: Yes, because the more you do it, the more you realize you can do it. It's fantastic. And it won't be just in garden clubs and PTA. Some women think they are powerful because they are running a PTA meeting with *Robert's Rules of Order*—that's not the same thing. The male structure says women can be as competent, as resourceful, as efficient as they want to be, as long as it's in areas that don't count too much.

M.C.: Do you expect a difference in values when women are more involved?

ANNE: Sure. I think the values will be much better. I'm appalled—it's frightening how much men are hung up on dominance and violence. They are obsessed with it. This is why we have wars, why men are behind sports. Until women can come along with our more humane values. . . . We don't need to go out and beat somebody up.

M.C.: Do you think that it's going to be a question of changing the institutions we have now or just working within them?

ANNE: They will have to be changed, because a lot of the problems we have now are due to the way men are raised, their home structure, early years in school where there are all women teachers.

M.C.: What is the future of the family? Do you see communal child-rearing really taking on? Or will the family of the future still depend on the essential pair? How would you like to see things evolve?

ANNE: I don't know. There is going to have to be some kind of a family, of course, because it takes so long for us to grow up. Children do require a lot of protection and guidance. I think that the child-care centers are going to be quite a big thing and the women are going to be out of the home more. I hope that men will take care of the children in the child-care centers. I think that the pair will never disappear. There will always be people who just want to have one mate. Communal marriage will probably be quite accepted—there are a lot of people who dig it. Actually, having one mate isn't normal. We're just going to have a more varied society, different types of things—if we can just keep ourselves alive and not blow ourselves up, and pollute ourselves, and poison ourselves.

M.C.: How do you feel about the attempt of a lot of young people to achieve a saner, more rational kind of life by escaping modern technology in its most obvious forms and leaving the cities for the country?

ANNE: I think it's great! Like my sister and her husband have got thirty-six acres in upstate New York, and they are trying to be self-sustaining.

M.C.: Do you think people like them are going to have much of an impact on society as a whole?

ANNE: Well, right now the whole communal thing is so dependent—it could never exist if it weren't for the support it gets from structured society. And besides, the women aren't getting anything out of it. They are just a bunch of shitworkers out on the farm. I think they are just doing what the housewives in the suburbs are doing, only under more primitive conditions. Ideally everything should be shared. There is no reason why women can't chop wood and the men cook.

M.C.: You mentioned that one of your original goals in the women's movement was to campaign against motherhood.

ANNE: Yeah. I really think motherhood should be abolished. Fetuses should be raised in test tubes. For one thing, you could totally eliminate birth defects. In the test tube you could control everything. There would be no thalidomide problem. The mother's state of mind affects the baby, the birth process affects the baby. We could guarantee every person born into this country a perfect body. Isn't that groovy? No brain damage because of a lengthy and difficult labor. And then women wouldn't be so masochistic about suffering through the birth process and wouldn't hate their children.

M.C.: Would you carry this mechanization further through child-rearing so that the child wouldn't be with its mother but at a day-care center most of the time?

ANNE: Well, if you're going to do that, there really isn't any point in having a parent, in the children knowing who their parents are.

M.C.: Or perhaps there isn't really any point in having a child.

ANNE: You have to generate the next generation. You could have exactly the number of people you want, the right number of each sex.

The kids would be raised in nurseries and the parents would go on their own way.

M.C.: Do you think people will accept that?

ANNE: I don't know. I don't know if it's a good thing. It's very provocative. How much of a need do human beings have to nurture and bring up a child? Is this inherent or induced? I personally can live without it.

M.C.: Have you decided categorically that you don't want to have any children?

ANNE: Oh, yes. But it's funny that I'm conditioned too. I was shocked when I read about a woman in the paper who said that she didn't want any children.

M.C.: How do you think the decision not to have children will affect the generation gap? It seems to me that a lot of the generation gap now is due to parent-child hostility that wouldn't exist under your system.

ANNE: I think being a parent makes people more conservative. They are forced to take positions and they can't change.

Not everyone has to renounce his or her family, get a divorce, wear bell-bottom pants, or throw bombs to feel free of some of the more oppressive aspects of life. Those willing to put out a little effort are finding that people, relationships, and even institutions are more flexible than expected. While revolution may still appear to be necessary at a certain point, means of evolutionary *change abound for people who recognize them. Marilyn and Ken, for example, have not only managed to keep their marriage in tune with their personal development for six years, but they have also brought about significant changes in their community by working with local government, school boards, and citizens groups. Marilyn, 27, is of Chinese extraction, grew up in South Africa, has a master's in English, and has taught remedial English to ghetto students. Ken is 37, returned to school for a master's in history after a successful stint in banking and stock brokerage, and now teaches history at a university. They are working on two books and contribute regularly to local newspapers.*

KEN: I think we are agreed that if there is to be change in this country, it has to come from the bottom up. Unless there is an economic catastrophe—which is always a possibility, from what we read. I don't see a revolution coming. But I see that if an economic catastrophe comes. . . . It is possible. First of all, the land system in California, as Nader has revealed, is far worse than it was in the times of the Spanish land grants, if you want to take a prerevolutionary period. The tax system in this country is far worse than it was before the Czarist regime collapsed. It's terrible, but most people are not aware of these things. I have thought that if a depression came, it would cause a radical restructuring of the economic system, which would be good. We cannot continue our corporations as they are.

M.C.: What kind of economic system would you like to see set up?

KEN: Without committing myself, because it could go in several ways, I'll say what we *cannot* have. What I would *not* have any longer is the kind of corporate structure which insists on growth. When I was in brokerage, the only thing you looked at was the growth in sales. The firm I worked for went bankrupt. You underwrote a firm because its growth was tremendous, and you forgot that profits were the important thing. This happens all the time. We're so growth-oriented. And we can't do it any longer, because of all the ecological reasons. And yet, our corporate form of capitalism is such that if it does not have growth, it is going to collapse. This to me seems to be the great dilemma. Some sort of economic setback will cause the collapse. And then maybe through the political process things could be revised.

M.C.: A graduate student I know said that most of the people she knew had been so discouraged by the inability to change anything through political action that they had retreated to a life of self-indulgence. I think its really scary that when you start scratching beneath the surface there are not so many active people out there.

MARILYN: I think the difference is, perhaps, this local-national split. When you talk about national politics, it's ridiculous. Why we have been so successful and so involved is that this is something close and tangible that we can actually achieve, and we *have* achieved. If you talk about something like the President of the United States, well, forget it. In fact, this is how they keep you weak. They focus your attentions on the people in the national elections and in Washington, but you can do nothing. You're not worth anything. You can write letters to congressmen until you're blue in the face. But on a local level. . . .

M.C.: So you think the only thing that will move people is if there's a dire catastrophe in their own area and they're forced to cope with it?

KEN: Yeah, maybe like the Radical Four getting on the Berkeley City Council. Even moderates and conservatives started taking an interest in politics, locally: "Gee, we can't have that happen!"

M.C.: Do you think there's going to be a lot of violence?

KEN: I don't think one can make a statement either way. There's so much that could happen.

M.C.: Have you felt close to violence?

KEN: Oh, yeah.

MARILYN: We passed that a year or two ago.

KEN: I felt very strongly, and I probably still feel, that there's a necessity for violence. I cannot, I know now, participate in violence. I can give passive support if someone else is doing it. But a year ago I was more inclined to violence.

M.C.: Do you see any parallels between the political system and the fact that most of America is primarily male-dominated?

KEN: I can mention Golda Meir, and Mrs. Indira Gandhi. They're very impressive, I think, in emulating their male counterparts. I don't know. I generally feel that women are far more tolerant, have a far better understanding of human nature, but that could get pretty elliptical too if you overgeneralize.

MARILYN: I think that, on the whole, a minority has better insights than a majority. In other words, a black man living in a white man's ghetto has to be able to understand both worlds, like a woman working in a man's world. But if you get blacks who are totally middle class, then they are even worse. But on the whole, if you get an intelligent woman in a man's job, she'll do better, because she's sympathetic to the other side.

M.C.: Do you think that there are any qualities which are inherently female, versus inherently male qualities?

MARILYN: No, but that's because I tend to think that ninety percent of that is environmental. I don't know if there are any inherently male or female qualities. Because all the things that I would name would be cultural. There's that old joke about my wife and me: "I make all the big decisions, like whether we're going to go to China or not, and she makes the small decisions, like what refrigerator we're going to buy." But that's cultural. I absolutely can't say.

M.C.: Are you more optimistic about changes in personal relationships?

KEN: Oh, yeah, from what we've seen in this community.

MARILYN: But it's not a typical community.

KEN: But it's an urban community. There's certainly a lot of restructuring going on. There's a lot of experimenting.

MARILYN: We're moralistic, we don't like promiscuity. We have to get over that.

M.C.: Do you feel that way, that it's something you have to get over?

MARILYN: No, not us, *they* have to get over it! The disillusionment of the kids that's seeping in is that their parents are so bloody hypocritical. They tell the kids to tell the truth. They then weasel out of a party, cheat on their golf scores, or have shady business deals. If you can't do it in your personal relationships . . . I feel very strongly about marriage. Nobody has to get married. If you don't want to stay with one person, don't get married, just sleep around. But if you get married, you make this choice and you make it freely. You make a promise and an obligation, and you should keep it. Businessmen don't back down on business deals—much—but they take more care to keep their businesses than they do their marriages, which seems to me totally wrong. A personal relationship should be more important.

M.C.: Marilyn, what do you think of women's liberation?

MARILYN: I think that the main idea is fantastic. But, like any other movement, it has a lunatic fringe. You have to have a lunatic fringe because reasonable people don't get on the front pages of the newspaper. The first thing you need is publicity. You need people to know what the issue is and to be interested in it. So you need freaky women going around burning bras. Unfortunately that is the image. But it's the same with the Black Panthers. It makes good newspaper copy. The nonpublicized image goes blank. I don't relate to women's liberation very much because we don't have a problem with it. The most important thing for us is our personal relationship, two people. Whoever is free at mealtime cooks and whoever is free when something else has to be done does it.

M.C.: Has becoming politically active in the community been the major factor in changing the allocation of your activities from the traditional male-female arrangement to a more flexible ad-hoc arrangement?

MARILYN: Ken activated me politically. When you knew me before I got married, I was never politically active. I didn't have the confidence. I only got the confidence after I was married. Partly I think this is what marriage does and partly it's who you marry. I think we did this for each other. There were certain things I didn't have confidence about and Ken just assumed that I could do those things: "Of course you can do it." We did this for each other. First of all, you build your own self-confidence, and then you get to the point where you say, "Damn it, I'm going to do it better." It's a development of your personality. I think there are women who need women's liberation because you have to get your own head together first.

M.C.: But you have never felt the urge to go join a women's meeting?

MARILYN: No, because you get all these freaky types like Germaine Greer mentions. I had an experience on campus where they wouldn't talk to me because I had a wedding ring and I wore a skirt. I explained that the reason I wore skirts was that I had two pairs of pants and I had lots of skirts. I didn't think it would prove that I was liberated for me to go and throw out my skirts and buy a whole bunch of pants.

M.C.: Do you have anything against joining groups of women, or is it just that the subject matter doesn't interest you?

MARILYN: It doesn't interest me for the same reason that I don't enjoy Asian groups. I think they do very unhealthy introspection. I think this is what Germaine Greer says about women taking judo so they can beat up construction workers who whistle at them: "If you think the body of the man next to you is your enemy, you're sick." I think what we're fighting for is a system that doesn't have a hierarchy where some people oppress other people. Whites oppress blacks and men oppress women, that whole method of thinking. The causes of the oppression are still there because they're in the mind of the people. You have to remove the system of thinking that there's a hierarchy, instead of just inverting the hierarchy. We have to get away from the mode of thinking that some groups of people are better than other groups of people, whether by race or occupation or birth, by money, by sex. And that's what the Cultural Revolution is. That's what you really need in this country. I don't think it helps for blacks to go around oppressing whites just because whites have always oppressed blacks, or women to oppress men. Men are oppressed too. I'm interested in the men's liberation movement—getting rid of this masculinity bag where you have to go out every night and screw women.

KEN: It's probably a lot harder for the man to break out of his mold than it would be for the woman to break out of her very boring housewife mold.

I have a feeling that 1972 might be one of those big years, like with Nixon going over to China. We're going to have a tremendous flow of ideas—Chinese medicine, equality of women, community participation, rationing of resources. It's going to shake up a lot of people. Maybe the two big events of 1972 will be women and Nixon in China.

MARILYN: For example, in China nobody throws away used light bulbs. They save them and take them back to the factory and drill a little hole and change the filament and seal them up again. At the supermarkets they wrap things in big leaves. And you throw them back into your garden and use them for compost. I am a grocer's daughter, so I think of these things automatically. But it has gotten really popular.

KEN: It makes you think of little things in this country, like nine different-colored boxes of Kleenex. We take so many of these things for granted! Can you just imagine the waste involved in that? There are something like fifteen different kinds of toilet paper here, excluding the scented ones!

Also, you see a fantastic amount of—I hate to use that word—participatory democracy going on in China, local activity at every level. No one can drop out and be a wallflower, saying that he doesn't want to participate. In this country you have a showing of democracy at the top, like a choice between a Humphrey and a Nixon! At the municipal-local level no one does anything. It is bankrupt at the local level in this country. It's just been the last couple of years since you've had any spirit. It's been basically just Boss Tweeds all over the place. If we could get some of that local energy that they seem to have over in China into this country. . . .

MARILYN: The work that we're doing now we're doing for the whole community. When *we* do it it's patriotism, and when *they* do it it's propaganda. I don't think that's so terribly reasonable.

KEN: They don't have the pursuit-of-the-profit ethic. Everything is geared towards improving individual economic welfare in this country. In China you have it almost ingrained that you try to better your family or your communal area. The final measure of success is not what you *earn*, as in this country, but it's something else—the community will place a high priority upon doing some activity. In this country again, it is converted into a Cadillac or a house or some kind of conspicuous consumption.

Fran and Alice see the women's movement as a source of creative energy, for society as well as individuals, and a way of revitalizing personal relationships. They are both active in "co-counseling" (a new kind of group therapy) and are instructors of "critical arts" at an experimental college, where they organized a women's group. Fran, 30, intends to continue training to become a family counselor. Alice, 27, is finishing a Ph.D. in sociology.

FRAN: I went to the first women's meeting in 1968 in Cambridge at MIT. I was teaching at the time and all of a sudden I started to think about my class that I was teaching and how I was completely involved with the male students, and the female students I thought of as dull and trivial. Then I started to feel terribly guilty. I realized that there was something important that was being said. At that meeting we broke down into little groups and I started to think about my feelings toward women. And then another girl and I formed a group, which was in some sense the only group I was ever in. That was a big deal for me, insofar as it was the first time that I ever had independent relationships with women where I felt I was an equal. I had always had one boyfriend, had been afraid of everybody else in the whole world. I was terrified of other people and I could only appear in a couple with a guy. In college I felt that I was a weird unfeminine person. There were all sorts of normal girls that I was friendly with, but I was never like them. So that group was a big deal. It was like a huge flash —there was a very major part of my life that I had never thought about. And my present life, which I had never thought about, was suddenly getting revised all over the place, by going to the group and having insights. What happened was that the group got bogged down and rigidified, and there were positions held, like people who were for marriage and people who were against marriage. And some people wanted to get more personal, and other people wanted to get more political and go into action. And it broke up after about three months. But the only thing that I can see that's the right thing to do now is co-

counseling. And that seems to me to be the most effective way to get at people now. It seems to me that the women's movement is closer to co-counseling than normal radical politics. The things from co-counseling are just more effective ways of doing what the women's movement is trying to do anyway.

If I think about the relationship between co-counseling and the normal women's group, it seems like the first step in a women's group is to realize that it's shared problems. And the second step is the self-affirmation thing, realizing that the problems aren't your fault and that you don't *have* to suffer under them—that you can make some attempt not to have that stuff happen to you. Usually what happens in a women's group is that people can identify their problems—their boyfriend sleeps around—but they don't know what to do. They can leave the guy, get involved with somebody else, various alternatives that do not touch the heart of it. They can also say, "All you have to do is change the system." But that's a dead-end—not that it's not true, but insofar as no one knows what to do. The thing about co-counseling is that it has a specific way of undoing this stuff and of actually changing you so that you can take the initiative in being different, which seems to be the major thing. It has two different aspects. First it has the theory that the person has all capacities and is intelligent and understanding and loving and lovable and smart and responsible; and all that is wrong with the person can be undone with discharge, like figuring out the right way to laugh about it, or cry about it, or whatever. In a women's group somebody says, "Men are always putting me down, and it hurts me." If I were doing co-counseling, then it would be a question of getting the person to cry that stuff out, but also getting the person to realize that theoretically it's not that men are the oppressors and are evil and that it's a hopeless situation, but that men do that out of their *own* hurts. There are very specific things that the woman can do: first, recognizing that what is said to her is not true; second, to parry the hurtful things that get said to her so that she is not just in a locked-in role of the oppressed; third, even to go out to the men and affect their behavior. The main thing, it seems to me, is that it makes the person much more *active*.

ALICE: The first stage of consciousness-raising, as I see it, is reducing, or breaking into, what has been considered totally private experience, and making people aware that they are not the only ones who have had it, becoming aware that there are social things that condition that. But then co-counseling takes up much more. Some of these groups are tremendously euphoric. Part of it is, I think, from being in very stimulating contact with other women, in fruitful, supportive relations. The whole thing about bonds with other women becoming highly libidinized and much more erotic—it's like getting the other half of the world that you can relate to in a very active way. You already had the male half of the world, only you didn't think you had it, and probably you didn't have it entirely. Then when she begins to establish relations with women, I sense a tremendous amount of energy. Also, more exciting things being attempted, like going around and speaking at schools, setting up a day-care center, which I did with one of the groups. Like very ambitious group projects that you would take on together, political action.

M.C.: So it's like going from the internal to the external?

ALICE: Yeah, much more like attacking the world, taking it on. A real feeling of narcissism, in the best sense, in the people who have had a lot of negative feelings about their own talents and capacities—to all of a sudden be active and be doing things with other people, having companionship. It was very stimulating.

M.C.: What about coverage by the media of the whole movement? Do you think that it has been accurate and beneficial or otherwise?

FRAN: I have the feeling that it's been very useful insofar as all people have an authentic impulse to liberation, which makes them capable of seizing an idea even if it's presented in a distorted form. The stuff gets presented in a very fucked-up way, but that doesn't matter because people still get the idea.

ALICE: I hadn't heard that expressed, but I think in general I agree with it. Like on the speaking tour I was with radicals, and they made it a policy not to talk to the media under any circumstances. I felt very uncomfortable with it, because I thought "why not?" I am basically for the greatest coverage. But I do think that coverage is very distorted and that there are very few attempts to develop the deeper train of thought.

M.C.: Why do you think that is?

ALICE: Because all news has that aspect, there's a desperate striving after sensation—"Am I alive or am I not?" The more sensationalistic you can make something, the more you might have the illusion of being alive. And about this in particular, it has something to do with sex.

M.C.: Do you have the feeling that it is a male counterattack?

FRAN: I have the feeling that the general function of the media is to keep people opinionated and slightly hopeless, and that's the way society is kept where it's supposed to be. The mass media translate the women's movement into "Are you for or against short skirts?" It makes it all trivial and without truth content. The thing in the media that I found most influenced people negatively is the impression that people in women's liberation are hostile to them, like the normal housewife feels strongly that she's being criticized all the time by the women's movement.

ALICE: Also that they would be personally disruptive. "We thought you'd come in with bras on sticks."

FRAN: Someone said, "I thought if I went to the meeting you would make me take my bra off."

M.C.: It's funny that people focus on the bra business. That seems to be the distorted image of the movement. I've noticed that if I ask people point blank what they think of women's liberation, they say, "Well, I don't approve of the bra-burning bit, but . . ." How many cases of bra-burning have actually taken place?

ALICE: The other side of that is like my sister-in-law and a friend of hers were telling me about their recent adventures. And they said that they knew that they had discovered soul sisters when they saw that the other wasn't wearing a bra. They looked at me proudly and one of them said, "When I saw her falling free like that, I was so impressed! I thought 'my God!' "

FRAN: Obviously it is a big deal or people wouldn't be so fucked-up about it. Getting over the taboo of presenting yourself in plain sexual terms instead of images. It has something to do with the fact of having your body more in direct contact with the world.

M.C.: How do you feel about the youth culture as far as the position of women is concerned?

ALICE: It strikes me that a lot of the youth culture doesn't share my goals for women. There is a lot of this "my old lady" stuff and "earth-mothering," getting into nutrition and things like that, which are really good, but which don't have confrontation with authority, a crucial element of women's liberation.

FRAN: They also don't have any emphasis on synthetic insight. It definitely allows people to sit around and try to figure stuff out and not be conventional. But it doesn't have a conception of people being strong and responsible and cooperative. It's sitting around doing nothing or doing your own weird thing. And neither one of those has much to do with the women's movement.

M.C.: What's going to happen when the kids who are now, say, in their first year of college get to the point where they could take over positions of authority in politics, or business, or whatever?

ALICE: It's going to be interesting to see if the people who are influenced by youth culture and are committing their lives to it indeed *take* those positions of authority, and whether those positions of responsibility are taken by people who are *not* touched by youth culture—that seems to me far more likely. It really could be that millions of kids would not step into standard roles.

FRAN: It seems to me that it's possible for those kids to make a pure switch back into the standard roles, like to completely become a normal guy but with long hair. The youth culture doesn't give them enough power to change any role that they would be in. They're just at the mercy of it.

ALICE: What would probably happen is that they would be in the role and experience a tremendous amount of conflict about being in it, feeling different values not terribly well formulated. I don't see how they can possibly go through the roles without having a lot more friction and stumbling blocks than their parents did.

FRAN: I think that they would experience a conflict in terms of *hassle*—which is not really perception of conflict!

M.C.: What about real conflict? Do you think there is going to be a lot of violence, either from grown up youth culture kids or even from women?

FRAN: No, I just think that violence is going to be the same old type of violence—from the authorities and the really oppressed people. I really have a sense that the plain radical stuff is not going to rise again in that form, that nobody has the energy to do that any more. My intuition is that the co-counseling thing is really going to work. As people get more into it, they're going to get much more powerful at reaching out and changing the stuff that they're in already and a lot of the people who have positions in the normal world, and that that is going to make a lot of difference. That is the kind of culture that's going to spread.

ALICE: Also, co-counseling opens up the directness of the gratification that the person can get from the people that he is with mainly, but also from his talents, his activities. That means a much more centered life, that you need much less, fewer material things. It's not that you go on an ascetic trip and deny yourself everything and start wearing a burlap bag. Far from it. You discover what you look good wearing and wear that a lot, or what you need to be comfortable in a house.

And also in terms of people and experiences. What strikes me about the most prominent aspect of the American experience is that we are deadened, we are unable to get gratification from the most direct things in life, like from the people we love, our mates. So we're constantly turning outward in hopes of getting the sensation that we're alive. That's what the entertainment industry is about. Instead of having more and more exotic, freaky, sex movies—they go farther and farther as people hope and hope that they are going to get *some* sensation—it would go more in the direction of letting people who have some degree of self-acceptance and self-joy get together with other people who have that too and make their own films. It would not involve nearly as much proliferation of hardware and goods.

M.C.: Fran, can you fantacize [*sic*] for a minute on what the future family is going to be like when women are truly liberated?

FRAN: I can think of two slightly different stages. One positive stage I imagine as people still basically getting paired off, but having much more positive relationships with each other—more loving and free-flowing, and very much more equal in the sense that it will be taken for granted that it's good for each person to go out into the world and love lots of people, lead a very creative life. People will be a lot less isolated from kids. There will be lots more adults around who can be tender and accepting to kids. Both of the parents will have that kind of relationship with them because neither one will be blocked off about kids. And I would imagine that the normal thing would be that all people would be active. There wouldn't be the choice of the dull job versus the dull home. The eventual thing, a hundred years from now . . . I was thinking about monogamy. Monogamy is completely satisfactory if you don't get barriers between the people. But ultimately that wouldn't be the case, when people aren't godlike and fucked-up. It may be that people would sleep together just as a way of being together.

ALICE: Very recently I started to have a set of thoughts related to this. I certainly had a period, very academically buttressed, where I was thinking that monogamy was on the way out and that was the cause of tremendous ill. I still support what I was thinking at that time. What I also think now, though, is that a lot of this emphasis on collective stuff. . . . If you cannot trust one other person, to hope to be able to trust a group is impossible. There is a tremendous amount of hope that, because people are so scared of each other, if they just get with enough people it will be okay. From myself, I know that the first thing is going to be being able not to have to defend myself from the most important people in my life, who are two or three. That's very hard. I don't want to say just one, because there are definitely problems with that—but maybe I do mean one, the person who I am with, the one I have the ultimate commitment to.

FRAN: What I imagine is different levels of commitment. Like the person that you lived and slept with would be the deepest level of commitment, but that it would be the normal thing for people to be committed to their friends.

ALICE: And committed to levels that are unheard of in bourgeois society, like economically committed, being there in time and space when you're needed. It's incredible to me, the isolation of each little pair in the whole bourgeois setup. I would definitely be for enlarging circles of commitment.

FRAN: But there's commitment and commitment. You can be committed to somebody who is continually borrowing money from you in a totally irresponsible way—that's valueless. I think that people will become much more responsible, but that won't mean that they aren't committed. It's like getting over neurotic dependency.

ALICE: It's definitely an after-the-cure commitment.

M.C.: Do you think about the future very much, Alice?

ALICE: Yes. But I don't even approve of thinking of the future. I think a lot about the future, and I'm very scared of the future. I always think about the future in the most traditional terms; what job will I have, will I have enough money, am I going to get sick and die? I think of it as these little future points in the time continuum about which I have these pre-set figures of imagined events, about which I can only have anxiety. That seems to me a very fruitless way, because the authentic way of thinking about the future is much more present-oriented, speaking out of things that I have my energy caught up in, that I know to be true—present fears and joys, perceiving directly out of them into the next moment. As long as I can do that and be fully engaged, I don't have to worry about falling out of the world or not having a job or money. That doesn't mean being stupid—of course, I'll not end up next year without having made my applications [for teaching positions]. It does mean that present involvement and engagement is worth all of my attention. It's a waste of time to build one's life around worrying about being broke. That's what I see happening a lot—people who never give a thought to the present moment. They're living all the time in their fears. The more conservative they get, the farther ahead their range is. Like my parents are really worried about the ultimate, the end—twenty years. I'm concerned about next year. A lot of people at our school are concerned about next week.

M.C.: Fran, do you consider yourself future-oriented?

FRAN: Yes. That's such an interesting thing. I used to think about the future in terms of catastrophe and anxiety. And now I have two different ways of thinking about the future. One is the coping way, like hedging: "If the world stays normal, I'll be safe, because in four years I'll be able to be a marriage and family counselor and I can make money that way." And the other perspective is that all horizons are opening up, there are more things that I can do, and everything is getting better and better. It seems to me that in my life everything is always getting better and better and working out.

ALICE: Another thing that I was going to say is that I think that this obsession with the future, born out of fear, is exactly one of the things that keep us from having direct experience. It takes you out of the present, it takes you out of the possibility of getting real gratification from whoever you are with and whatever you're doing. So when I'm anxious, I spend a lot of time thinking about my applications and my bank balance and what I'm going to be doing next year. I have gone through two or three days without registering a single thing that happens to me. I'm just not a centered human being. When I'm not anxious, I'm very much concentrated in the present and getting gratification out of it. So insofar as I have control over it, I tend to center myself in the present. Also it seems to me that you just cannot tell anything about the future insofar as you divorce yourself from the present. If anything, it is more important to look to the past so that you can discern direction. I do find that important in getting a handle, a perspective on things. The most hopeful and positive way of thinking about myself is to realize that I have been improving. If I can really understand in sophisticated terms what the nature of that improvement has been, then the future is disarmed, it no longer scares me.

Jenny, 3, and David, 5, have already developed some definite ideas about the differences between males and females in our society, even though their parents say they have raised them the same way and have taught them to have the same expectations from life.

E.C.: What do you kids think the world is going to be like when you're ten?

JENNY: I think it's going to be like a table, a red table.

E.C.: Well, what's it like right now?

JENNY: Oh, the world is like a fish now.

DAVID: No, I think it's like a big light, shining, glowing.

E.C.: How about when you're fifty?

DAVID: I think it's going to be like nightmares.

E.C.: How come it's going to be like nightmares?

DAVID: Because! Because I dream of so many things. Sometimes I get scared like mad.

E.C.: What's the difference between boys and girls?

DAVID: They're sort of different because girls have vaginas and boys have penises.

E.C.: Is that the only difference?

DAVID: Yeah.

E.C.: Are there some jobs that men do and some jobs that women do?

DAVID: Dads come home late.

E.C.: Jenny, if you could be anybody in the world, who would you be?

JENNY: A bear.

E.C.: Would you be a man bear or a woman bear?

JENNY: A man bear. No, a woman bear. Womens and sisters are mommies. I'm going to be a mommy when I grow up.

E.C.: Are you going to have babies?

JENNY: Yeah, two babies.

E.C.: Why not more?

JENNY: Because I don't like to have more.

E.C.: Are you going to have a husband?

JENNY: I do have forty. But I don't want to have a husband when I have babies.

E.C.: You don't want to have a man around the house?

JENNY: No.

E.C.: Do you like boys or girls better?

JENNY: Girls better.

E.C.: Why?

JENNY: Because girls have vaginas and boys have penises. I just like vaginas, not penises.

E.C.: Why don't you like penises?

JENNY: Because penises go potty on me.

E.C.: David, if you could be anybody in the world, who would you be?

DAVID: My friend Steve, 'cause he climbed a mountain and I didn't.

E.C.: Who would you be if you could be a grownup?

DAVID: Nobody!

E.C.: Would you be a woman?

DAVID: I'd be a worker from the store. A man worker.

E.C.: Why not be a woman worker?

DAVID: The women worker is too funny! I don't like women because they do silly things. They take people to bed. Wowee—that's so silly.

E.C.: Is your father silly too?

DAVID: No, he's not silly!

E.C.: If I were a magician and changed you into a woman, what would you do then?

DAVID: Nothing.

E.C.: Would you have babies?

DAVID: No, I don't like babies.

E.C.: Would you get married?

DAVID: No.

E.C.: Would you work?

DAVID: No. I'd get somebody to change me into a frog.

E.C.: You'd rather be a frog than a woman?

DAVID: Yeah.

Notes

NOTES

Introduction

1. Elizabeth Gould Davies, *The First Sex* (New York: G. P. Putnam's Sons, 1971), pp. 3–7.

Chapter 1

1. Alvin Toffler, *Future Shock* (New York: Random House, 1970).

Chapter 2

1. Jacques Ellul, *The Technological Society*, trans. by John Wilkinson (New York: Alfred A. Knopf, 1964).
2. See, for example, Lionel Tiger and Robin Fox, *The Imperial Animal* (New York: Holt, Rinehart & Winston, 1971).

Chapter 3

1. Antony Jay, *Corporation Man* (New York: Random House, 1971), p. 93.
2. Toffler, p. 83.
3. Jacques Ellul, *The Political Illusion*, trans. by Konrad Kellen (New York: Alfred A. Knopf, 1967).
4. M.F. Ashley Montagu in *The Saturday Review Treasury* ("Selected from the Files by John Haverstick and the Editors of the *Saturday Review*") (New York: Simon & Schuster, 1957), p. 474.
5. Barry Farrell, "You've Come a Long Way, Buddy," *Life*, August 27, 1971.

Chapter 4

1. Patricia Cayo Sexton, *The Feminized Male* (New York: Vintage, 1970).
2. Liz Smith, "Gloria Steinem, Writer and Social Critic, Talks about Sex, Politics and Marriage," *Redbook*, January 1972.
3. "Anaïs Nin Talks About Being a Woman," *Vogue*, October 15, 1971.
4. Jean-François Revel, *Without Marx or Jesus* (Garden City: Doubleday, 1971).

Chapter 6

1. Vivian Estellachild, "Hippie Communes," *Women: A Journal of Liberation*, Winter 1971.
2. Coleman McCarthy, "The Abandonment of America's Aged," *Los Angeles Times*, December 5, 1971.

Chapter 8

1. Mr. & Mrs. K as told to Monte Shertier and Alfred Pulca, *The Couple* (New York: Berkeley Medallion Books, 1971); Peter and Barbara Wyden, *Inside the Sex Clinic* (New York: World, 1971).

Chapter 9

1. John F. Trimble, *The Group Sex Scene* (New York: Pinnacle, 1971).

Chapter 10

1. Norman Mailer, *Why Are We in Vietnam?* (New York: G. P. Putnam's Sons, 1967), p. 114.
2. "J," *The Sensuous Woman* (New York: Dell, 1971).
3. Martha Weinman Lear, "Q. If You Rape a Woman and Steal Her TV, What Can They Get You For in New York? A. Stealing Her TV," *New York Times*, January 30, 1972.
4. Eldridge Cleaver, *Soul on Ice* (New York: McGraw-Hill, 1968).

5. Kate Millett, *Sexual Politics* (New York: Doubleday, 1970), pp. 3, 7.
6. *Ibid.*, p. 313.

Chapter 11

1. Desmond Morris, *The Naked Ape* (New York: Dell, 1967).

Chapter 12

1. Stanley Cohen, "Directions for Research on Adolescent Group Violence and Vandalism," *The British Journal of Criminology*, October 1971.
2. Roy R. Silver, "15 'Sentenced' by a Judge Investigate Jail in Nassau," *New York Times*, April 13, 1972.

Chapter 13

1. The précis of the play is adapted from Rev. W. Lucas Collins, *Aristophanes* (Edinburgh, 1872).
2. See Konrad Kellen, *Khrushchev: A Political Portrait* (New York: Frederick A. Praeger, 1961).
3. James B. Rule, "The Problems with Social Problems," *Politics and Society*, Fall 1971.
4. Stephen Schlesinger, "The Good Young Guys," *Vogue*, August 1971.

Chapter 14

1. James F. Hollingsworth, quoted in "Generals Comment on Killing," *Los Angeles Times*, April 16, 1972.
2. Richard Barnet, "The Game of Nations," *Harper's*, November 1971.
3. Dr. Peter A. Corning, quoted in "Women May Have to Rule, Scientist Says," *Los Angeles Times*, December 29, 1971.
4. Barnet, *loc. cit.*
5. Bella Abzug quoted in "People," *Time*, February 28, 1972.

Chapter 15

1. Sidney J. Slomich, *The American Nightmare* (New York:

Macmillan, 1971); the excerpt in the present text appeared in "An Expert's Warning: Beware of Experts," *Los Angeles Times*, October 31, 1971.

Chapter 16

1. See Mike Rokyo, *Boss: Richard J. Daley of Chicago* (New York: Dutton, 1971).
2. Theodore H. Rosebury, *Life on Man* (New York: Viking, 1969).
3. Dan Greenburg, "Shelley," *Playboy*, December 1971.
4. "Is America Entering Age of Depression?" *Los Angeles Times*, April 13, 1972.

Conclusion I

1. "What U.S. Women Believe and Want Disclosed by [Harris] Poll," *Los Angeles Times*, March 24, 1972.

Conclusion II

1. Interview by Vivian Gornick of Dr. Horner in *Ms* (Winter 1971–72).

Appendix

1. The essay appeared in *Neue Zürcher Zeitung*, July 5, 1966, and was translated for the present text by Konrad Kellen.

Index

INDEX